Naval Battles

of the

Twentieth Century

Naval Battles

of the

Twentieth Century

Richard Hough

THE OVERLOOK PRESS
WOODSTOCK & NEW YORK

First published in the United States in 2001 by
The Overlook Press, Peter Mayer Publishers, Inc.
Lewis Hollow Road
Woodstock, NY 12498
www.overlookpress.com

Library of Congress Cataloging-in-Publication Data

Hough, Richard Alexander.
Naval battles of the twentieth century / Richard Hough
p.   cm.
Originally published: London : Constable and Co., 1999.
Includes bibliographical references and index.
1. Naval art and science—History—20th century. 2. Naval battles—
History—20th century. 3. Naval history, Modern—20th century. I. Title.
V53 .H68 2001   359'.009'04—dc21   00-051565

Book design and type formatting by Bernard Schleifer
Manufactured in the United States of America
ISBN 1-58567-040-5
1 3 5 7 9 8 6 4 2

For my wife

Contents

ILLUSTRATIONS

All photographs are the property of the Hulton Getty Picture Library

INTRODUCTION

I HAVE SELECTED fourteen naval battles of the twentieth century to include in this book. They range from the Battle of Tsu-Shima in 1905 to the Battle of the Philippines in 1944. These two battles are separated by almost fifty years and mark the rise of the Japanese Navy to become a great naval power; and then later its destruction. Both these battles took place in the eastern hemisphere, and the British Navy, having been the dominant naval power in the nineteenth century, took part in neither.

However, all but four of the other battles recounted in this book involved the Royal Navy, including the second biggest, the Battle of Jutland in 1916.

Between the World Wars it became increasingly evident that the nature of war at sea was changing radically, and that air power might become the dominating factor. Gone were the days when a naval battle featured a line of battleships firing their guns at one another from, say, a range of 200 or 300 yards, stretching to 12,000 or 15,000 a hundred years later.

Now, as became evident from 1940 onwards, battle fleets might destroy one another from ranges limited only by the amount of fuel in the tank of an aircraft. These battle fleets did not use range-finders because they could not even see one another.

At the Battle of Jutland in 1916 battleships of 25,000 tons, costing about £2,000,000, pitted themselves against one another, firing shells weighing anything up to 2,000 pounds. When these large-calibre shells made a hit in the right place, just one might suffice to destroy an enemy ship of equal size, as happened several times at Jutland.

Twenty-five years later a handful of aircraft, each costing about £10,000 to build, crippled an entire fleet with the loss of only two of them. At the Battle of Midway in the Pacific, four Japanese aircraft carriers were destroyed in one day for the cost of a handful of bombers, meanwhile altering the balance of power in that war. Yet no heavy guns had been fired and the enemy had been located by scouting planes or radar.

By 1940 the battleship was obsolescent, as predicted by General 'Billy' Mitchell years earlier, as well as by other far-sighted authorities. The battleship and its cousin, the battle-cruiser, had become useful only for bombarding land targets and providing protection for the new dominant warship — the aircraft carrier.

Attempts by Germany in the Second World War to use battleships and battle-cruisers for commerce raiding turned out disastrously, the biggest of them, the *Bismarck*, being crippled by a single plane before being sunk by guns and torpedoes.

The torpedo as a weapon of sea warfare had been invented many years earlier. Destroyer-borne torpedoes had crippled the Russian Fleet at the outset of the Russo-Japanese war of 1904–5. The torpedo was rapidly developed; ten years after that event one torpedo sank the only German battleship to be destroyed at Jutland. Only one torpedo was needed for the *Pommern* to blow up and immediately sink.

A torpedo carried by a plane, secured under its belly, made a lethal combination. This was developed in the 1920s and 1930s, and all major naval powers used it in the Second World War.

The dive-bomber was also a new weapon widely used in that war. At the surprise attack on Pearl Harbor by the Japanese Navy in 1941, dive-bombers and torpedo bombers all but wiped out the American battleship fleet. But it was not the stunning victory the Japanese claimed it to be because there were no carriers there; moreover this 'sneak' attack so stirred the pride and anger of the American people that the industry of that nation, the greatest in the world, before long was launching a new carrier every week.

All of the battles fought in the Pacific and described in this book feature the carrier, and it was the skill and courage of American air crews, flying from carriers, which turned the tide in the battle to control this enormous, 70,000-square-mile ocean.

I have not chosen to discuss in detail the submarine-launched torpedo, except incidentally. It did indeed have successes against carriers and all types of warship, from battleships to destroyers, and it can be argued that the greatest battles of the twentieth century were fought by submarines operating in the Atlantic and Pacific Oceans.

Certainly the German U-boat operations in both World Wars in the Atlantic came nearer to bringing Britain and her allies to their knees in this new form of commerce warfare — the *guerre de course*. But that, perhaps, might be the subject of another study.

This book tends to concentrate its attention on battles on the sea rather than beneath the waves, and to illustrate the development of sea warfare, from the ironclads through the all-big-gun dreadnought to the aircraft carrier — the 'Queen of the Seas' even before the end of the twentieth century.

Naval Battles
of the
Twentieth Century

I

....

THE BATTLE OF TSU-SHIMA, 26 MAY 1905

By 1900 the eastward expansion of the Tsarist Russian Empire had reached the Pacific and, in extending its influence into Manchuria, Russia sought the eviction of Japan from its occupation of Port Arthur, an ice-free port on the Yellow Sea. Japan, a rapidly rising imperial power in the Far East, had fought a war with China between 1894-95 largely to gain a hold over the lucrative trade of the decaying Chinese Empire. Victory had left Port Arthur in Japanese hands, but pressure from Russia, with diplomatic support from Germany and France, forced Japan to relinquish it. The Russians next persuaded China to lease Port Arthur and the Dairen Peninsula to them, chiefly to enable their navy to supplement its main base at Vladivostok. The Russian position was further strengthened by the Boxer Rebellion of 1900, in which the Chinese sought to oust all foreigners from their country, but which, in the end, exacted punishing retribution from all the western powers and Japan, and left Russian troops in Manchuria. Japan for her part dominated Korea and considered Manchuria within her own sphere of influence. Humiliated by her eviction from Port Arthur, she viewed the presence of a Russian army in Manchuria with suspicion. During protracted negotiations Japan secured an alliance with Great Britain and an understanding that the Russians would withdraw their troops by 1903. Moscow defaulted on this promise, providing the Japanese with the pretext to make their surprise attack on Russian naval vessels at Port Arthur on February 8, 1904, precipitating the Russo-Japanese War of 1904-1905.

Command of the sea was vital to the Japanese, and the annihilation of Russia's naval forces was paramount. A cruiser squadron operating from Vladivostok inflicted considerable damage on Japanese supply routes, but Admiral Togo succeeded brilliantly in neutralizing the Russian navy in the Far East. While the opposing armies slaughtered each other on land, the Tsar dispatched the Baltic Fleet to regain Russian sea power in the Far East. Admiral Rozhestvensky' ships steamed 18,700 miles to meet their nemesis at Tsu-shima – the first steam battle-fleet to be replenished at sea, by colliers hired from the German navy. It was to be their only achievement. Togo's fleet annihilated the Russian navy and the Tsar, faced with revolution at home, accepted the American offer to mediate the peace. The Treaty of Portsmouth was signed in New Hampshire in December 1906.

·····················

ONE HUNDRED YEARS after victory at the Battle of Trafalgar had given Great Britain control of the seas, there took place on the other side of the world one of the most decisive sea battles of all times. The victors, this time, were the Japanese.

Japan, historically a shut-off and secretive nation, had come out into the real world less than fifty years earlier. In 1867 the Shogunate was abandoned and the Emperor was returned to his divine status. At the same time Japan followed the Western policy of nationalistic imperial aggression. Formosa was annexed in 1894, and the economy of Korea was dominated by Japan. Industries, also based on Western practice, sprang up. Men-of-war were ordered from British yards, and when they arrived in Japan were closely studied and imitated. Guns of all calibres were made at the new ordnance shops.

Training of officers and men, and their ranks and uniforms, were based on the British way, too. Emulating Western practice, there developed in Japan a lust for expansion, for imperialism. In Japan's case there was some justification because, like Britain, the Japanese islands were overcrowded and a foothold on the Asian land mass would relieve some of the pressure. The war with China in the 1890s was an overture to the more formidable and risky enterprise against Russia.

The Imperial Japanese Navy's Commander-in-Chief was Admiral Heihachiro Togo. He was a fierce and feared officer, dedicated to his service and the Mikado, a patriot respected by all those serving under him, but much loved by them, too.

Like many Japanese naval officers, Togo was sent to England, which possessed the largest and most admired navy in the world, for his training. Here Togo learned not only the language but about Britain's naval heroes of the past, and especially Horatio Nelson, whose flagship, *Victory*, he visited in Portsmouth harbour. Thereafter, Togo based his strategic and tactical principles on those of the great master. He spent two years as a cadet on board the three-masted sailing ship *Worcester*. This was followed by a round-the-world cruise on board the training ship *Hampshire*, with a long spell ashore at Melbourne, Australia. He then returned to London by Cape Horn, completing a voyage of 30,000 miles.

Togo concluded his studies at Cambridge University and was about to return home when a signal from Japan ordered him to monitor the construction of one of the first warships to be ordered from Britain, the *Fuso*, building at Poplar on the River Thames.

This he did, learning a great deal, but it delayed his return, on the completed *Fuso*]r[, until February 1878. He had been away seven years, and in his absence his country had been transformed from a feudal society into a modern industrial state.

Togo rose swiftly in the infant Japanese Imperial Navy. He became C.-in-C. by the time of the Sino-Japanese war, and witnessed the Japanese Army's bloody capture of Port Arthur, Korea, the most northerly ice-free port in eastern Asia. He also took note of the Russian and international pressure exerted on his country to pull out. It was, therefore, with great keenness that Togo participated in the staff talks making plans for all-out war against Russia. Nothing could be done, he was told, without gaining control of the sea. Togo planned to do this in early 1904 with one knock-out blow. He intended to rely on a new weapon of sea power — the torpedo boat and the British-designed Whitehead torpedo. He had plenty of both, and he intended to use a third weapon, that of surprise. His objective was Port Arthur.

Briefing his commanders, he told them, 'We sail tomorrow, and our enemy flies the Russian flag.' Then to his torpedo boat commanders, 'Show yourselves worthy of the confidence I place in you. We go in at 10.30 at night on 8th February.'

And so they did, just as a later Japanese C.-in-C., Admiral Yamamoto, descended upon Pearl Harbor almost half a century later, also without warning but using bombs and airborne torpedoes.

The Russian men-of-war had all their lights blazing and Togo took the precaution of using the Russian signal code to reassure the enemy. Neither the shore batteries nor the ships' guns were manned, and the first wave of torpedoes was delivered at point-blank range. When they withdrew, two of Russia's best battleships and a heavy cruiser were crippled. The next day Togo, firing at maximum range, bombarded the surviving ships, damaging four more.

The Imperial Japanese Navy now controlled the seas about her coast, allowing her armies to be reinforced and equipped with the supplies to keep them in the field in Manchuria and Korea. In August 1904 the Russian Fleet twice ventured to sea, and on both occasions was discovered and defeated by Togo's excellent gunnery.

To set against these successes, Togo suffered the misfortune of losing two of his battleships on a minefield, depriving him of one-third of his front-line strength.

Shortly after this catastrophe, word reached the Japanese High Command that more ships were leaving the Baltic Sea in Europe to reinforce Russian naval strength in the Far East.

The Imperial Russian Navy at the beginning of the century was divided into three commands. These were the Far East Fleet, operating out of Vladivostok and Port Arthur, but now neutralized by Admiral Togo. There was another force in the Black Sea to protect the Crimea and southern Russia. And finally there was the Baltic Fleet, with its bases at Kronstadt, Reval and Libau.

After the Russian naval failures against Japan, the Tsar and the Russian High Command determined to dispatch the Baltic Fleet halfway round the world to 'wipe the infidels off the face of the earth', as Tsar Nicholas expressed his instructions. The timing of this reinforcement was decided by the completion of four battleships of the newest type. They were the *Suvoroff*, *Alexander III*, *Borodino* and *Oryol*. On paper these were formidable men-of-war of 15,000 tons, armed with four twelve-inch guns, capable of firing shells to a range of ten miles. There were numerous smaller-calibre guns to beat off torpedo boat attack; and to resist enemy shellfire there was ten-inch-thick hardened steel armour plate on the ships' waterline and other vulnerable parts. All four battleships could sustain a speed of eighteen knots.

These battleships formed the core of what was now grandly named the Second Pacific Squadron. But the rest of he fleet was made up of heterogeneous warships, most of great age and of doubtful use in battle. The men who were to man them were equally ineffective, or worse than that — revolutionary. Marxism had taken a strong hold on Russia's armed services, and mutinous mutterings were heard long before the Second Pacific Squadron sailed.

The Tsar of Russia had selected Admiral Zinovi Petrovich Rozhestvensky as C.-in-C. of this Second Pacific Squadron. Born in 1848, and therefore a year younger than Admiral Togo, Rozhestvensky was a tall, impressive figure with a fine record, including combat in the Black Sea, where he had acquitted himself bravely and skilfully. He was also renowned for his administrative powers. He would need all these in abundance if he was to complete his task successfully. His commission was, no less, to prepare a fleet of some forty-five vessels not including the attendant auxiliaries. Then to sail it over a distance of 18,000 miles, link up with what remained of the Far Eastern Fleet, and then seek out and destroy Admiral Togo's fleet.

There was no precedent for such a task, even with a well-equipped fleet manned by experienced officers and men, with coaling bases *en route* and a secure anchorage at its destination. The British Navy had set up coaling stations all over the world to feed the appetite of its far-flung men-of-war protecting its world-wide possessions. Rozhestvensky would have to make rendezvous with colliers in sheltered waters.

Reflecting his undeterrable optimism, the Admiral announced to the world that he would sail on 15 July 1904. 'But of course this is going to be a long voyage taking many weeks, and there will be nothing for me to do in the Far East by September. The Japanese will have capitulated long before then.'

The reality was not so rosy. By the end of September, Rozhestvensky ordered a period of manoeuvres and gunnery drill in the Baltic for those of his vessels that were ready, and many were not. One of the manoeuvres included a dummy night torpedo attack. Rozhestvensky's report the following morning suggested that Admiral Togo had little to fear from this huge armada:

> Today at 2 a.m. I instructed the officer-of-the-watch to issue the signal for defence against a torpedo attack. Eight minutes afterwards there was no sign of anyone taking up his station. All officers and men were sound asleep. And when at last a few hands of the watch did appear, what did they do? Nothing. It seemed that they did not know where to go, nor was there a single searchlight ready for use.

Almost a hundred similar orders were issued. The results gave little encouragement to the C.-in-C., but the departure of the Second Pacific Squadron could be delayed no longer. The ships returned to port, first to take on supplies, and then to be painted and polished for inspection by their 'most gracious Majesties', the Tsar and Tsarina. Knowing nothing of the problems that lay ahead and the unfitness of the fleet for the long journey, let alone its battle-worthiness, the people of Russia were excited beyond measure about the departure of the 'fleet of revenge'. This was to be a crusade against the 'infidels of the east' who had dared to challenge the might of Imperial Russia.

There followed a flurry of ship inspections, cries of 'Long live your Imperial Majesties', farewell banquets and the consumption of much champagne (by the officers) and vodka by the men.

At last, on 8 October 1904, Rozhestvensky gave orders for the departure. As the Second Pacific Squadron made its way across the North Sea, restlessness and mutiny were the preoccupations of the lower deck; among the officers, from Rozhestvensky down, superstition governed their feelings. In the weeks before their departure, there had been alarming reports from neutral nations, Norway and Denmark in particular, of the arrival of flotillas of Japanese torpedo boats intent on intercepting units of the Russian Fleet and its four new battleships.

Tension approached breaking point when one of Rozhestvensky's scouting ships reported torpedo boats ahead. The *Suvoroff* switched on her searchlights, and the other big ships followed. Soon, the midnight North Sea resembled the scene of a firework party with starshells adding to the display. One of the searchlight beams settled on three small vessels. Without even waiting for orders, the gun barrels followed the searchlight beams and fire was opened at short range. The gun layers concentrated their fire on the largest of the three vessels, the trawler *Crane* of the Gamecock fleet out of Hull and trawling the rich waters of the Dogger Bank.

In a moment the *Crane* began to assume a list. Two of her crew were killed and the rest wounded, some seriously. One of the survivors reported later, 'To show what we were, I held a big plaice up. My mate, Jim Tozer, showed a haddock.' But it would take more than a fish or two to silence these excited gunners.

However, what did cause the battleships to break off the action was serious fire from short range from the cruiser squadron, which had turned through 180 degrees on sighting the gunfire, and had immediately opened fire on its own battleship squadron. At first, Rozhestvensky believed that the Japanese torpedo boats had summoned reinforcements. Then he identified his own cruisers and ordered the buglers to sound the cease-fire. The battleship division steamed away at full speed to the south-west. Rozhestvensky was aware that fishing trawlers had been among their targets, but he and his staff were certain that there had been torpedo boats among them. No doubt the British, who were sympathetic to the Japanese cause, had encouraged the torpedo boat flotillas to blend in with the Dogger Bank fishing fleets.

The Russian gun crews could scarcely contain their excitement and satisfaction. They had been blooded. They had engaged the enemy and won. The battered Gamecock trawler fleet had lifted the morale of the Second Pacific Squadron to an unexpected high level. It was not until the squadron reached Vigo in Spain that they learned that they were the cause of an international crisis. Here in the wide harbour they had a rendezvous with colliers bearing their life-blood — coal. But the Spaniards were having none of it. It was contrary to international law for warships of a belligerent nation to remain in a neutral port for longer than twenty-four hours, and it was also forbidden to replenish stores of any kind, including coal.

Rozhestvensky went ashore to protest, but the Spanish authorities were unbending. He returned with nothing but newspapers. All told of the international crisis brought about by the action in the North Sea. Britain was on the verge of war, and to confirm this there, clearly visible, were ships of the Royal Navy's Channel Fleet with its power to blow Rozhestvensky's Second Pacific Squadron out of the water.

For forty-eight hours it was touch-and-go, while cables flashed between London and St Petersburg. But then the crisis began to cool. The Spanish Government relented to the point of granting Rozhestvensky permission for the four *Suvoroff*-class battleships to take on 400 tons of coal from the colliers. Disregarding this limit and working through the night, the battleship took on 800 tons, with the reward for every officer and man of two extra tots of vodka.

Shadowed day and night by British men-of-war, Rozhestvensky now worked down the Spanish and Portuguese coasts towards the Straits of Gibraltar. By contrast with their Spanish reception, at Tangier they were warmly received, the Sultan of Morocco being delighted to show his indifference to the politics of the great powers. They could coal at leisure from the colliers that awaited them by prior arrangement. The men went ashore, the senior officers dined with the hierarchy, and everyone felt much better.

This motley collection of warships, headed by the *Suvoroff*, now headed south down the west coast of Africa and into tropical heat that none of these Russian peasant sailors had ever before experienced. Slowly, and with frequent break-downs, the Second Pacific Squadron reached Dakar, where ten colliers awaited them. No less than 30,000 tons of coal had now to be shifted, by lighters and human muscles from colliers to bunkers. The bunker capacity of the *Suvoroff* was 1,100 tons, but all ships were instructed to take on board twice their official tonnage.

The reason Rozhestvensky issued this order was that he had received intelligence that their next two coaling ports, which were French, had been closed to them. He issued three pages of instructions on where the coal was to be stored: on the upper deck, lower deck, gun deck, twelve-inch gun passages, officers' cabins (up to the rank of commander) ... in fact any corner of the ship so long as the engines continued to operate. They could then proceed to their next destination — round the Cape to Madagascar in the Indian Ocean.

Conditions were appalling, life scarcely supportable. The combination of tropical heat, high humidity and the presence of coal dust in every breath they breathed, every mouthful of food, and even in their vodka ration, was almost beyond bearing. Conditions improved slightly as they entered the more temperate region of South Africa, and coal consumption diminished the stocks of coal. When they passed Cape Town and doubled the Cape of Good Hope, they caught tantalizing glimpses of green fields and vineyards.

[

Off Japan, Admiral Togo and his staff were kept well supplied with intelligence of Rozhestvensky's whereabouts. They knew to the day when the Russian Second Pacific Squadron arrived in Madagascar, and how there was a rendezvous with the squadron's detached warships, which had been sent through the Mediterranean and the Suez Canal.

While Admiral Rozhestvensky had been preparing his Second Pacific Squadron in the Baltic, firing on British fishing trawlers in the North Sea, receiving inhospitality from the French and the Spanish, and then working his way for month after month down the African coast, Togo had completed his destruction of the Russian Far East Fleet at the Battle of the Yellow Sea, although this had been a hard-fought engagement and Togo's flagship *Mikasa* had been badly damaged. That victory had taken place in August 1904, shortly before Rozhestvensky's departure from the Baltic. The most specific reports of Russian progress came from Singapore, at that time a British naval base of great importance. Here Japanese observers were welcome, and everyone turned out to watch the astonishing sight of some forty men-of-war of all classes from modern battleships to ancient coastal defence vessels, all belching smoke. It was also possible to make out great stacks of coal on the decks. Many of the ships were not keeping formation, which accounted for their lying so low in the water, the battleships' armoured belt being below the waterline and their secondary armament on the lower gun deck therefore unworkable. The speed of this vast mixed fleet was estimated at no more than five knots. The intelligence cabled back to Japan was therefore favourable, and must have reassured Admiral Togo.

'Poor bastards, they haven't a chance against the Japs!' was the consensus of opinion among the observers.

What these observers could not know was that many of these 'poor bastards' were on the verge of mutiny, and that on one ship at least full-scale mutiny had broken out before the fleet had left Madagascar.

Admiral Togo, in his flagship *Mikasa*, received this latest intelligence at his base, Chin-Hei bay on the south-eastern coast of Korea. Over the preceding months he had refitted his fleet's ships and carried out numerous exercises. His officers and men were cheerful and optimistic, eager to meet this new foe about whom they had heard so much.

Now that Port Arthur was in Japanese hands, the Russians must certainly head for Vladivostok, where lay the few surviving men-of-war, Togo calculated. The Russians were most unlikely, Togo figured, to follow a route on the Pacific side of Japan, which would entail a much longer journey, and therefore the consumption of much more coal. On the assumption that Rozhestvensky would proceed north-east through the Korea Straits, Togo calculated that he could choose his time to intercept and give battle. But intelligence about the Russian Fleet's progress was of vital importance.

Togo formed a 'Special Service squadron' composed of fast merchantmen and a few light cruisers. Each of these Special Service ships had a chart identical to Togo's, which showed the approach marked in numbered squares.

Late in the evening of 26 May 1905, Togo received a faint radio signal from one of these Special Service ships: 'Enemy sighted in square 203 steaming north-east, speed seven knots.'

Meanwhile, Rozhestvensky had sighted at last light on that same day the dim outline of the island of Tsu-Shima, midway between the west coast of Japan and the east coast of Korea. He calculated that if there was a dawn mist he might get his fleet through the Tsu-Shima straits and escape to Vladivostok. However, by contrast with his opponent, his Fleet Order No. 294 was heavy with foreboding and emotion:

I have sworn to God to accomplish my task. He has already strengthened and has in His infinite mercy protected us in the stress of the operations we have already accomplished. I pray that God may strengthen my right hand, and if I fail to fulfil the oath I have sworn, He may purge my country from shame with my blood.

The C.-in-C. stayed up late on the bridge of the *Suvoroff*, peering into the darkness ahead, but was at length prevailed upon to sleep in an armchair on the bridge. On paper, the Japanese fleet was greatly inferior to Rozhestvensky's. Against the *Suvoroff* and her three sister ships, all of them fitted with the latest equipment and twelve-inch guns, Togo had only his flagship *Mikasa* as a modern battleship. Togo's strength lay in his cruisers, which were numerous, armoured, fast and fitted with six-inch and eight-inch guns. In numbers, the Russian fleet was superior by almost two to one, but Rozhestvensky had begun his 18,000-mile voyage with some slow, inferior ships, and had been further burdened by the arrival *en route* of what was grandly called the Third Pacific Squadron, made up of long-obsolete ships which should have gone to the breakers years ago. Instead, they had been refitted and dispatched as unwanted 'reinforcements' for Admiral Rozhestvensky, whose fleet would be further slowed as a consequence.

The entire Japanese fleet was sighted on the starboard bow shortly before 1.30 p.m. on 26 May 1905, steaming at a higher speed than Rozhestvensky could ever achieve and on an opposite course to the Russian Fleet. But as the Russian commander studied the units of the fleet he had been sent to destroy, they suddenly turned starboard ninety degrees, impudently crossing the Russians' line. In rising seas and clear visibility, the Japanese, led by Togo's *Mikasa*, then turned to port together until they were on an identical course to Rozhestvensky's. The Russian admiral had never before witnessed such immaculate station-keeping in an evolution of great complexity.

At 1.55 p.m. the two fleets were uncompromisingly committed to battle. There was now no question of the Russians' steaming off to reach Vladivostok, and no question of the Japanese

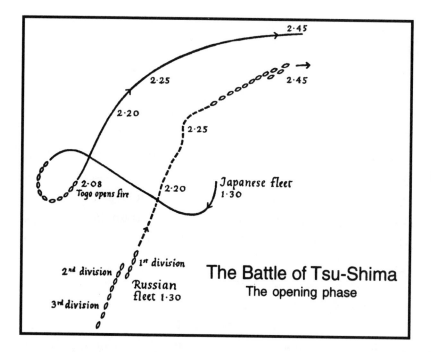

The Battle of Tsu-Shima
The opening phase

failing to intercept Rozhestvensky's fleet. Gunnery would be the final arbiter, together with a measure of luck, good or bad.

The first surprise to both admirals was the high quality of the Russian shooting. All four of the Russian *Suvoroff*-class battleships ranged with unexpected accuracy with their twelve-inch guns on the vanguard of Togo's fleet while it was still completing its 180-degree turn. Some ten minutes passed, during which time the Japanese guns were masked by their own ships, while the Russian gunners were presented with the leading Japanese ships in turn and at the same range.

The Russian gunners took full advantage of this situation, and at length both sides were committed to a gunnery duel while steaming on roughly parallel lines.

'This was the scenic part of the battle,' wrote a Royal Navy observer on board the *Mikasa*. 'Two long lines of ships attacking one another vigorously, formations as yet unbroken, and the fate of the day seemed to hang on every shot.'

To the unconcealed admiration of the crew of the *Mikasa*, this British observer, Commander W. C. Pakenham, RN, had sat in a deck-chair on the quarter-deck of the flagship, jotting down notes with supreme insouciance and regardless of the flying shell fragments. When he was seen to go below at the height of the fighting, his shirt covered in blood, it was assumed he had had enough. Not a bit of it; he had returned to his cabin to change his shirt and generally spruce himself up, then returned to his deck-chair. The blood originated from a Japanese sailor killed close to him.

After the battle the Mikado ordered Admiral Togo to send to him the bravest man on the flagship. Without further thought, the admiral produced Pakenham, or 'Paks' to his friends.

By contrast with this Royal Navy officer, Admiral Rozhestvensky went into battle in the armour-plated conning-tower of the *Suvoroff*. It was only ten feet in diameter but had all the equipment to handle the ship, and the fleet. Secure passage, at least from flying shell splinters, to the bridge below and the ship's upper deck, was ensured by a steel tube, lined with ladder rungs. Peering through his binoculars from this conning-tower, the Admiral watched with satisfaction the effect of his fleet's fire as the Japanese line completed its 180-degree turn.

A few minutes later, after a few sighting shots, serious Japanese fire opened until the whole line, led by the *Mikasa*, sparkled from end to end with the muzzle flashes of some five hundred guns. The Japanese gunners' aim was sublime, one over, one short, then, splitting the difference on the range-finders, a hit. The Japanese were clearly concentrating their fire on the *Suvoroff* and the leading ship of the second division, the old

Oslyabya. These bore the brunt of the fire from twelve-inch, eight-inch and six-inch shells.

The conning-tower of the *Suvoroff* was twice hit by shells. The heavy armour prevented them from penetrating, but splinters entered through the narrow sighting port and screamed round and round, killing the helmsman and the senior flag gunnery officer at his range-finder, and wounding several other officers and Rozhestvensky himself. As the Japanese Fleet closed the range, 'bending' the Russian line to starboard, there was only one way to avoid annihilation: this was to cut behind the Japanese and, in doing so, concentrate fire on the tail-end of the Japanese line, and with luck then escape north.

Now it was too late. Togo had succeeded in accomplishing the classic tactical movement of 'crossing the T' of his enemy. At the same time, he ordered the firing of armour-piercing

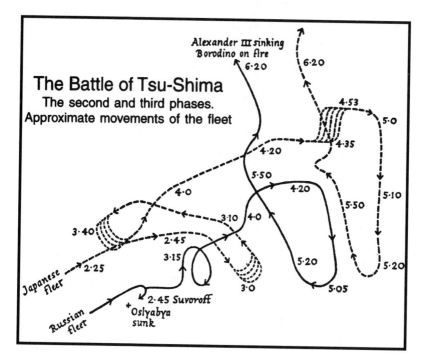

The Battle of Tsu-Shima
The second and third phases.
Approximate movements of the fleet

Alexander III sinking
Borodino on fire
6·20

shells. At 2.20 p.m. the range was now little more than a mile, and almost every shell found its target. The *Suvoroff* was hit time and again, with fires breaking out from stem to stern. There was no point in Rozhestvensky remaining in the conning-tower and being roasted alive. A twelve-inch shell hit on the stern had jammed the rudder hard to starboard. All the signal halyards had been destroyed, preventing the last means of communicating with the fleet. Rozhestvensky, wounded again by splinters in the head, the back and right leg, was helped by surviving members of his staff to the escape hatch. But how could the half-conscious Admiral negotiate the rails for thirty feet?

With an officer leading the way and another at the Admiral's head, they somehow managed to drag Rozhestvensky down the tube without any thought for his dignity, and in spite of the smoke and choking fumes from the fires got him on to the upper deck, and then carried him into a disabled six-inch gun turret. They laid him on the steel base of the turret. After a few moments the Admiral recovered consciousness, and even above the sound of the fires cried out clearly and angrily, in a voice that was all too familiar, 'Why aren't the guns firing? — man the guns instantly.' Another hit near by provoked Rozhestvensky's relapse into unconsciousness again.

The *Suvoroff* was not the first to go down. It was the old *Oslyabya* which capsized, exposing its red barnacle-covered bottom and then disappearing, giving no chance of escape to the engine-room crew, all two hundred of them. The *Suvoroff*'s three sister ships were in a bad way but were still able to fire some of their guns and keep the enemy at bay.

From the quarter-deck of the *Mikasa*, Pakenham took note of every shell hit on the Russian battleships. Of the *Suvoroff* he wrote,

Her condition seemed infinitely deplorable. Smoke curling round the stern rolling horizontally away on the wind. If the absence of funnels contributed much to her air of distress, the now extensive conflagration raging amidships showed its reality. Less than half the ship can have been habitable; yet she fought on.

He also observed a destroyer almost alongside the wretched flagship as if about to give her the *coup de grâce*. Then the *Mikasa* drew away and Pakenham lost sight of the outcome. The destroyer was in fact Russian, the *Buiny*, and she had been summoned to take off the gravely wounded C.-in-C. This was accomplished with the utmost difficulty and against the protests of Rozhestvensky himself.

When the destroyer drew away, the surviving senior officer remaining on board was Midshipman Werner von Kursel, a young man of immense courage. He brought fresh spirit to the fire-fighters and manned the remaining undamaged gun, a 75mm quick-firer. He used this so effectively that when a division of Japanese destroyers approached like hungry curs, he fended them off, giving the *Suvoroff* a longer life by a few hours.

She went down at last at seven o'clock as the mist and dusk closed in, her fires extinguished at last by the waters of the Tsu-Shima straits. Not a man on board survived.

The only incident of luck that Rozhestvensky experienced in the battle was the passage north in darkness unmolested through the entire Japanese fleet. At dawn, they chanced upon three of the few survivors of the Russian Fleet, the old cruiser *Donskoy*, and two destroyers, one of them with two hundred survivors from a Russian battleship packed on board.

The Russian Admiral's luck was compounded by the destroyer's lack of coal. Coal! That black mineral which had been their enemy long before they had arrived in Japanese waters. They would never have reached Vladivostok with the amount left in the *Buiny's* bunkers. Rozhestvensky was therefore painfully transferred to the destroyer *Bedovyi*, which had adequate fuel for the dash north. But almost at once the remnants of the Russian Fleet were intercepted by two Japanese destroyers which opened accurate fire while the Russian destroyer and the *Buiny* made off at top speed.

Rozhestvensky had lapsed into a coma again, and his chief of staff calculated that, in his admiral's condition, the vibration of the *Bedovyi* at full knots would kill him. He therefore ordered a white flag to be hoisted and the Russian national flag to be hauled down. While one of the Japanese destroyers pursued the two fleeing Russian ships, at the same time firing at them, the second destroyer hove to and launched a boat.

The Russian crew were alarmed to observe that the Japanese lieutenant in command had unsheathed his sword. When he leapt on to the *Bedovyi* he ran straight for the wireless aerials which he slashed down in a series of strokes. This same lieutenant was astonished to discover that the C.-in-C. of the Russian Fleet was on board this little destroyer, which was now nominally the flagship. As almost all the forty other ships were already at the bottom of the sea, this could be called an annihilating victory.

The destroyer *Bedovyi*, now flying the Japanese flag, was later towed into the Japanese port of Sasebo. There Rozhestvensky was carried ashore, half conscious with a bloody towel wrapped round his head, and a bandage round his right foot where he had suffered a ruptured nerve as well as a broken bone.

Rozhestvensky was treated with great respect by the Japanese authorities. In the naval hospital, after a period of rest, a surgeon operated on the wound in his head, extracting a sliver of bone from his broken skull. With his tough constitution, Rozhestvensky recovered rapidly, cheered by a message from the Tsar:

> I heartily thank you and all the members of your squadron who have loyally fulfilled your duty in battle for your service to Russia and myself. It was God's will not to give you success, but the country is proud of your courage. I wish you a speedy recovery. May God console all of us.

Admiral Togo, now an even greater hero in his country, paid his respects to his old enemy. 'You performed your great task valiantly until you were incapacitated,' he told him.

At length, when Rozhestvensky was strong enough, he was released and took the long journey overland back to St Petersburg.

The Battle of Tsu-Shima decided the conclusion of the Russo-Japanese war in Japan's favour. Japan took her place as a major naval power, which she retained until 1945; while Russia lost for the same period her status as a great naval power.

Admiral Rozhestvensky, on returning home, was retired on a generous pension and survived until 1909, a forgotten and tragic figure.

2

···

THE BATTLES OF CORONEL
AND THE FALKLAND ISLANDS,
1 NOVEMBER 1914
AND 7 DECEMBER 1914

At the outbreak of the First World War, Great Britain's world-wide trade, carried in her vast merchant fleet, was vulnerable to destruction by surface raiders as well as the new submarine. The concept of a war against trade was well established and, in the days of sail, had been successfully countered by sailing merchant ships in convoy. Convoy was not introduced by the British until 1917, by which time Germany's submarine war had almost reduced to her knees what had been the world's pre-eminent sea-power. In 1914, however, the submarine had yet to prove its effectiveness, and commerce raiding was carried out largely by cruisers.

In peacetime, used singly or in squadrons, cruisers traditionally exerted influence in their own national interest, and in China most European powers maintained a number in the Treaty Ports they had extorted from the ramshackle Chinese Empire. One such German squadron was based in Tsingtau on the Shantung Peninsula. Commanded by von Spee, in August 1914 it lay in the Caroline Islands, poised to adopt a predatory role and fall upon the extensive trade of Great Britain.

The British position was more complex. The cruisers of the Royal Navy, while directed to destroy enemy trade, were also required to protect British merchant shipping. This was an awesome responsibility, with a multitude of laden ships plying the trade routes of the extensive British Empire, many of which were still sailing vessels. British interests, moreover, went beyond the frontiers of empire; there was heavy investment in South America, and consequently British merchantmen plied the waters of the Pacific and South Atlantic Oceans. This world-wide commitment required the deployment of numerous British cruisers, many of increasing obsolescence, such as those under Craddock which, in October 1914, left the Falkland Islands and steamed into the South Pacific.

Although not a major maritime power, Germany, had, in addition to her interests in China, major trading links with South America, in particular Chile. Von Spee had also been warned that, under the terms of the Anglo-Japanese treaty, Japan would enter the war and render his position at Tsingtau untenable. Thus, having crossed the Pacific to the Chilean coast, on November 1, 1914, von Spee fell upon Craddock's squadron off Coronel.

The German victory caused a furious reaction in London, where a squadron of battle-cruisers under Sturdee was sent south to extract vengeance for this humiliation. A month later, Sturdee caught von Spee off the Falklands.

....

AT THE OUTSET OF the war of 1914—18 the world's oceans suddenly became dangerous, to men-of-war and commercial traffic alike. From his base at Scapa Flow in the Orkney Islands off the north coast of Scotland, Admiral Sir John Jellicoe attempted to impose a blockade on Germany with his Grand Fleet, while the German High Seas Fleet was content to remain in its base at Kiel and Wilhelmshaven — 'a Fleet in Being'. The only other German base outside the homeland was on the other side of the world, at Tsingtau in China. Here was stationed the German East Asiatic Squadron composed of modern armoured cruisers of high speed and heavy gunpower. This squadron posed a serious threat to the trade of Britain and her allies in the vast wastes of the Pacific and Indian Oceans.

The Commander-in-Chief of this squadron was Vice-Admiral Maximilian Graf von Spee, a Prussian of ancient descent who had grown up, like Admiral Togo, during the years of industrial, colonial and military expansion of the newly unified German nation. Also like Togo, he had been drawn to the sea as a boy at a time when the Navy was a small coastal force, but saw it grow around him as he rose through the ranks. The explanation Germany offered to the outside world for this growth was that she required an ocean-going navy for the protection of her colonies. These colonies were expanding at a great rate, to the consternation of the old imperialists, France and Britain. Spee himself, as a young lieutenant, took part in one of Germany's great acquisitions, that of South-West Africa.

By the last years of the nineteenth century Kaiser Wilhelm II was turning his eyes to farther horizons, to China and the islands of the Pacific. Like the other European powers and Japan, Germany relied on a blend of cunning, diplomacy and sheer force to acquire concessions or colonies. Having 'acquired' dozens of islands including the Solomons and a great number north of New Guinea, which were honoured with the collective title the Bismarck Archipelago, what was now urgently needed was a base for men-of-war to protect this German Pacific empire. The French had acquired Tonkin for this purpose, the British Hong Kong.

After much consideration and exploration, the Germans settled on Shantung Province with its Bay of Kiaochau and its port of Tsingtau. This choice was enhanced by the discovery of mineral wealth inland. Germany therefore insisted that the ninety-nine-year concession wrung out of the Chinese include the right to build a railway system to service the mines.

Germany then set about developing Shantung with the same Teutonic efficiency and speed as she had displayed in South-West Africa and the numerous Pacific islands. Spee was a witness to these hectic activities when he was serving aboard SMS *Deutschland*, the flagship of the first German Pacific Squadron to arrive in China under the command of the Kaiser's son, Prince Heinrich.

Later, Spee saw action for the first time in what came to be known as the Boxer Rebellion. The German Ambassador in Peking had been assassinated, and the nationals of Germany, Britain, France, Russia, America and Japan were all besieged in the British Legation. The fighting to relieve them was intense and long.

Meanwhile, on his return to Germany, Spee was promoted Captain and given command of a new battleship. He was now a married man with two boys who were to follow in their father's profession. Spee in middle age was an impressive figure, tall and erect with a neatly trimmed beard and moustache, both going white, and piercing blue eyes that missed nothing.

At the end of 1912, Count Maximilian von Spee, now a vice-admiral, was appointed to command the South-East Asia Squadron, an enviable post indeed. After a short time at Tsingtau, in order to settle into his appointment, he arranged for his two sons, Count Otto and Count Heinrich, to join him from Germany. Heinrich served in his flagship, Otto in the light

Nürnberg. The flagship was SMS *Scharnhorst*, named after the great Prussian reformer of the Army. The *Scharnhorst* represented the ultimate in her class of armoured cruiser, faster than any battleship and capable of destroying with her 8.2-inch guns any other cruiser. The only British man-of-war capable of catching and destroying her was the new battle-cruiser, the 'greyhound of the seas', but these were needed in home waters as an integral squadron of the British Grand Fleet.

Under Spee's command was a sister ship, the *Gneisenau*, and three very fast and modern light cruisers, capable of about twenty-five knots and armed with the quick-firing and highly effective 4.1-inch gun. These five ships made a homogenous and formidable squadron, whose duties included protecting German interests in the Pacific, putting down any native insurrection, and in time of war pursuing and capturing or destroying enemy merchantmen.

During the two years and eight months of peace after Spee hoisted his flag as Commander-in-Chief, the squadron was brought to a peak of efficiency, winning the German Navy's prize for accurate long-range shooting for two years in succession. In July 1914, word reached Spee that there was a serious crisis back home in Europe. Then in early August he received a cable informing him that a state of war existed between the Central Powers (Germany and Austro-Hungary) and the Allied forces of France, Britain and her empire, and the Russian Empire.

Maximilian von Spee had for long expected and prepared for this event. It was, after all, the culminating point of his professional career. He was on a training cruise with his squadron at the time, and had arrived at Ponapé in the Caroline Islands when the message about the outbreak of hostilities was received. He was also alerted to the ominous news that Japan was likely to enter the war on the Allies' side — as indeed it did on 23 August. In the ten years since the Russo-Japanese war, Japan had built or purchased a major fleet. There was, therefore, no question of Spee returning to Tsingtau. Now without a base, he decided to head for the west coast of South America where, he knew, Chile was sympathetic to the German cause and he would doubtless find plenty of plunder in the form of British shipping. Partly in order to deceive the enemy of his intentions, Spee detached the light cruiser *Emden* and a collier with instructions to disrupt British shipping in the Indian Ocean. He then set forth on his lonely and anxious voyage south-east across the Pacific with his supply ships and colliers, taking a roundabout route, from time to time detaching one of his light cruisers both to pick up supplies and to confuse the enemy.

The *Nürnberg* saucily steamed into the American naval base at Honolulu and negotiated, with some difficulty, to take on coal. The armoured cruisers anchored off Bora Bora in the Society Islands and took on fresh fruit. They then daringly headed for Papeeté, the capital of French Tahiti. Here, though, they heard for the first time guns fired in anger.

The French authorities had been warned of the possible arrival of enemy warships, and the defending batteries in the hills above the town were manned. Nor, when they opened fire, was the aim bad. The first salvoes straddled the *Scharnhorst* and Spee ordered return fire. Within two minutes all the guns had been destroyed. The armoured cruisers now closed the harbour, where they were met by a French gunboat, the *Zélé*. The 8.2-inch guns opened fire at point-blank range, and in a few moments she, too, had been destroyed.

This event, this 'victory', cheered the German crews beyond the reality of the destruction of a few old coast defence guns and the sinking of a 600-ton gunboat. But with the 'Battle of Tahiti' behind them, everyone looked forward to bigger prey. After rendezvousing with the *Nürnberg* at the Marquesas Islands, Spee again headed south-east for lonely Easter Island, one thousand miles off the coast of Chile. Here they could coal from their colliers in a sheltered bay, and communicate with German agents at Valparaiso. Better than that, they learned that another light cruiser, the *Dresden*, which had been operating in the Atlantic, was on its way to reinforce Spee, and that the *Leipzig* which he had detached earlier, was hastening south to rejoin him.

Thanks to the German agents, and the efficiency of German radio, Spee also learned of the arrival in the Pacific from the Falkland Islands of a British naval force dispatched to search for him. The ships were named, but not the commander of this hostile squadron. His reference books could tell Spee the details of the ships, but not of the C.-in-C. Refreshed and coaled, Spee departed from Easter Island with its giant, sinister statues, and continued his odyssey south-east.

Rear-Admiral Sir Christopher ('Kit') Cradock had much in common with Vice-Admiral Count Maximilian von Spee. They were born within a year of one another, had advanced in step up the promotion ladder and had similar temperaments and also similar appearances. Both wore full beards, Cradock's darker than his counterpart's, both had piercing blue eyes. Moreover they were well acquainted with one another. As young lieutenants they had fought side by side in an international force putting down an insurrection in China. They were both in the thick of the fighting, and Cradock was later given a German decoration for his bravery.

Cradock's courage was further confirmed on the hunting field, where he went straight at the fences with almost rash abandon. He used to say that there were two ways he would be glad to die — 'Breaking my neck on the hunting field, or at sea in battle.'

Cradock regarded himself as a lucky man, at least until the outbreak of war in 1914, when he seemed suddenly to be deprived of it. He was serving as C.-in-C. of the North America and West Indies Station. His responsibilities were heavy, but he was ill equipped to carry them out. His flagship was the *Good Hope*. He had under his command another old armoured cruiser, the *Monmouth*, armed with six-inch guns, and dating back to 1903, and a fast and modern light cruiser, the *Glasgow*.

Cradock's first duty after the declaration of war was to protect the large convoys of Canadian troops for France which began to leave Halifax within weeks. His only likely protagonists were two German light cruisers, the *Karlsruhe* and *Dresden*, both similar to Spee's light cruisers in the Pacific. Cradock, only weeks earlier, had been working harmoniously with the officers and men of these ships, protecting German and British citizens caught up in the Mexican revolution.

Now the hunt was on for the two German cruisers. Less well informed by agents ashore than Spee, Cradock was told that the *Dresden* was off New York when she was in fact off the Amazon estuary *en route* to the Pacific to reinforce Spee. Cradock came close to catching the *Karlsruhe*, but she was faster than all his ships and fled among the West Indies islands at a stunning twenty-seven knots. She never was caught but was blown up by an internal explosion. No one learned about that at the time, so she remained a threat.

Then Cradock had surprising orders from the Admiralty in

London. He was to quit the Atlantic altogether, proceed down the South Atlantic to the Falkland Islands, await reinforcements, then proceed into the Pacific, seek out the German East Asiatic Squadron and destroy it.

Cradock, therefore, made his way south, but his bad luck continued implacably. He tried to coal in the estuary of the River Plate but was delayed by terrible weather. When he cabled the Admiralty in London asking what reinforcements he could expect, he was informed that a modern armoured cruiser, the *Defence*, would be sent to join him at Port Stanley in the Falkland Islands. Greatly cheered by this news, Cradock headed south to rendezvous with his reinforcement. *En route* he was told that Spee's squadron was no longer a menace and he should therefore proceed to the Pacific and attack German shipping. But the only German shipping was Spee's supply ships and his colliers. Nor did the Admiralty bother to inform Cradock that the *Defence* had been diverted elsewhere. But they did inform him that a battleship was hurrying to the Falklands as a heavy reinforcement.

The Admiralty's intelligence had again been at fault. Far from retiring west to Australian waters, as they had been wrongly informed, Spee was already off the Chilean coast, taking on supplies at Valparaiso before heading south with the intention of doubling Cape Horn and then heading north-east to destroy the British base at Port Stanley. It was at Port Stanley that Cradock had been ordered to await his battleship. He did so, but with increasing impatience as rumour told him that Spee was certainly not heading west but, as was the case, heading south down the coast of Chile.

On 15 October the captain of the battleship, *Canopus*, sent Cradock a signal saying that he was delayed by serious engine trouble and could manage only eleven knots. Cradock decided to press ahead without her. There was an element of bizarre tragedy in this piece of additional bad luck. As the battleship's Captain Grant was to discover, too late, there was nothing at fault with the battleship's engines. The engineer commander had experienced a nervous breakdown, perhaps caused by the imminence of battle, and had falsified the engine room reports. The *Canopus* could manage at least 16.5 knots, almost her speed when new.

But even at maximum speed, the *Canopus* could not hope to catch up with Cradock, who had passed through the Magellan Straits and was on a northerly course along the fractured coast of southern Chile. Instead, on hearing the news from Port Stanley, the battleship was ordered to follow in his wake while escorting Cradock's supply ships and colliers.

Spee made use of his radio to deceive the enemy. The German admiral ordered complete radio silence except for the light cruiser *Leipzig*, hoping to give the impression that she was the only ship in these waters. The *Glasgow*, commanded by Captain John Luce, which had been detached to the little port of Coronel to glean any available intelligence, was returning to Cradock when the radio operator picked up powerful signals with the call sign of the *Leipzig*. These became so loud that they could only indicate the near proximity of the German cruiser. The time was midday, the date 1 November 1914. Nothing could be seen owing to the thick mist.

To the *Glasgow*'s signalmen the Morse code was resembling machine-gun fire. A few minutes later the mist cleared and revealed a three-funnelled light cruiser. For a moment Captain Luce considered opening fire, but it was his duty first to inform his flagship and then rejoin her at top speed.

But there was more to report than the sighting of an enemy light cruiser. The look-out suddenly reported more heavy smoke — and within seconds, out of it there emerged the dark silhouette of another three-funnelled light cruiser, and two bigger four-funnelled silhouettes. They had found their quarry: the German East Asiatic Squadron was steaming south in heavy seas on a parallel but opposite course to Cradock's squadron.

'General Quarters' was sounded on the *Glasgow*, and on the *Good Hope* and *Monmouth* as soon as Luce's signal was received.

The sighting of the enemy was almost simultaneous on both sides. Spee surveyed the scene with satisfaction. His two armoured cruisers were superior to the enemy's in every department. He was faster, and the weight of his broadside was twice that of the enemy's, whose main-deck six-inch guns would probably not be able to fire in these high seas. He had total confidence in his ships and in his men, who had worked together for more than two years. Moreover, there was no sign of the battleship he had been informed was joining the enemy. If the enemy had the twelve-inch guns of a battleship it could be a tough fight. Without them Spee knew he could sink the lot.

The afternoon sun was low on the horizon, dazzling his gun layers. It was not yet the time to strike, and Spee ordered a turn to port, opening up the range. He could just make out the English squadron countering by attempting to close the range. But the old English ships did not have the speed, and for an hour and a half, through tumultuous seas, which threatened to swamp the light cruisers, the two squadrons thundered south as if afraid to commit themselves while the sun sank lower and lower and at precisely 7 p.m. touched the horizon.

Spee waited two more minutes, while his 8.2-inch gun crews elevated their guns close to the maximum. The range was 12,500 yards. Commander Pochhammer of the *Gneisenau*, whose target was the *Monmouth*, later wrote, 'Not long since we had fraternised with her officers at Hong Kong, and, in all friendliness, drunk the health of our respective sovereigns at meals. Those were happy days. Now we were ready to celebrate again, but only when she had sunk beneath the waves.'

The silhouettes of the English cruisers were now sharply etched against the afterglow of the sunset, while Spee's cruisers were almost lost against the darkness, only the white-topped Andes being clearly visible fifty miles distant. It was the final and devastating piece of Kit Cradock's bad luck.

But why, it was asked time and again after the battle, had Cradock sought battle at all with his vastly superior enemy? The answer must be speculative, but there are many possible reasons. The first is the nature of the man, who was ardent in the pursuit of his duties, and his duty was clear — to seek and destroy Admiral Spee's East Asiatic Squadron. The fact that he had been promised an armoured cruiser at least as powerful as the enemy's armoured cruisers, and then had it withdrawn, to be replaced by an old and hopelessly slow battleship, was exasperating but did not affect the issue.

Then there was the Troubridge precedent. Admiral Sir Thomas Troubridge was second-in-command of the Mediterranean Fleet and had given up the pursuit of a single German battle-cruiser, the *Goeben*, under doubtful circumstances, which had led to his court martial and disgrace.

Perhaps the most likely theory is that Cradock had calculated that, before his own destruction, he might sufficiently damage the enemy's armoured cruisers to make the task of his successor less difficult, and at the same time cause Spee to use up a significant number of his shells, which could not be replaced. Nor did he have any docking facilities if his ships were to be damaged.

In spite of the advantage of light, conditions for accurate gunnery remained appalling, the big ships rolling near to ten degrees. The *Scharnhorst* was the first to open fire, flagship to flagship. From the bridge of the *Glasgow*, Captain Luce watched in awe as the heavy shells fell 500 yards short — at a range of 7.5 miles. The next salvo, which followed less than a minute later, was about the same distance beyond its target. Luce could hardly believe his eyes — one under, one over, and then a hit. It was the classical pattern of gun laying. The hit on the English flagship was on the forecastle, wiping out its 9.2-inch gun and its crew. Cradock now had only one remaining gun capable of firing at this range.

The *Monmouth* was suffering as badly from the *Gneisenau* as the flagship was from the *Scharnhorst*, a great fire amidships telling of her suffering. Nor could she effectively reply. The darkness was complete, the only evidence of the enemy being the gun flashes of her broadsides, half seen through the splashes of near-misses by the enemy's guns.

The *Good Hope* was the first to sink, though no one saw her go down with her crew of 900 officers and men, and the unlucky Admiral.

The *Monmouth*'s fires had somewhat abated meanwhile, but only for the sinister reason that a hit on the waterline had caused an abundance of sea water to pour in. When the shipyard workers were securing the four-inch hardened steel armour back in 1902, they could hardly have credited that a single German shell could have pierced it with such impunity.

Captain Luce, whose *Glasgow* had been fired on by two of the German light cruisers without damage, now brought his ship as close alongside his wrecked cohort as he dared. By signal lamp he asked the *Monmouth*'s captain of her condition. The latter replied that he wanted to get her stern first to the sea because she was making water badly forward.

Some unwounded ratings on the upper deck gathered together and cheered the *Glasgow*. At that moment the scudding clouds cleared to reveal a full moon, like the footlights in a stage melodrama. They also revealed the silhouettes of the German armoured cruisers hastening for the *coup de grâce*. Luce was ordered to leave the wrecked *Monmouth*. With the utmost reluctance, he ordered, 'Hard a starboard, full ahead together.' The clouds closed over the moon, and the little cruiser disappeared into the darkness of the Pacific.

The *Glasgow*'s place alongside the wreck was replaced by the light cruiser *Nürnberg*, her captain demanding that she should lower her flag. She refused to do so, and so the cripple was subjected to a raking fire from stern to stem of 4.1-inch shellfire. Spee's son, Otto, later wrote home to his mother, 'It was dreadful to have to fire on the poor devil no longer able to defend herself, but her flag was still flying.' After a second run, he observed by the light of her fires the armoured cruiser rolling slowly over, revealing keel and red underside, and then she buried herself and her 800 men in the depths of the ocean. The seas were far too high to consider lowering boats for possible survivors.

Making free use of searchlights now that there was no danger, the German Admiral gathered the *Gneisenau* and his smaller cohorts about him in the darkness, and steamed north for Valparaiso. It was close to midnight. At dawn, Spee ordered a victory ceremony. The sun was out, the sea calm. The three light cruisers and the *Gneisenau* hove to in a line while the *Scharnhorst* steamed slowly down the line, the message of her signal halyards reading, 'By the Grace of God, a fine victory. My thanks and good wishes to you all.'

A great cheer rose from the officers and men of his squadron, which the Admiral, in full dress uniform, acknowledged with a salute.

While Spee and his men were celebrating, Luce was making contact with the *Canopus*, fearful that the old battleship would steam north and be found by Spee, who would certainly take on the ship in spite of its twelve-inch guns. Luce rendezvoused with the battleship and its attendant supply ships at noon, and after a conversation between the two captains they all steamed south at economical cruising speed for the western entrance to the Magellan Straits. Halting only to pick up any information or messages at the Chilean port of Punta Arenas, the most southerly town in the Americas, Luce led them north-west to the Falkland Islands.

The Admiralty in London had long since heard the news of Cradock's defeat. The loss of the two armoured cruisers and all their men created a sensation among the British people. They had invested so much money and faith in the Royal Navy, and their expectations were proportionately high. Instead of the great victory at sea, there had been disaster after disaster: the *Emden*, which had been detached by Spee on a raiding mission in the Indian Ocean, had sunk twenty-eight merchantmen with a total tonnage of 58,000 before being sunk herself by an Australian cruiser of superior firepower. In the North Sea, three armoured cruisers were sunk in succession by a U-boat. And now this disaster in the Pacific. The First Sea Lord had already resigned by this time, to be replaced by that old war-horse, that dynamo of energy, Admiral Sir John 'Jacky' Fisher. He owed his appointment to Winston Churchill as First Sea Lord. The two men admired one another and worked well in harness. The moment Fisher heard the first news of Coronel, he recognized that to pursue and annihilate Spee's squadron, armoured cruisers were inadequate. Only battle-cruisers would do the trick.

Fisher detached from the Grand Fleet not one or two but three of its battle-cruisers. Two of them, under the command of Vice-Admiral Doveton Sturdee, were to go down south to the Falkland Islands, and the third, the *Princess Royal*, was to make her way to the Caribbean to intercept Spee if he progressed through the recently opened Panama Canal to raid North Atlantic shipping.

All this was to be carried out at the utmost speed; Fisher was a great hustler. When Sturdee's *Invincible* and *Inflexible* arrived at Devonport from Invergordon to coal, the Admiral Superintendent of the dockyard attempted to carry out some minor engine repairs. Fisher was having nothing of that; the two battle-cruisers were to leave in forty-eight hours, if necessary with dockyard staff on board.

Fisher had emphasized to Admiral Sturdee, too, the need for haste, realizing that if Spee got into the South Atlantic he could cause mayhem to British shipping out of the River Plate and then move north into the Caribbean. But Sturdee was not a hustler; he was a cautious commander, anxious not to strain the engines of his two big ships, to economize on coal and preserve the strengths of his stokers for the combat ahead. He therefore cruised south at the economical speed of ten knots. He topped up his coal at the Portuguese island of St Vincente in the Cape Verde Islands, which lost him twenty-four hours and gave every opportunity for the German agents to report on the presence of the ships, with their names.

Sturdee seemed as unaware of the need for security as he was of that for speed. When he resumed his voyage, he hove to time and again in mid-ocean to halt and search for contraband in neutral vessels. He lost another twelve hours when a target-towing cable wrapped itself around the flagship's propellers. The battle-cruisers were therefore late at the rendezvous with the other ships of his squadron, consisting of three armoured cruisers and two light cruisers, including Captain Luce's *Glasgow*, which were awaiting him at Abrolhos Rocks off the coast of Brazil.

Here Sturdee in the most leisurely manner coaled and shipped stores, then convened a meeting of his commanders. John Luce was the key figure at this meeting, being the only officer who had already fought Spee and escaped. He was convinced that the enemy was even now working his way through the Magellan Straits, and then would head for the Falkland Islands in order to destroy the coal stocks at Port Stanley, and the wireless station. Luce was as clear in his mind as Fisher was that speed was of the essence. When he heard that Sturdee intended to spend three days at this anchorage he was appalled. He returned to the flagship after the meeting had terminated and apologetically and respectfully suggested that they should sail as soon as possible.

'But dammit, Luce,' Sturdee replied, 'we're sailing the day after tomorrow. Isn't that good enough for you, Luce?' It was not, and the difficult meeting ended with Sturdee saying, 'Very well, Luce, we'll sail tomorrow.'

* * *

After enjoying the acclaim of the citizens, especially the German citizens, of Valparaiso, and after taking in stores and coal, Spee, with his force intact, cruised down the west coast of South America, heading for Tierra del Fuego. He had no intention of using the Magellan Straits, where he would certainly be reported by enemy agents in Punta Arenas. Instead he followed the course of Francis Drake in 1778 and met the same strength of storms that the circumnavigator had suffered. One or two of his light cruisers nearly capsized in these high seas because of the weight of the spare coal carried on their upper decks.

It was with immense relief that they threaded their way through the islands of 'the land of fire' and anchored in the Beagle Channel, named by the naturalist Charles Darwin after his ship. Here they anchored, and with an equal lack of urgency as displayed by Sturdee, Spee encouraged his men to go ashore, relax and play football. Spee himself and Captain Maerker of the *Gneisenau* enjoyed themselves botanizing, an enthusiasm of both these German officers.

By 5 December Spee judged it was time to proceed, and he called a meeting of his commanders to discuss plans. He proposed to steam straight for Port Stanley in the Falkland Islands, bombard the wireless station and raise the German flag over the British colony. It would be some sort of recompense for the loss of the German colonies in the Pacific and would provide a great boost to German morale at home. Some of his commanders, including Captain Maerker of the *Gneisenau*, were more cautious. They preferred that they should head at top speed for the River Plate estuary and destroy British trade and then steam north to European waters. They pointed out that they had exhausted almost half their 8.2-inch ammunition at Coronel, and it would be highly unlikely that they would reach home without meeting some opposition. Spee countered that he had picked up signals from the German consul in Punta Arenas confirming that there were no enemy warships in Port Stanley: it was too good an opportunity to miss. He had the final word, and they would clear the Beagle Channel at noon the following day.

Although that one important signal had got through from Punta Arenas, for some reason — perhaps the mountainous nature of Tierra del Fuego or the storm through which they had passed — no other signals had reached the German C.-in-C. Although German consuls and agents from sources as far apart as Valparaiso and Montevideo had full knowledge of a powerful British force, including two battle-cruisers, on its way south, the pricelessly accurate German intelligence before the Battle of Coronel had, this time, utterly failed Spee.

The *Canopus*'s engines, which had earlier been falsely reported as defective, genuinely became so on the passage south with the *Glasgow*. Both ships eventually ended up in Stanley harbour, when the battleship was instructed by the Admiralty to 'moor the ship so that your guns command the entrance ... Be prepared for bombardment from outside the harbour: send down your topmasts.' Her captain was also instructed to arrange observation stations to enable the ships to direct fire by land line on ships outside.

The *Glasgow*, meanwhile, was sent north to rendezvous with the armoured cruisers and light cruisers at Abrolhos Rocks, arriving before the battle-cruisers.

Admiral Sturdee's combined force arrived off Port Stanley at 10.30 a.m. on 7 December. He approved of the measures already taken to defend Port Stanley, although he believed that Spee was still on the Chilean coast as there were no reports of German warships entering the Magellan Straits. But a belated sense of urgency had suddenly overcome Sturdee, and he ordered coaling at once with a view to leaving for the south in forty-eight hours. The light cruisers *Glasgow* and *Bristol* therefore went into the inner harbour where the battleship lay, and the armoured cruisers and battle-cruisers began coaling in the outer harbour.

Nights are short in summer in these latitudes and the look-outs on Spee's ships sighted the outline of the Falklands as early as 2.30 a.m. on 8 December. He then detached the *Gneisenau* and the light cruiser *Nürnberg* to reconnoitre before bringing up the rest of the squadron. Captain Maerker of the *Gneisenau* had been the leading opponent to this enterprise, and it was not long before he was satisfied that he was right. By 9 a.m. the *Gneisenau*'s look-out could see a thick black cloud of smoke, which Maerker interpreted as the burning of coal stocks, but then, five minutes later, Maerker was told that the funnels and masts of warships could be identified. Mile by mile, the news became worse. The next report was chilling and scarcely credible. From the control position high up in the armoured cruiser's foremast, the gunnery officer, with powerful binoculars, identified and reported tripod masts — four of them. Maerker refused to believe the report and told the officer that the nearest battle-cruisers were in the Mediterranean.

Maerker therefore reported to Spee that there were warships in the harbour and that they were probably three 'County'-class cruisers and one light cruiser. Maerker then proceeded on his way, preparing to open fire on the wireless station which was clearly visible on a hill behind the town.

Sturdee, in his report, compared his situation to Drake's on Plymouth Hoe as the Spanish Armada approached: 'Admiral von Spee came at a very convenient hour because I had just finished dressing and was able to give orders to raise steam at full speed and go down to a good breakfast.' This was not strictly true. The colliers were still alongside the battle-cruisers. Two of the armoured cruisers had not started coaling, and only the *Glasgow*, *Carnarvon* and *Kent* were ready to put to sea.

Tactically, there was nothing to prevent the entire German squadron from approaching within gun range and raking Sturdee's ships before they could put to sea, damaging the battle-cruisers and the other cruisers, then retreating south hoping that the weather would close in as it nearly always did in these waters.

If this move was considered by Spee, it was frustrated by the one warship in Stanley harbour that could not put to sea. A look-out on a hill behind the harbour, linked by telephone to the *Canopus*, reported, 'A four-funnelled and two-funnelled man of war in sight SE steering northwards.'

As they approached, the *Canopus*, informed by land line of the range and bearing of the German ships, brought her old twelve-inch guns to maximum elevation, and when the range came down to 11,500 yards, she fired the first salvo, the noise of the discharge shattering the relative silence of the harbour. The two shells, with a total weight of over 6,000 pounds, soared into the early morning sky, and then, by an amazing chance of fate, one of them struck the *Gneisenau* just aft of her fourth funnel. Maerker sheered aside like a whipped horse.

Spee had observed this alarming turn of events from his position five miles astern of Maerker's ship, and immediately cancelled the bombardment and told Maerker not to accept action and to steer east by south and at full speed. Later, all five German cruisers formed up in line ahead and attempted to work up to twenty-two knots.

Looking anxiously astern from the *Scharnhorst*, Spee observed one enemy ship after another emerge from Stanley harbour entrance. Then, to his horror, he identified not one but two battle-cruisers. He knew at once that they had twelve-inch guns and could outpace him by at least five knots. His only salvation from total annihilation lay with the weather, but for the present the sun blazed down and visibility was unlimited.

When Sturdee was clear of Stanley harbour and working up speed to the ship's maximum of twenty-six to twenty-seven knots, he was able to make out Spee's squadron hull down on the southern horizon under a huge pall of black smoke. He ordered that most exciting general signal, 'Chase!', to be hoisted from his flagship. He calculated that he needed only two hours to get the German squadron within range of his twelve-inch guns. Sturdee remained calm and confident during this race, as indeed he had every right to be.

Since time immemorial it had been the custom before a sea battle for the men to wash and don clean clothes in case of being wounded. This was all the more necessary under these circumstances, as many of them were still covered with coal dust. It was equally important for them to have hot food as well as fire in their bellies before action. There was just time for this to be accomplished, and the men were in an excited frame of mind at the prospect of action against an enemy that could hardly hope to win.

Sturdee's three armoured cruisers were doing their utmost to catch up. The *Carnarvon* could not make more than eighteen knots, and the other two were not much faster. Sturdee therefore decided to detach these ships altogether and continue alone at full speed, keeping only the *Glasgow* with him. The battle-cruisers' 'white streaks at stern and the water boiling in their wakes, often higher than the after decks, masses of black oily smoke from the funnels which the many white ensigns showed up in striking contrast', had signalled 'action stations' by noon. At 12.47 the *Invincible* signalled, 'Open fire and engage the enemy.' Their target was the light cruiser *Leipzig*, last in the German line.

Observing calmly from the bridge of the *Scharnhorst*, Spee made the desperate decision to detach his three light cruisers in the hope that they could escape and renew their depredations, while he and Captain Maerker took on the battle-cruisers alone. The term 'self-immolation' would not have crossed his lips, but suicide it was. As soon as they broke away, the commanders of the three light cruisers observed two armoured cruisers and a light cruiser (John Luce's *Glasgow*) following them. The chase had become two chases, while the engine room staff on both sides slaved to find a touch more pressure, giving a knot or two more speed.

The fight between the four big ships took on the nature of a classic gunnery duel, the first and the last in the war unimpeded by mines, submarine torpedoes or aircraft. As the firing at great range began, a full-rigged sailing ship appeared on the port beam, an unwilling and shocked spectator at this awful drama in a remote sea. She was a Frenchman who had left her port before the war had broken out, and had no means of knowing about it. She now went about and disappeared thankfully from the scene.

Sturdee attempted to keep within the comfortable range of his twelve-inch guns and beyond the range of Spee's 8.2s. To counter this the Germans closed the range to 10,000 yards when Sturdee's 5.9s were within range. This gave them a singular advantage because the British battle-cruisers had only four-inch guns to deal with destroyer attacks at close range. Sturdee was further handicapped by his own dense smoke, Spee being in the lee of the battle-cruisers. Moreover, the German shooting was as outstanding as it had been at Coronel. 'It was magnificent to watch,' according to one observer, 'perfect ripple salvoes all along their sides. A brown coloured puff with a centre of flame marking each gun as it fired.' After a few salvoes, they were straddling the British ships.

Sturdee, exasperated by his gun layers' blinding by his own smoke, ordered a thirty-two-point (360-degree) turn, which gave him two advantages, opening the range and clearing the sky. It was now 3.15 in the afternoon and the twelve-inch guns were having a telling effect on the German armoured cruisers, especially as the British shells were filled with newly introduced lyddite. Besides, the broadside of the battle-cruisers was more than twice the weight of the *Scharnhorst*'s and *Gneisenau*'s. The flagship was holed fore and aft below the waterline, letting in water and reducing her speed. She was also on fire in several places. Admiral Spee's signal to Captain Maerker was characteristically generous: 'You were right after all.'

The *Inflexible* was now concentrating on the German flagship, hitting her all over, and yet she continued to fire perfect salvoes. The gunnery officer was asking 'What the devil can we do?' when *Scharnhorst* shut up 'as when a light goes out ... Then she turned towards us and we could see that she was listing heavily, funnels all awry. As she was obviously sinking we checked fire.' She disappeared at 4.15 p.m. No attempt to pick up survivors was made as the *Gneisenau* was still firing and had to be dealt with first.

The *Carnarvon* had now at last caught up and added the fire of her six-inch guns to the rain of shells on the unfortunate ship. But the surviving German armoured cruiser continued to fire and at 5.15 made a hit on the *Invincible*'s armour plate. But according to Sturdee's report, at 5.30 'She turned towards the flagship with a heavy list to starboard and appeared stopped, with steam pouring from her escape pipes, and smoke from shell and fires rising everywhere ... At 5.40 the three British ships closed in ... and the flag flying at her fore-truck was apparently hauled down, but the flag at the peak continued flying.'

By 6 p.m. the *Gneisenau*'s guns ceased firing: there was no more ammunition and most of the gun crews were dead anyway. There was no more steam for her boilers either. Captain Maerker ordered all his crew who could do so to come up on deck. The captain called for three cheers for the Kaiser, then ordered the ship to be scuttled by opening the underwater torpedo tubes. It was now every man for himself. Those who could threw themselves into the icy water with whatever they could grab to support them. Between two and three hundred succeeded in getting away before the ship capsized and disappeared. While all three of the British ships lowered boats, three cheers for their ship were called by the men in the water. Many of them drifted away and drowned before help could arrive, and those who were saved were in a parlous condition, half dead from the cold, and many of them wounded in the action. But the two battle-cruisers got 170 safely on board, where they were immediately given hot drinks and blankets; and the *Carnarvon* picked up another twenty.

Admiral Sturdee later learned how the pursuit of Spee's light cruisers concluded. The pursuers had not had an easy time. Not only were the German ships faster than expected, but the foul weather which Spee had prayed for arrived an hour or two after he had gone to the bottom. Mist and rain and rising seas made shooting very difficult, and the German 4.1-inch gunnery proved as sustained and accurate as that of the armoured cruisers. It was a wonderful piece of artillery with a range almost equal to the British six-inch. The *Kent* caught the *Nürnberg* and after a ferocious gunnery duel sent her to the bottom at 7.26 p.m.

Two more of the German light cruisers were sunk, but the *Dresden* succeeded in getting away in the mist and rain and failing light. Both the *Nürnberg* and the *Leipziq* put up gallant fights to the end against overwhelming odds. A handful of survivors were picked out of the freezing water, but Otto von Spee was not among those from the *Nürnberg*. His mother had lost both sons and her husband in these lonely, inhospitable seas.

As for Sturdee, on learning to his chagrin that the *Dresden* had escaped, he took the two battle-cruisers far south, intending to hunt for her among the islands of Tierra del Fuego. But in view of the reduced visibility and the darkness, he reversed course and headed back to Port Stanley. There he cabled London with the news of the victory, and set about servicing his ships. He was certainly not in a condition to face a foe equal to the one he had just crushed because he had used up nearly all his shells. He determined to return home and rejoin the Grand Fleet, which had sorely missed his ships.

There was great jubilation at home at the victory. 'Kit' Cradock had been avenged; Sturdee was given an immediate baronetcy, the first time this had occurred since the honour conferred on Admiral Hoste after the Battle of Lissa in 1811. The First Sea Lord, Jackie Fisher, though delighted at the victory and the justification of the design of these battle-cruisers, which had been his conception, was less pleased that one of Spee's ships had escaped. But the *Dresden* was soon hunted down and destroyed in an obscure Chilean bay. Winston Churchill later commented:

> No German ships of war remained in any of the oceans of the world ... The consequences were far-reaching, and affected our position in every part of the globe. The strain was everywhere relaxed. All our enterprises proceeded in every theatre without the slightest hindrance ... The public, though gratified by the annihilating character of the victory, was quite unconscious of its immense importance to the whole naval situation.

3

The Battle of the Dogger Bank January 1915

The enmeshing web of alliances that had divided the nations of Europe into two camps and then drawn them into the First World War in August 1914, had been fuelled by a naval arms race between Germany and Great Britain. The empire of the latter excited the jealousy of the German Kaiser, Wilhelm II, who was aided by the aggressive nationalism of his newly created state in general and of his naval chief, von Tirpitz, in particular. An honorary admiral in the British fleet, Wilhelm II approved the building of the High Seas Fleet, intended to oppose the Grand Fleet of Great Britain.

The cockpit of this confrontation was the North Sea. The High Seas Fleet had its base at Wilhelmshaven; with the Strait of Dover rendered impassable, the Grand Fleet lay at Scapa Flow in the Orkney Islands. A fast squadron of battle-cruisers under Beatty was based at Rosyth in the Firth of Forth, with British light squadrons at Harwich, just north of the Thames Estuary.

British strategy relied upon Beatty locating any German incursion and luring it onto the guns of the Grand Fleet under

Jellicoe. Despite the fact that German officers drank frequently to Der Tag, "The Day" upon which they would humiliate the might of the Royal Navy, the German plan called for an avoidance of action with superior forces. To maintain their fleet, the Germans carried out hit-and-run raids, designed to weaken and demoralise their enemy. One such sortie was made by von Hipper's battle cruisers against British fishing vessels on the Dogger Bank in January 1915.

Learning of this, the British Admiralty dispatched Beatty from Rosyth and Tyrwhitt from Harwich. The two forces were to rendezvous and then cut von Hipper off from Wilhelmshaven.

....

THE BATTLE-CRUISERS that had defeated Spee at the Falkland Islands battle were the first generation of a new class of warship which combined the gunfire of a dreadnought battleship with superior speed but less protective armour. They were the natural successor to the dreadnought and followed hot in the wake of the *Dreadnought* itself. This all-big-gun ship put an end to generations of mixed-armament ironclads, later renamed battleships. The typical battleship building throughout the world at the turn of the century had a main armament of four heavy guns in two turrets, fore and aft, with batteries of secondary weapons sited on either beam. These were the type that fought at Tsu-Shima, where many lessons were learned from the findings of such observers as Captain Pakenham.

Both sides at Tsu-Shima found it difficult to observe the fall of the heaviest shells because of the curtain of splashes created by the secondary guns. Several navies, including the American, Japanese and Russian, were working on this problem in the early years of the twentieth century, and designs were in hand when Sir John ('Jacky') Fisher was appointed First Sea

Lord in 1904. He convened a committee on designs at the end of that year, and under the strong influence of Fisher, politically supported by Lord Selborne, the First Lord of the Admiralty, the first all-big-gun battleship was put in hand. It was built at neck-breaking speed (Fisher was a great hustler) and was on its trials less than a year later. She was named *Dreadnought*, the tenth Royal Navy ship of that name, by King Edward VII. She combined a speed of twenty-one knots with ten twelve-inch guns, adequate armour protection, and batteries of four-inch guns to deal with destroyers. Overnight, it made obsolete all earlier battleships, including those of the Royal Navy.

There then ensued what became known as 'the dreadnought race' between Germany and Britain — an immensely costly race it was, too. By October 1914 Britain had completed twenty-four dreadnoughts, the gun calibre increasing from twelve-inch to 13.5-inch, and finally to fifteen-inch. The displacement of the *Queen Elizabeth* class was 27,500 tons, compared with the *Dreadnought's* 17,900 tons. During the same period Germany completed sixteen dreadnoughts, all with eleven-inch or twelve-inch main batteries.

The race between the two navies in the construction of battle-cruisers was equally tense. The side armour of the *Invincible* was only seven inches thick, whereas that of the *Von der Tann*, Germany's first battle-cruiser, was eleven inches. In every respect, the German Navy's battle-cruisers were stronger than their British counterparts, but the British ships were marginally faster and boasted heavier broadside: the eleven-inch guns of the *Van der Tann* firing shell weighing a total of 5,400 pounds, the *Invincible's* equivalent 6,800 pounds. At the outbreak of war, Germany had completed six battle-cruisers while the Royal Navy had commissioned nine.

The battle-cruiser rapidly asserted itself as the predominant warship in the early months of the First World War. The Battle of the Falkland Islands exemplified its speed and power, and the Germans used their battle-cruisers aggressively in the North Sea from the early days, while the High Seas Fleet's battleship squadrons remained in port without showing any signs of facing the British Grand Fleet. The German battle-cruisers were commanded by the very able and positive Admiral Franz von Hipper. In England he earned the sobriquet 'baby-killer Hipper' after his bombardment of undefended east coast towns contrary to the Hague Convention. He was nearly caught by Admiral Sir David Beatty's Battle-Cruiser Fleet in mid-December 1914, but escaped owing to a signalling failure by the Admiral's signal officer, Ralph Seymour.

Signalling was not a strong point in the Royal Navy during the First World War. It certainly did not match the capabilities of the Intelligence Department, which, with the aid of powerful radio stations on the east coast, could intercept German signals which were then decoded at the Admiralty. On 23 January 1915 the Admiralty deciphered a signal to Hipper authorizing him to proceed to sea that evening after dark to reconnoitre the Dogger Bank and return to port the following evening.

When he left the Jade estuary at 5.45 p.m., Hipper could have had no idea that his movements were being followed as if an enemy ship were shadowing him. His force consisted of three battle-cruisers armed with eleven-inch or twelve-inch guns, and the *Blücher*, which was the most powerful armoured cruiser ever laid down, but without the speed and gunfire of its cohorts. Her main armament was of 8.2-inch guns, which had proved themselves at Coronel and the Falklands but lacked the weight, penetrating power or range of the larger-calibre German guns.

On 23 January 1915, at the Admiralty, Churchill had spent a part of the morning with Fisher at his bedside; he had a cold but clearly enjoyed his talk with his First Lord. When Churchill returned to his office at around noon:

> I had hardly sat down when the door opened quickly and in marched [Admiral] Sir Arthur Wilson unannounced. He looked at me intently, and there was a glow in his eye.
> 'First Lord, these fellows are coming out again.'
> 'When?'
> 'To-night. We have just got time to get Beatty there.'

Signals were at once sent to Commodore Tyrwhitt commanding the light forces at Harwich, saying, 'All your destroyers and light cruisers will be wanted tonight.'

Another urgent signal was sent to Admiral Sir David Beatty at the battle-cruiser base at Rosyth near Edinburgh on the Forth: 'Get ready to sail at once with all battle cruisers and light cruisers and sea-going destroyers.'

A rendezvous for Tyrwhitt's and Beatty's forces was fixed for dawn at the point where the Admiralty had predicted Hipper's battle-cruiser force would be at sunrise.

Beatty sailed with his big ships down the Forth, under the famous railway bridge and out to sea late in the afternoon of 23 January. He was flying his flag in the *Lion*, which with the *Tiger* and *Princess Royal* formed the 1st Battle-Cruiser Squadron, each ship armed with ten 13.5-inch guns. He was followed by Admiral Moore with the 2nd Battle-Cruiser Squadron. Moore flew his flag in the *New Zealand* and had with him the *Indomitable*, both older battle-cruisers similar to those that had fought at the Falklands. This mighty force, accompanied by light cruisers and fleet destroyers, sped south-eastward through the night

A journalist, Filson Young, who was temporarily on Beatty's staff, observed:

> From the signal bridge of the *Lion*, when I went up at 6.30 a.m., the eastern horizon showed light and the sea was beginning to grey over, but it was still dark night about us. The Admiral was already there, at 6.45 signals were beginning to come in from the Harwich flotillas indicating that the rendez-vous chosen by the Admiralty had been hit off exactly ... at ten minutes to seven I went down to breakfast; and when I returned fifteen minutes later the daylight was beginning to spread and the cloud banks to roll away. It promised to be an ideal morning, with a light breeze from the NNE and a slight swell on the sea. At seven the bugles sounded off Action, and in a few minutes came, with a thrill to all of us, the flash of gunfire and a signal from Aurora that she was in action with enemy forces.

The trap had sprung, and Hipper reversed course as soon as the smoke and dim silhouettes of the British battle-cruisers were reported a few minutes later. Meanwhile, Beatty called for a speed of twenty-seven knots and made all preparations for a running battle. The two ships of his 2nd Battle-Cruiser Squadron could not manage this speed and fell behind Beatty's 'big cats', as he called them.

The same situation applied to Hipper's force, the *Blücher* proving unable to keep up with the newer, faster *Derfflinger*, *Moltke* and the flagship *Seydlitz*. By 9.10 a.m. the *Blücher* was just within range of Beatty's *Lion*, which opened fire at 20,000 yards. The poor *Blücher* never had a chance. She was abandoned to her fate by Hipper, who had made a blunder by bringing her with him.

But there was a comparable British blunder when the Germans opened fire. Beatty signalled, 'Engage corresponding ships in the enemy's line.' This ambiguous signal led to both the *Lion* and *Tiger* firing on the second German ship, while the *Moltke*, the second in the German line, was left unmolested. She took advantage of this by concentrating her fire on the *Lion*, which suffered some twenty heavy shell hits. By unhappy chance *Lion* suffered two almost simultaneous hits by the *Derfflinger's* twelve inch guns. One of them struck the flagship's nine-inch-thick armour on the waterline, which let sea water into the port engine feed tank. This led, half an hour later, to the stopping of the port engine. As a result, the *Lion* fell behind the other battle-cruisers, except the older *Indomitable*, which was ordered to finish off the sorely damaged *Blücher*. To his other ships, Beatty signalled, 'Close the enemy as rapidly as possible consistent with keeping all guns bearing.'

A sailor in the *Tiger* recalled:

Now the enemy began to hit us. Up in Q turret, the well-drilled crew had been at cannonade with the enemy for some time, and the rhythm of the crews was remarkably good; the shells and cordite cartridges were coming up from the shell rooms and magazines via the loading room, and hoist with regularity to be loaded into the breach. The shells were handled by hydraulic grab and the chain rammer uncoiled with a hiss to ram the great projectiles into the rifling of the guns. The steady gun drill of the crews manning levers, watching electric instruments with grim determination to do their best; the firing of the huge guns, recoiling to the explosion of the cordite charges, the smooth running out again with the recoil system — suddenly all this was interrupted by a noise like an express train overhead. There was the shattering roar of an explosion, the ship reeling to a direct hit on the roof on the turret which rolled the armour back like a piece of canvas...

More misfortune for Beatty followed. Just before eleven o'clock he thought he sighted the periscope of a U-boat off his starboard bow. The Admiral was suffering from a new and infectious naval disease dubbed 'periscopitis'. In the early weeks of the war, U-boats had penetrated the Grand Fleet's base at Scapa Flow in spite of all the precautions taken, and had sunk in succession three armoured cruisers in the North Sea. Unknown in the South Atlantic, the new underwater weapons were to have a profound influence in home waters and affect tactics in battle.

Fearing a trap of a concentration of U-boats against which he had been warned, Beatty therefore ordered an eight-point turn to port *away* from this threat, thus putting his ships astern of Hipper and bringing about an additional fear of another new weapon, the mine, dropping from the stern of destroyers. He therefore determined, when clear of the wakes of the German ships, to swing round and engage Hipper on his port side.

There now followed a series of signal failures and misunderstandings which led to Admiral Moore, now in command, breaking off the action with Hipper's surviving battle-cruisers, and instead turning north-east to engage in the final destruction of the *Blücher*. The complexity of the occasion was compounded by the crippled *Lion*'s signal halyard being shot away, and as a result of that waterline hit, all electricity either for wireless or signal searchlights ceased. Beatty watched the turn of events in horror. Seymour managed to call a nearby destroyer alongside, into which Beatty transferred and at top speed caught up with the *Princess Royal*, in which he raised his flag to continue his control of the battle. But it was too late. The enemy was at least twelve miles distant and there was no question of catching Hipper before he was in heavily defended home waters, and in range of the guns of Heligoland.

Back in the battered and disabled *Lion*, there was a real fear that she might capsize. Filson Young thought 'she was in a quite sinking condition'.

> The list to port was increasing steadily, and as we came down from the foretop we left our oilskins and other gear there, in order to be more free in the water, as it seemed possible that the end might come at any moment. The decks presented an extraordinary spectacle, battered and littered with fragments of smashed and twisted steel, with here and there yawing gashes where heavy shell had burst or fragments penetrated ... Meanwhile, [men] had been working hard in the damaged part of the ship, shoring up bulkheads, getting out collision mats and doing what they could to see that the damage inflicted did not go any farther. It was found that the water was not increasing...

Later, Filson Young reached the conclusion that the German fire was better initially, and that they got sooner on to the target, and that the British improved later while theirs deteriorated. The reason for this, which was first demonstrated at Coronel, was that the Germans used stereoscopic range-finders, which demanded identical eyesight in both eyes, and were, moreover, extremely tiring. But they gave superior initial estimation of the enemy's range as compared with the coincidence range-finders used by the British. The Germans tended to tire from the great concentration required, and by this time the simpler British system was getting the range more accurately.

The *Blücher* was fought with the same tenacity and high discipline as Spee's armoured cruisers but, like them, battered by heavy shells, in the end she heeled over and sank to the bottom. The battle greatly lifted the spirit of the British people, who hailed the Dogger Bank fight as a great victory, but Beatty observed in a letter to a friend, 'The disappointment of that day is more than I can bear to think about. Everybody thinks it was a great success when in reality it was a terrible failure.'

But Beatty himself should share some of the blame for failing to obtain a knock-out victory. Even if there had been a U-boat in the vicinity (and there was not), he should have turned towards it to comb the tracks of its torpedoes. Nor was he right to assume that Hipper had mine-laying facilities. He did not. But it was his false assumptions from the interpretation of his own signals, which were insufficiently clear, which must be most blamed.

For Hipper and the Germany Navy there were benefits as well as losses. There could be no doubt that, for the loss of an old armoured cruiser, the three pricelessly valuable modern battle-cruisers were saved from almost certain destruction. In the event only three heavy shells struck the German battle-cruiser *Derfflinger*. One of the 13.5-inch lyddite shells fired by the *Lion* struck the barbette of the after twelve-inch turret, penetrating the nine-inch armour and igniting the waiting charges in the working chamber. From there it flashed down to the ammunition chamber and then horizontally to the handing room of the adjacent (superimposed) turret. Both turrets were thus put out of action and 159 men killed. Thanks to swift action, however, the after magazines were saved by flooding. Otherwise the ship would certainly have blown up. Even so, flames rose up to 200 feet in the after part of the ship. It was a high price to pay, but it was also a blessing in disguise. The German naval command at once put in hand anti-flash protection in all their heavy ships.

Although the Germans made more than twenty hits with heavy shell, mainly on the *Lion* and *Tiger*, none involved flash risk to the magazines. The Germans were very depressed by this first meeting between dreadnought battle-cruisers. The C.-in-C. of the High Seas Fleet was sacked, and the Kaiser called for an even more cautious naval policy.

The British public were elated, and, as the *Indomitable* towed the battered *Lion* up the Firth of Forth, the waiting crowds gave welcome cheers. The newspapers, too, were elated. 'It will be some time before they go baby-killing again,' the *Globe* thundered. As it transpired, there was no further contact between dreadnoughts for a further sixteen months.

4

....

THE BATTLE OF JUTLAND
31 MAY–1 JUNE 1916

Despite the early clashes between surface squadrons at Coronel, the Falklands, the Dogger Bank and elsewhere, there had been no mighty clash of battle-fleets, no battle of annihilation comparable with Trafalgar one hundred and ten years earlier. Both the German High Seas Fleet and the British Grand Fleet yearned for such a day, the former to establish their superiority over the decadent British, the latter to refute the charge of degeneration and to re-establish the rule of Britannia over the waves. The engagement between the battle-cruiser squadrons at the Dogger Bank had been frustrating for both parties, not merely for the inconclusive nature of the action, but for the failure of the main battle squadrons to engage. The Commander-in-Chief of the High Seas Fleet, Admiral Ingenohl, was removed from his command for failing to sail in support of Hipper, while in the Grand Fleet Admiral Jellicoe itched to try the mettle of his heavy squadrons of battle-ships. By 1916, with the armies of both nations bogged down in the mud and blood of the Western Front, there was an ominous lack of action in the North Sea and a spreading perception (on the British side at least), that the Royal Navy was not pulling its weight. This feeling was supported by Hipper's second bombardment of England's eastern coast in April, a further humiliation for a country that had, since

1905, invested vast sums of money for a new fleet of Dreadnought battle-ships.

Behind the public's perception, the naval high commands of both sides had been seeking an advantageous opening and both depended upon luring the enemy's battle-fleet to sea, where it could be overwhelmed by a superior force. Such was the state of play by May 1916.

．．．．．．．．．．．．．．．．．．．．．

HISTORY DOES NOT always record the influence, however indirect, of the United States on the greatest clash of arms at sea in the First World War. On the one hand, American protests had become so loud at the effects of unrestricted U-boat warfare on American lives and shipping that orders had been given to the numerous U-boat flotillas to withdraw from this practice. This gave the C.-in-C. of the High Seas Fleet, Admiral Reinhard Scheer, a sudden gift of this powerful weapon.

On the other hand, Great Britain was also in trouble with the American administration. This, again, concerned American trade, a sensitive subject to America since the War of Independence. The tight British blockade of Germany, instituted from the outset of the war, demanded the halting of countless American merchantmen and escorting them into a British harbour in order to search for contraband. This could be done at sea, contended the Americans, thus saving time. The British argued that this was far too dangerous, providing sitting targets for marauding U-boats.

Jellicoe wrote later:

I had been informed, both by the Foreign Office and Mr Page, the United States Ambassador, that the relations between the two countries on the blockade question were in a very strained condition. Hence there was reason to fear the outcome of this position, and reasonable caution was a necessity.

The consequence of this warning to Jellicoe sharply intensified his determination to avoid risks. His Grand Fleet Battle Orders, GFBOs, featured such phrases as, 'Too much not to be left to chance in a fleet action, because our fleet was the one and only factor that was vital to the existence of the Empire, as indeed to the allied cause...'

This was a long way from Nelson's 'something must be left to chance' in his Battle of Trafalgar Memorandum. Churchill's rendering of Jellicoe's role, 'He was the only man on either side who could lose the war in an afternoon', had not yet been coined, but it applied in May 1916, as before and after. He was also the only commander on either side who could *win* in an afternoon. Finally, he was the first admiral to fight dreadnought battleships against enemy battleships.

Jellicoe's GFBOs were based on the old principle of a formal, long-range navy duel on parallel lines in daylight. (There was no provision for night fighting, which was considered far too chancy.) The only admiral who dissented was Doveton Sturdee, who had been given command of the 4th Division of Jellicoe's battleships. Since the Falklands battle and all the praise, and honours, heaped upon him, Sturdee had become rather big-headed and had started to throw his weight about. He argued for more flexibility and independence for divisions under certain circumstances. But as Jellicoe was heard to remark, 'Sturdee often goes off at half-cock.' The dangers of over-centralization of command were compounded by radio, which had already played a part at the Battle of Coronel.

Peacetime manoeuvres of the Grand Fleet's battleships were conducted with divisions (usually four battleships) in line ahead, the divisions themselves disposed in line abreast, the C.-in-C. leading the centre division. When in sight of the enemy, according to circumstances, the divisions deployed into a single line, to port or starboard, or possibly straight ahead, in which case the divisions to port or starboard of the flagship would fall in and turn behind the C.-in-C. This deployment to a single line had been practised on numerous occasions, and by May 1916 Jellicoe was satisfied that it could be carried out to port or starboard with complete confidence and safety.

The German Navy was newly built and possessed the advantages and disadvantages of having no tradition or history. It was the product of recent German unification and of Kaiser Wilhelm II's ambition for Germany to become a leading world sea power. On a personal level, the Kaiser had been acutely jealous of his late uncle, King Edward VII's, predominance at sea. The man who recognized his master's ambition and implemented it was Admiral Alfred (later 'von') Tirpitz. He was the German leader in the dreadnought race with Britain, and was the German Jacky Fisher. He was determined and soaringly ambitious, not for himself but for his Kaiser and *Vaterland*. It was Tirpitz who ensured that the High Seas Fleet was equipped with the finest ships and imbued with strong patriotism and discipline of the first order. It was his achievement that the 40,000 officers and men never waned (until almost the end of the war) in their self-belief and confidence that they could beat any British naval force they faced.

At the time of Jutland, the German Navy, at the Falklands

and the Dogger Bank battle, had already proved that its ships were built to the highest standards. By comparison with the ships of the British Grand Fleet, Tirpitz's ships were stronger, more heavily armoured and as fast as their British counterparts. Only in gun calibre did the German Navy fall behind the Royal Navy. While the British were arming their dreadnoughts and dreadnought battle-cruisers with the twelve-inch gun, the Germans were content with the eleven-inch. The Royal Navy swiftly advanced to the 13.5-inch gun as main armament; the Germans countered with the twelve-inch. At Jutland, seven British super-dreadnoughts (as they were named) were armed with the magnificent fifteen-inch gun, hurling a projectile weighing 1,920 pounds a distance of 24,400 yards, or fourteen miles. The German Navy had no fifteen-inch-gunned ships at Jutland. Its first was on trials in the Baltic. There were scare stories in England that the Germans were casting 17.1-inch guns, but they never did.

Vice-Admiral Reinhard Scheer, the C.-in-C. of the High Seas Fleet, inspired fierce loyalty from his staff and officers and men in spite of the heavy demands he made on them. He liked everything done immediately and accurately; but, having followed his wishes, his staff might see their plans impatiently discarded. In action, Scheer was cool and decisive, as he needed to be under the circumstances of Jutland.

Rear-Admiral Franz von Hipper, the commander of Scheer's scouting forces, had already shown his mettle at the Dogger Bank battle. He was as quick-thinking as his superior, and many have classed him as the finest admiral at Jutland on either side. Grand Admiral Erich Raeder described Hipper as 'an energetic and impulsive individual, with quick perception and a keen "seaman's eye". Theory was not his forte; he hated paperwork.' Professor Arthur J. Marder, the leading historian of the dreadnought era, considered him 'the outstanding sea officer of the war'.

In April 1916, the land war had been raging for twenty months, but at sea the anticipated clash of the great fleets had still not occurred. During the dreadnought race before the war, the people of both Germany and Britain had held great expectations of these expensive fleets. But, apart from side-shows and the inconclusive Dogger Bank battle, a silence reigned over the grey North Sea. From the British view, the German Navy had given the impression that it could strike at will down the east coast of the country. Hipper's raids had been highly disillusioning.

Then, early on the morning of 25 April 1916, Hipper struck again, this time at Yarmouth and Lowestoft, wrecking houses and killing civilians. 'And where was the Navy?' people demanded.

Both sides had been searching for a plan to bring about a decisive conclusion in the North Sea. It had been standing policy in the German admiralty to niggle away at the Grand Fleet, to sink individual dreadnoughts, or cut off a detached force and attack it with a superior force. They had succeeded in mining and sinking one new British dreadnought — the *Audacious*; they had had no further success, though they claimed they had sunk the *Tiger* at the Dogger Bank.

Towards the end of May 1916, the British and Germans coincidentally drew up plans of a similar nature. The Germans proposed to dispatch a scouting force up the east coast of Denmark, to a point near the southern tip of Norway, hoping to lure a British counter-force which would then be set upon by Scheer's High Seas Fleet following up from the rear. The plan could not be implemented according to schedule because the weather proved too rough for advanced scouting zeppelins, thought essential, to carry out their task. Meanwhile the U-boat flotillas, which had been withdrawn from their commerce raiding, were to position themselves off the British bases as traps to seize on any heavy forces putting to sea to counter the German action.

On the British side, intelligence from Room 40 (the decoding department at the Admiralty) led to the sending of a warning to Jellicoe and Beatty that the High Seas Fleet would probably come out early on the morning of 31 May. When the probability became a certainty, the two admirals were ordered to get up steam for full speed urgently and put to sea. There had been too many false alarms in the past, but this time a belief ran through all the ships and all ranks that this was to be the real thing, and there was great excitement. That same evening, as darkness began to fall, the Grand Fleet was at sea, two and a half hours *before* Hipper with his battle-cruiser scouting fleet left his base in the Jade river estuary. Another battle squadron with a cruiser squadron and attendant destroyers left Invergordon on the Firth of Cromarty further to the south. When they rendezvoused, Jellicoe, the C.-in-C., had with him a total of twenty-four battleships, three battle-cruisers, eight armoured cruisers, twelve light cruisers and fifty-one destroyers.

Farther south still, Beatty's Battle Cruiser Fleet had already steamed down the Forth under the railway bridge, past Edinburgh, past the islands of Incholm and Inchkeith and through a cleared passage in a minefield and out to sea. Beatty had with him the 5th Battle Squadron, the jewel in the crown of the Grand Fleet. These were Admiral Sir Hugh Evan-

Thomas's four fifteen-inch-gunned fast battleships. The 5th Battle Squadron was with Beatty by chance, and greatly strengthened him. His requests to Jellicoe for these twenty-five knot, heavily armoured super-dreadnoughts had been turned down in the past as Jellicoe valued them as a fast wing of his battle fleet, but by chance a few weeks earlier, Beatty had dispatched to Scapa Flow for gunnery practice his three 'I' class battle-cruisers, which, though they had done well at the Falklands, were more fragile and slower than his other battle-cruisers. In exchange he was lent the 5th Battle Squadron, whose influence on the forthcoming battle was to be profound.

Beatty was supported, also, by fourteen light cruisers in three squadrons commanded by Commodores Sir Edwyn Alexander-Sinclair, Sir William 'Barge' Goodenough, and Vice-Admiral Sir D. W. Napier. He also had with him the seaplane carrier *Engadine*, a new phenomenon in naval warfare. (It could be defined as an aircraft carrier but its three seaplanes had to be hoisted out by crane, and subsequently plucked back again at the conclusion of their flight. They could not operate in heavy weather, but they did have two-way radio, albeit of a primitive and unreliable nature.)

Jellicoe, too, had an aircraft carrier, the *Campania*, an ex-Cunarder which was rather more advanced than Beatty's. It carried six seaplanes, which could be flown off by means of a disposable trolley down a ramp aft but had to be lifted on board again when they returned. Unfortunately she was anchored distant from the main body of the fleet and had not seen the critical signal to raise steam for full speed; nor, in the twilight, did she observe Jellicoe's main fleet departing. It was not until nearly midnight, two hours behind Jellicoe, that the *Campania* cleared the anchorage. When Jellicoe was informed, he ordered the seaplane carrier to return, fearful of her being the target of a U-boat and wrongly calculating that she could not catch him up. (He had been misinformed about the *Campania*'s speed, and did not learn that it was twenty-three knots until seven years *after* the war was over!)

By chance both the German and British Fleets had similar orders, Hipper to proceed to a point south of the tip of Norway where he would rendezvous with Scheer's main force at 2.30 p.m. on 31 May. Beatty was to proceed to a point slightly south-west of the enemy's rendezvous, then alter course to the north to rendezvous with Jellicoe's main battle fleet, farther west of the Skagerrak than Scheer. By the time dawn broke on 31 May, neither Scheer nor Hipper with the Scouting Fleet had any knowledge that the Grand Fleet was at sea. On the other hand, Jellicoe had been told by the Admiralty that Scheer with the main German Fleet remained still in his base, though they had good reason to believe that Hipper's Scouting Fleet was at sea. Thus it came about that these four fleets were steaming about the eastern North Sea with no knowledge of the others' where-abouts. It is hard to believe that scouting frigates would not have better informed their C.-in-C.s in the Napoleonic War or even the Dutch wars of the seventeenth century.

The 31st May 1916 was a day of ironical as well as tragic incidents. Beatty's entire force was already turning north and thus out of range of the unseen enemy when a keen-eyed look-out on the masthead of Beatty's easternmost scouting cruiser, the *Galatea*, spotted at a range of some twelve miles a small merchantman hove to and blowing off steam. At almost exactly the same time, the most western of Hipper's scouts sighted the same steamer to the west. The *Galatea*, in company with the light cruiser, *Phaeton*, closed the merchantman at full speed, at the same time signalling to Beatty the stirring words, 'Enemy in sight', followed by, 'Two cruisers, probably hostile, in sight bearing ESE, course unknown.'

As the two British light cruisers closed the enemy, they opened fire with their six-inch guns at 2.28 p.m. A German light cruiser returned the fire, immediately straddling the *Galatea* at 15,000 yards. Characteristically, the next German salvo made a hit on the cruiser. Uncharacteristically, the shell was a dud. A few minutes later, Alexander-Sinclair reported to Beatty that he could observe much heavy smoke to the north-east, indicating a strong force of big ships. The merest glance at the chart showed that, whatever strength the force reported by the *Galatea*, it was certainly enemy and it could be cut off from its base.

At 2.32 p.m. Beatty made the general signal by flags to turn south-east. Again there was a breakdown in signalling and the order never reached Evan-Thomas, flying his flag in the *Barham*, and the all-powerful fifteen-inch-gunned 5th Battle Squadron continued to stream north for the rendezvous with Jellicoe. The first tragedy of the battle was that instead of supporting Beatty, Evan-Thomas was soon ten miles distant from the Battle-Cruiser Fleet before Alexander-Sinclair reported the enemy south-south-east. The 5th Battle Squadron at once turned sixteen points or 180 degrees and ordered full speed of twenty-five knots. A few minutes later the *Galatea* reported that the German light cruiser seen had reversed course to the south-east. At 3.45 p.m. Alexander-Sinclair observed distant flickers of yellow light on the south-eastern horizon, which could only mean the firing of heavy guns. Under the most dangerous conditions the Commodore had brought the two fleets together, and called up reinforcements in the shape of the 5th Battle Squadron.

Hipper was elated at the situation. He not only had the best of the light but also knew that his enemy would have great difficulty in assessing the range of his ships against the darker sky in the east. Moreover, it seemed possible that he might achieve the purpose of this operation by drawing this battle-cruiser detachment of the British Fleet into the hungry jaws of Scheer's battle squadrons, which were less than fifty miles to the south. For the present, Hipper closed the distance between his ships and the enemy, knowing that the British 13.5-inch guns could outrange his twelve-inch and eleven-inch guns.

Beatty's flag-captain, and members of his staff who had observed this shortening of the range, wanted Beatty to open fire while his ships had the advantage of this greater range. Beatty, however, was too preoccupied with trying to signal Jellicoe by wireless telegraph (W/T). It was, therefore, Hipper who opened fire first, and Beatty's flag-captain took it upon himself to give the order to the chief gunnery officer to open fire. The German gunnery, as at the Dogger Bank fight, was deadly, the *Lion* being hit twice with heavy shell within five minutes.

Beatty ordered the distribution of fire signal at 3.46 p.m. It hardly seemed possible that the signalling failure at Dogger Bank could be repeated, but so it was. Beatty ordered his flag-ship and the *Princess Royal* to concentrate on Hipper's flagship, *Lützow*, at the head of the German line, and the other ships to engage ship for ship. But Seymour, the signals officer, dispatched the order *by flags only*, making no use of the lamps at his command. And these flag signals, in the smoke and splashes of German gunfire, were missed by both the *Queen Mary* and the *Tiger*, and thus the most modern German ship, the *Derfflinger*, enjoyed for ten vital minutes uninterrupted firing practice. But the *Moltke* suffered the fire of two of Beatty's ships, while the two oldest battle-cruisers present, the *Von der Tann* and the *Indefatigable*, fought a private duel of their own.

The gunnery duel rose to its climax, conditions on the bridge of the British flagship became ever more daunting. As Lieutenant W. S. Chalmers later wrote:

All round us huge columns of water, higher than the funnels, were being thrown up as the enemy shells plunged into the sea. Some of these gigantic splashes curled over and deluged us with water. Occasionally, above the noise of battle, we heard the ominous hum of a shell fragment and caught a glimpse of polished steel as it flashed past the Bridge.

The *Lion* received its most serious hit a few minutes after 4 p.m. but officers on the bridge, including Beatty, were unaware of it. This can be accounted for by the noise caused by the firing of her guns, the scream of the wind from her twenty-eight knots speed and sundry other noises, including enemy near-hits.

The first news of this serious hit was delivered by a sergeant of the Royal Marines, who staggered on to the bridge in a terribly burned condition, his face black, his uniform singed, and barely able to stand from shock. But he drew himself to attention, saluted and reported crisply, '"Q" turret knocked out, sir. All the crew are killed, and we have flooded the magazines.' He was the only survivor, though the Major of Marines, F. J. W. Harvey, mortally wounded, just managed to reach a voice pipe to order the handing-room crew to close the magazine doors and flood the magazines. (Harvey was later awarded a posthumous VC.).

A heavy German shell had penetrated the armour plate of the 'Q' turret, amidships, at the joint with the roof plate. The roof plate was blown off and fell back on the deck, while the twelve-inch shell penetrated the turret and exploded. Thanks to the gallant major, the *Lion* did not blow up, though Hipper thought he had got her.

It was a different story at the tail of the two lines of combatants, where the *Von der Tann* and *Indomitable* had been fighting a private battle. The shooting on both sides was first class, and the British ship scored several hits; but the *Von der Tann* shrugged off the effect of these twelve-inch armour-piercing shells, thanks to her ten-inch-thick armour plate. Then, just after 4 p.m., the *Indomitable* was struck on the upper deck by three eleven-inch shells. They had to pass through only one-inch thick deck armour, and all three penetrated into the bowels of the battle-cruiser before detonating. The effect was appalling; she was thrown out of line, at once sinking by the stern.

From the *Lion*'s bridge, Beatty's attention was drawn to the rising cloud of smoke where so recently the *Indomitable* had been steaming. To ease the pressure on his surviving ships, the admiral ordered out the 9th Destroyer Flotilla. Hipper countered by sending out to meet them a light cruiser and her attendant destroyers, which were less heavily gunned than their British counterparts but carried more torpedoes. Julian Corbett, in his history, described the chaos that followed:

> It was a wild scene of groups of long low forms vomiting heavy trails of smoke and dashing hither and thither at thirty knots or more through the smother and splashes, and all in a rain of shell from the secondary armament of the German battle cruisers ... with the heavy shell of the

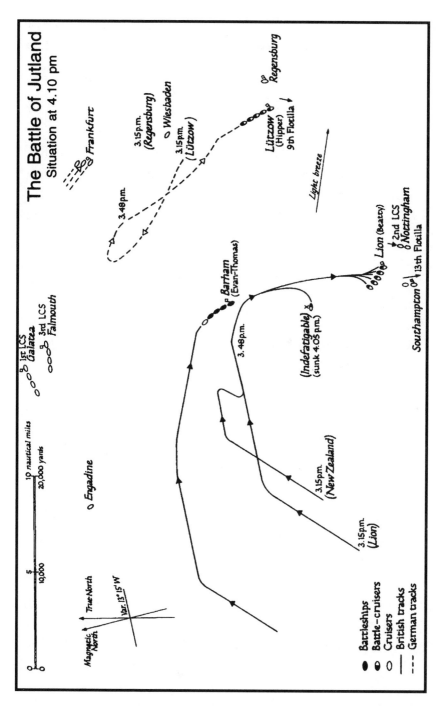

The Battle of Jutland
Situation at 4.10 pm

contending squadrons screaming overhead. Gradually a pall of gun and funnel smoke almost hid the shell-tormented sea, and beyond the fact that the German torpedo attack was crushed, little could be told of what was happening.

New actors now entered the stage from the wings. By a stupendous effort, the 5th Battle Squadron had brought itself within range, and the splashes from her first salvoes of fifteen-inch shell appeared to be twice as tall as the battle-cruisers'. Moreover, the shooting of Evan-Thomas's gun layers was as accurate as that of any of Hipper's ships. The squadron flagship, *Barham*, was already straddling the *Von der Tann*.

Hipper was concerned by this new reinforcement to the enemy's fleet; on the other hand it increased the value of the force which would shortly be facing the overwhelming gunfire of Scheer's battle fleet when they fell into the trap. Meanwhile, with satisfied relish, he witnessed another triumph by his gunners. The *Queen Mary*, the third ship in Beatty's line, had been taking a number of hits from the *Seydlitz*, but giving as good as she got with full eight-gun broadsides with her 13.5-inch guns when the *Derfflinger* shifted her aim from the *Princess Royal* on to her. At 4.26 p.m. she took a full salvo of four twelve-inch shells forward. The *Queen Mary's* end was mercifully swift. There were two massive explosions and the 26,000-ton battle-cruiser was folded in two like a discarded paper bag. Her masts and funnels collapsed inward. Some observers thought they caught a glimpse of her keel through the smoke and falling debris, and then she was gone. The following ships, the *Tiger* and *New Zealand*, had no time to turn aside, and they steamed at full speed through the suffocating smoke, their decks becoming littered with all that remained of their cohort.

Looking back from the bridge of the *Lion*, Beatty was heard by his flag-captain to utter what was to become one of the famous comments of the sea war: 'There seems to something wrong with our bloody ships today, Chatfield!'

In spite of this catastrophe, with the reinforcement of the great fifteen-inch-gunned 5th Battle Squadron, Beatty must eventually destroy Hipper's battle-cruisers before sunset. But shortly after Beatty's remarks about his own ships, *Lion* took in a wireless signal as cryptic as his recent comment. It was from Commodore Goodenough carrying out his scouting duties two and a half miles ahead of the flagship. He first signalled 'enemy light cruiser to SE.' Then, three minutes later, Goodenough signalled by searchlight, 'Battleships SE'; and five minutes after that a fuller wireless report to both Beatty and Jellicoe: 'Have sighted enemy battle fleet bearing approximately SE course of enemy N.' The German battle fleet was *not* still in the Jade as the Admiralty had incorrectly signalled.

After altering course towards the *Southampton*, and when he could make out through the funnel smoke the masts and funnels of German battlehsips, Beatty hoisted the general signal to his surviving battle-cruisers and the 5th Battle Squadron to turn in succession sixteen points to starboard, i.e. to the north-west. His primary duty now was less to strike at the enemy but to lure him north into the arms of Jellicoe's battle squadrons. Six minutes later he altered course to the north. Jellicoe was now less than fifty miles away, steaming at twenty knots and with expectations high. Meanwhile, the 3rd Light Cruiser Squadron led by Goodenough in the *Southampton* was having a rough time. They were in range (16,000 yards) of almost the entire German battle fleet. Eleven-inch and twelve-inch shells burst all around the *Southampton*, soaking those on deck and on the bridge.

Goodenough continued south, reporting in detail on the nature, course and speed of the German battle squadrons. It was not until 4.48 p.m. that he ordered the helm to be put over and then set off in pursuit of the 5th Battle Squadron, which was five miles to the north-west. But the enemy fire continued as fiercely as ever. The light cruiser's navigator had a theory that if he steered the ship in the direction of the last splash 'the enemy having registered an "over" would reduce [increase, in the case of an "under"] the range for the next salvo, by which time our range would in fact have increased'. But they were never out of danger until they met Jellicoe, for whom Goodenough had provided so much vital information.

The German C.-in-C. never recorded his reaction to the report from one of his scouting cruisers that the entire Grand Fleet was racing head-on towards his battle squadrons. But Scheer was known and admired for his steadiness, and we can be certain that he took the threatened catastrophe calmly, listening to the more detailed reports coming in by wireless. There appeared to be six squadrons of dreadnoughts each of four ships advancing line abreast, preceded by scouting light cruisers and armoured cruisers, while Hipper and his battle-cruisers were already 'bending' starboard on an easterly course.

Scheer's own dreadnoughts, sixteen of them, were formed in line ahead, headed by the *König*, while taking up the rear were his six pre-dreadnoughts, harshly referred to as 'five minute ships', that being the time they were expected to last in battle. The commander of this squadron had begged to be taken along, and as Hipper had been handicapped by the obsolete *Blücher* at the Dogger Bank, so Scheer's speed was reduced by these old vessels. But if it came to a ding-dong gunnery battle, even if he lost some of them, their total of twenty-four eleven-inch guns could make a useful contribution.

The sun was now, at 6 p.m., much lower in the sky, but there were still some three hours of daylight remaining. Nevertheless, at high summer at this time of the year, mist patches could form and as quickly dissolve, so accurate gunnery could still be difficult.

Through yet another signalling failure by the *Lion*, Evan-Thomas's 5th Battle Squadron was the last to reverse course to the north in the face of Scheer's battle fleet. At 4.55 p.m. Evan-Thomas at last received the order to turn sixteen points in succession (ship by ship) to conform to the battle-cruisers' northerly course. It was as well that these new ships were so stoutly built because each of them in turn received the full attention of Hipper's battle-cruisers and the leading squadrons of Scheer's battleships. *Barham*, the flagship and the first to turn, was hit four times by heavy shell. The next two ships were luckier, but the last, *Malaya*, was the object of close attention. All the starboard six-inch secondary guns were wiped out, and a hit below the waterline caused the entry of hundreds of gallons of water, which gave her a four-degree list, affecting the elevation of her guns. One heavy shell landed on the roof of 'X' turret, but failed to penetrate owing to its twelve-inch-thick armour, in contrast to the unfortunate *Invincible* and *Queen Mary*. Nevertheless, this super-dreadnought kept up a steady rate of fire herself, and the *Von der Tann*, already severely damaged, did not now have a single operating heavy gun.

At 5.35 p.m. Beatty altered course to the east, and at the same time the 5th Battle Squadron drew itself out of range of all the German heavy guns. This brought about a light advantage at last in favour of the British, with the German gun layers having the low sun straight in their eyes.

A new factor now entered the battle, which had lasted two hours with scarcely a pause. Hipper noted the flash of heavy gunfire from a new quarter. He wrote later of a 'many-headed hydra'; however many battle-cruisers he sank, more appeared to reinforce the enemy. This time it was the 3rd Battle-Cruiser Squadron, led by Admiral Horace Hood, a magnificent officer, whose three 'I'-class battle-cruisers had earlier been detached from the Battle-Cruiser Fleet in order to practise gunnery at Scapa Flow. This was the reason why Beatty had the 5th Battleship Squadron, which had saved him from likely annihilation. Hood was now scouting for Jellicoe and was leading him towards the High Seas Fleet.

Hood spotted ahead of him, zigzagging frantically and surrounded by shell bursts, his light cruiser *Chester*, being pursued by four of Hipper's scouting cruisers. As she raced across the bows of the *Invincible*, Commander Dannreuther, who had been in this ship's fore control at the Falklands battle, ordered the twelve-inch guns to open fire on the pursuing German cruisers. They did so with devastating effect, severely damaging two and reducing the third, *Wiesbaden*, to a wreck.

This was the beginning of a simultaneous subsidiary battle as the opposing battle fleets were fast approaching one another. Hipper's battle-cruisers, now on an easterly heading, became the object of a ferocious British destroyer attack led by Commander Loftus Jones in the *Shark*. They were met by a German counter-attack aimed at the three battle-cruisers. It was frustrated, but at some cost. The *Shark* took the brunt of the German fire, and was sunk, with Loftus Jones, one leg severed, encouraging his men to keep firing the destroyer's only remaining gun.

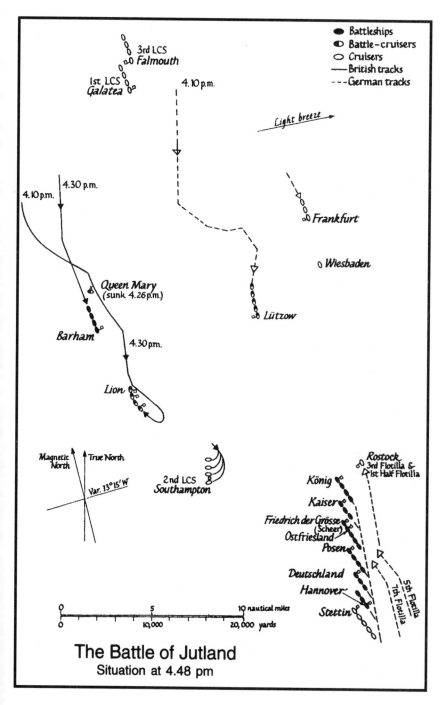

Battleships
Battle-cruisers
Cruisers
British tracks
German tracks

3rd LCS
Falmouth

1st LCS
Galatea

4.10 p.m.

Light breeze

4.30 p.m.

4.10 p.m.

4.10 p.m.

Frankfurt

o *Wiesbaden*

Queen Mary
(sunk 4.26 p.m.)

Lützow

Barham

4.30 p.m.

Lion

Magnetic North

True North

Var. 13° 15' W

2nd LCS
Southampton

Rostock
3rd Flotilla &
1st Half Flotilla

König

Kaiser

Friedrich der Grösse
(Scheer)

Ostfriesland

Posen

5th Flotilla

7th Flotilla

Deutschland

Hannover

Stettin

0   5   10 nautical miles
0   10,000   20,000 yards

The Battle of Jutland
Situation at 4.48 pm

Two posthumous VCs were earned during this phase of the battle: by Loftus Jones, and by sixteen-year-old Boy Cornwell of the *Chester*, found still manning his six-inch gun when the rest of the crew were dead, and he mortally wounded.

By 6 p.m. Jellicoe had been standing on the compass platform of the *Iron Duke* for many hours, his flag-captain and senior staff around him. He had spoken little, perhaps commenting favourably or unfavourably on the disposition of certain of his ships. To port of the flagship the two divisions were led by the *Orion* and *King George V*, while to starboard the three divisions were led by the *Benbow*, *Colossus* and *Marlborough* — all twenty-four dreadnoughts mounting twelve-inch or 13.5-inch guns, all coal-burning and for this reason leaving an immense cloud of black smoke as they tore through the water at eighteen knots. The visibility was variable, one minute clear to the west, with the sun becoming low in the sky, and a moment later smoke forming like lace curtains and then unpredictably drawing aside again. At best gunnery was going to be difficult.

Jellicoe knew that the enemy was approaching from the south, but no report told him of his exact whereabouts in relation to his fleet. Then one minute later, at exactly 6.01 p.m., he caught sight of the *Lion* at a distance of five miles, steaming fast and turning on an easterly heading. There appeared to be a turret missing amidships, and through binoculars there was more evidence of damage.

Jellicoe's flag-commander, thirty-eight-year-old Charles Dreyer, described this crucial moment later:

> Beatty in the *Lion* appeared out of the mist on our starboard bow, leading his splendid battle cruisers, which

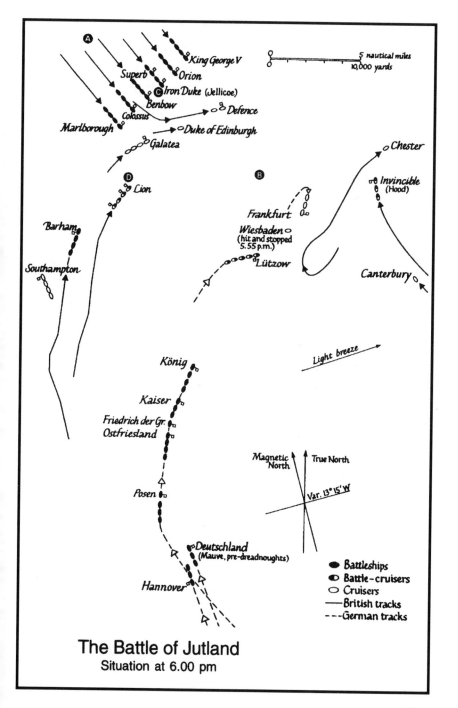

The Battle of Jutland
Situation at 6.00 pm

were engaged to starboard with an enemy invisible to us. I noted ... ghost-like columns of water thrown up by heavy enemy shells pitching among those great ships.

'Where is the enemy's battle fleet?' Jellicoe signalled by lamp.

'Enemy battle cruisers bearing SE' came the unsatisfactory answer.

Jellicoe repeated his question, and because Beatty by chance had at that moment caught a glimpse of the dreadnought *König* leading Scheer's battle fleet, signalled, 'Have sighted enemy's battle fleet bearing SSW'.

There was no indication of distance, but Jellicoe must now, urgently, deploy his fleet from cruising formation, which he had held since leaving Scapa Flow, to single line ahead. But would he deploy his squadrons to port or starboard? The fate of the Empire might depend on his decision. He stepped quickly on to the platform round the compasses and looked in silence at the magnetic compass card for about twenty seconds. I watched his keen, brown, weather-beaten face with tremendous interest, wondering what he would do ... I realised as I watched him that he was as cool and unmoved as ever. Then he looked up and broke the silence with the order in his crisp, clear-cut voice to Commander A. R. W. Woods, the Fleet Signal Officer, who was standing a little abaft me: 'Hoist equal-speed pendant SE.'

So Jellicoe was going to deploy to port. Already his ships were answering the signal, and he turned to his flag-commander saying, 'Dreyer, commence the deployment.' Dreyer did so by sounding two short siren blasts, which were immediately echoed by Jellicoe's division leaders.

For the few men of the Grand Fleet above deck who witnessed this deployment, it was a noble and awe-inspiring sight: twenty-four dreadnoughts of 20,000 tons or more, their white bow waves and stern wash contrasting with their black smoke above, forming themselves into a single line, headed by the *King George V*, the division flagship, in the centre.

This deployment heralded the climax of the battle. Already Hipper and Beatty had renewed their gunnery duel, with the 5th Battle Squadron again belatedly entering the fray.

On the other side, Hipper, who was suffering badly in this renewed duel, observed flashes of heavy gunfire in the east, where Hood was savaging his light cruisers. In a battle full of wrong conclusions and misunderstandings on both sides, Hipper thought that this was the van of the British Battle Fleet. It was no business of his to become embroiled in an exchange of fire with the entire Grand Fleet. He therefore ordered his fleet to turn sixteen points, or 180 degrees; at the same time, he recalled a destroyer attack against Beatty and directed it towards the wrongly identified Grand Fleet, i.e. Hood and his three battle-cruisers.

If Hipper had persevered with the destroyer attack against his antagonist, Beatty would have had to turn away to comb the tracks of the German destroyers' torpedoes, and in doing so revealed the presence of the deploying Grand Fleet to Scheer; for this reason this was the most advantageous moment for the Germans and the worst, nightmare moment for Jellicoe.

Rear-Admiral Sir Robert Arbuthnot, commanding Jellicoe's 1st Cruiser Squadron of outdated armoured cruisers, was an officer of courage bordering on rashness. He was the fourth baronet of this distinguished family. His favourite recreation was motor-cycling, a hazardous business in those pre-1914 days. Arbuthnot flew his flag in the armoured cruiser *Defence*, the ship earlier offered to Admiral Cradock, and then denied him. In terms of 1916 she and the other similar ships of her squadron had no business in the vulnerable van of the Grand Fleet. The *Defence*, laid down in 1905, was heavily enough armed with four 9.2-inch and ten 7.5-inch guns. But she had light armour on the waterline and deck armour averaging less than one inch.

The Admiral, instead of sticking to his task of reporting to the information-starved Jellicoe, spotted German light cruisers to the south (Scheer's scouting force), and in company with the *Warrior* set off after them. In doing so he obscured the enemy from the deploying dreadnoughts of the Grand Fleet, and, more importantly, from Beatty, who also was forced to swerve to port, away from the enemy, to avoid a collision.

So swift and precipitate was Arbuthnot's charge that within minutes he spotted ahead, through the mist and smoke of the gunnery duel, the awesome silhouettes of Scheer's leading battleships as well as Hipper's battle-cruisers. Arbuthnot calculated their range as under five miles. It was the last calculation this bold man made, for within less than a minute his ship became the target for numerous eleven-inch and twelve-inch guns. The *Defence* was straddled at once. The few who witnessed the execution recounted how the armoured cruiser and 856 officers and men appeared to suffer an 'absolutely instantaneous destruction'; one observer reported later, 'the ship seeming to be dismembered at once'.

The *Warrior*, Arbuthnot's accompanying cruiser, suffered similar devastation but was almost miraculously fortunate not to blow up. Instead, she was the subject of one of the most remarkable pieces of good fortune in the battle. The 5th Battle

Squadron, at full speed of twenty-five knots, had to put the helm hard over to conform to Evan-Thomas's efforts to form astern of Jellicoe. But the steering engine of the *Warspite* failed at that moment, perhaps from an enemy hit. Whatever the cause, the consequence was hard on the ship, which received the full attention of Scheer's battleships, suffering at least six hits by heavy shell. But it was fortunate for the *Warrior*, which was inside the two complete circles made by the *Warspite* and so relieved of further suffering.

Evan-Thomas ordered the battered *Warspite* to return to Rosyth, and the *Warrior* limped away, to bury her seventy dead. She was later taken in tow by the seaplane carrier *Engadine*, which took off her survivors when the *Warrior* began to sink.

As for Admiral Sir John Jellicoe, completing the deployment of his fleet into a traditional single line, so for Admiral Reinhard Scheer, driving his fleet north, the first enemy was the weather and failing light. Conditions were as vexatious and confusing as they could be, and Admiral Sturdee, commanding the 4th Battle Squadron, noted the contrast with the clear blue skies of the South Atlantic at his Falklands victory. So did Commander Dannreuther, gunnery officer of the *Invincible* high up in her foretop.

At this time, about 6.15 p.m., Scheer was as ill served by his scouting cruisers as Jellicoe had been. He had yet to be informed that the entire British Grand Fleet, and not just the battle-cruisers, were in the vicinity. The shock, therefore, was that much more severe when Rear-Admiral Behncke, in his flagship *König* and in the van of the High Seas Fleet, signalled that there was an endless line of British dreadnoughts 'crossing the T' of the advancing German Battle Fleet.

From the bridge of his flagship, *Friedrich der Grosse*,

Scheer could confirm the truth of Behncke's alarming reports seconds later.

Admiral Hipper, with his battered battle-cruisers, suffered almost simultaneously an equal shock. He had begun this engagement against six enemy battle-cruisers, had sunk two of them without loss, and then had suddenly faced a reinforced squadron of fifteen-inch-gunned fast battleships. He had, seemingly, knocked out one of these — and now, out of the mist and smoke, three *more* enemy battle-cruisers had appeared as if by magic. Many-headed hydra indeed!

This addition to Beatty's force forming immaculately in his van was Hood's 3rd Battle-Cruiser Squadron, scouting ahead of Jellicoe and now, quite rightly, joining in Beatty's ding-dong gunnery duel with Hipper. At once, Beatty recognized the quality of the shooting of Hood's three battle-cruisers. And now, at last, the light was favourable for Beatty and Hood, the low sun clearly etching the German ships against the western sky. Dannreuther, in the *Invincible*'s foretop, noted several hits in the first minutes on the *Derfflinger* and the already battered *Lützow*.

But, once again, the weather proved to be the final arbiter. The low mist and cloud that had protected Admiral Hood suddenly cleared — momentarily only, but long enough for the gun layers of the *Derfflinger* and several of the leading German dreadnoughts to swing first their sights and then their guns on to the *Invincible*.

Hood had been congratulating Dannreuther on the voice pipe, 'Keep at it as quickly as you can. Every shot is telling', when a shell hit 'Q' turret amidships, penetrated the seven-inch armour and exploded inside. The sequence was identical to that which had ended her sister ship, *Indomitable*. The twelve-inch shell charges were ignited, and the flash thrust down to the magazine below, the simultaneous explosion splitting her in two. It was 6.33 p.m. The official British naval historian wrote:

> Flames shot up from the gallant flagship and there came again the awful spectacle of a fiery burst, followed by a huge column of dark smoke which, mottled with blackened debris, swelled up hundreds of feet in the air, and the mother of all battle cruisers had gone to join the other two that were no more.

It was a near-miracle that there were seven survivors, one of them the gunnery officer. Shortly before he died, Dannreuther recounted to this writer how he was hurled into the sea and swam about until he and several ratings found some floating debris which they clung to until a destroyer, the *Badger*, came alongside and picked them up. The *Badger*'s commander said that Dannreuther 'stepped on board, wet from the sea but showing no other evidence that this was any different from a courtesy visit to another ship'.

Beatty did not repeat his comment, but there was certainly 'something wrong with his bloody ships'. There was something wrong with the bloody weather, too. Although they had the light advantage and the benefit of surprise, no sooner was a reading obtained on a target than a curtain of smoke or mist obscured it. In the van of the British line when its deployment was completed at 6.40 was, appropriately, the *King George V*.

Like Scheer's *Friedrich der Grosse*, Jellicoe's flagship was the centre of his line of dreadnoughts. Jellicoe himself and his flag-commander, Dreyer, with binoculars clamped to their eyes, realized that, before darkness closed about this armada, they had the power to crush the German High Seas Fleet and end the war in an evening. The British position was a tactical ideal — crossing the enemy's 'T' while possessing a great advantage in heavy weapons.

Scheer later wrote of his situation:

> It was now quite obvious that we were confronted by a large portion of the English Fleet, and a few minutes later, their presence was indicated on the horizon directly ahead of us by firing from heavy calibre guns. The entire arc stretching from north to east was a sea of fire. The muzzle flashes were clearly seen through the mist and smoke on the horizon, though there was still no sign of the ships themselves.

The British battleships opened fire as and when they could, made some hits on the leading German ships, the ship in the van, the *König*, taking the worst knock. But the gunnery officers of the British dreadnoughts afterwards asserted that they could never make out more than four enemy ships at a time. There were, however, two exceptions: the 5,000-ton cruiser *Wiesbaden*, which had been hammered to a standstill by Hood's battle-cruisers, and an unidentifiable vessel which many of the British ships passed close by. It was unidentifiable because only the two ends stood up out of the water, the broken amidships ends resting on the shallow sea bed. Those above deck who witnessed this gruesome sight presumed it was a sunk German battle-cruiser and cheered as they swept past. Only later did they learn that these were the twin gravestones of the *Invincible*.

But there was no mistaken identity in the case of the

Wiesbaden, and for lack of a better target twelve-inch and 13.5-inch fire struck this ruined vessel. Never was the correctness of von Tirpitz's principle of making his ships virtually unsinkable better exemplified. It seemed impossible that anyone could remain alive amid the twisted, smoking steel and the flattened remains of her three funnels. Yet, as a last gesture of defiance, the *Wiesbaden* contrived to launch one remaining torpedo attack which struck the *Marlborough*. The water poured in and reduced the battleship's speed — it was leading the 6th Division — to sixteen knots.

Scheer's next move was as urgent as had been Jellicoe's in deciding how to deploy. To continue north and be 'bent' farther and farther east was to court catastrophe. On manoeuvres he had frequently practised an evolution which he called the *Gefechtskehrtwendung* or simultaneous turn-away through 180 degrees. It was a tricky manoeuvre, with a high risk of collision. Jellicoe knew about it but it did not appear in his Grand Fleet Battle Orders. Scheer now ordered this turn-away, at the same time sending in his flotillas as a distraction and to lay smoke.

This German destroyer attack, though not successful, added to Jellicoe's uncertainty and also to his visibility. The German turn-away took place at 6.35 p.m., but it took nearly ten minutes for Jellicoe to become aware of it. Several units of his battle fleet had discerned what was happening, but neither they nor the scouting forces, whose function this was, sent a report to their C.-in-C., assuming, as had so often occurred in this engagement, that what they could observe Jellicoe could also see.*

---

*Jellicoe commented after the Battle of Jutland, 'Never imagine that your C.-in-C. sees what you see.'

The first intimation of what was happening was a sudden silence from the leading units of Scheer's fleet. When it was confirmed that the German Fleet had suddenly turned through 180 degrees, Jellicoe did not give the order to pursue Scheer, fearing that the Germans would cast mines astern. This continuing fear, stemming from the Russo-Japanese War twelve years earlier, was without foundation, for there were no facilities for mine-laying in any of the German heavy ships. Jellicoe, however, ordered a change of course to the south, with the intention of cutting Scheer off when he attempted to make for his home ports.

The final phase of this long engagement was as critical as anything that had gone before. Scheer had anticipated Jellicoe's counter-move, and now turned the High Seas Fleet on a reverse course with the intention of getting behind Jellicoe and heading for the Skagerrak between north Denmark and south Norway, or slipping down inside the minefields running parallel with the Danish coast. But he overestimated Jellicoe's speed, and by 7.10 p.m., an hour before sunset, he found himself driving towards the Grand Fleet in a repeat of his first encounter. This time, besides again sending in his destroyers to make smoke and discharge their torpedoes, Scheer ordered his mauled battle-cruisers to *ran an den Feind, voll einsetzen* — 'charge the enemy regardless'.

Simultaneously he ordered a second turn-about. This time, under the pressure of fire from Jellicoe and while still in irregular formation, it lacked the neat seamanship of the first turn-about, and it was a near-miracle that there were no collisions. Nevertheless, the manoeuvre was completed and again saved Scheer from disaster, while Hipper, observing the retreat of the High Seas Fleet, was thankful to be able to call off his charge. He had been within less than 8,000 yards of the leading

British battleships and was being hit again and again. At the conclusion only the *Moltke* was in a condition to defend herself, Hipper's other ships having had all their main armament put out of action.

As for Scheer's destroyer attack, it was met by a counterattack by Jellicoe's destroyer flotillas. The mêlée that followed was as chaotic as the earlier destroyers' engagements, with individual ships avoiding one another, sometimes only by yards, through water churned white by bow waves and stern wakes while the firing by their guns was continuous. The scene was not dissimilar to the air battles over the Western Front, or cavalry charges in wars gone by. Some ships were forced to a standstill, but only one German ship was sunk, by a British torpedo launched at point-blank range.

A number of German torpedoes were fired at the advancing British Battle Fleet, causing Jellicoe to order in succession two 2½-point turns to port, combing the tracks. Thus the British C.-in-C. was not prepared to risk the loss of any of his ships for fear of this underwater weapon.

According to the clock, there still remained half an hour of daylight, but with dusk there came an increase in the degree of mist and low cloud, making accurate gunnery well nigh impossible. The turn also had the effect of the two battle fleets steaming in opposite directions for a time, and at a combined speed of twenty knots.

When Jellicoe was satisfied that he was out of danger from the destroyers' torpedoes, he turned onto a south-westerly heading, the *King George V* again leading. She was a mere six miles from the leading German dreadnought, *Westfalen*. They were on converging courses, too, but as 9 p.m. approached the darkness was almost complete. No heavy guns opened fire on either side, and while Jellicoe was full of hope and expectation that there would be a renewal of the engagement at dawn, in fact it was the end of the fighting between the heavy ships.

The night of 31 May/1 June was one of tumult and uncertainty. Light cruisers and destroyers flitted about like moths in the darkness, occasionally switching on their searchlights to illuminate friend or foe. The German light cruisers *Frauenlob*, *Rostock* and *Elbing* were all sunk by torpedo, gunfire or collision. But the British 4th Flotilla lost five destroyers while attacking the German dreadnought line at point-blank range. That any survived under the circumstances was another miracle of that night, but they did succeed in ramming the dreadnought *Nassau*, which lost speed. The *Warrior*, the armoured cruiser of Arbuthnot's 1st Cruiser Squadron, which had lost contact at dusk after the annihilation of her flagship, *Defence*, was completely lost in the darkness and had the misfortune to find the wrong fleet. A look-out in the *Thüringen* spotted her at a range of about 1,000 yards. The battleship switched on searchlights; the twelve-inch guns opened fire and set the *Warrior* on fire while shattering her upper deck. Then she suffered an explosion in her magazine, just like her flagship.

A similar fate struck the German battleship *Pommern* when the British 12th Flotilla struck the German line at 1.45 a.m. A single torpedo sufficed to blow her up. There was a flash and then she was no more. This 'five minute' ship had not lasted five seconds. The *Pommern* was the only battleship lost on either side. Of her crew of 844 none survived. Although a pre-dreadnought, the *Pommern* was laid down in the same month, December 1905, as the *Dreadnought* herself.

Scarcely an hour after this spectacular sinking had lit up the night sky, Scheer, with Hipper, had reached the safety of

Horns Reef and his own minefields. He was lacking the *Lützow*, which had sunk earlier, the *Pommern*, four light cruisers and five destroyers.

As for Jellicoe, he had been informed by the Admiralty as early as 10.41 p.m. that the German Fleet had been ordered home. Jellicoe knew that Scheer could fulfil this order by doubling back behind him and heading for Horns Reef. But he was not listening to the Admiralty after the signal blunder earlier which had informed him that Scheer was still in his base when he had long been at sea and driving north.

When a misty dawn broke, Jellicoe headed for home with a heavy heart. There was much to do *en route* to Scapa Flow, all of it sad or disagreeable: the surgeons attending to the wounded, the chaplains supervising the burying of the dead in the traditional manner, and everyone attending to repairs.

Officers and men alike of Jellicoe's battle squadrons experienced a mixture of elation and disappointment. For almost two years they had all wondered privately how they would respond when they at last faced combat. Now they had been through the fire and found themselves 'not wanting'. The future King George VI, a midshipman in one of the turrets of the battleship *Collingwood*, always said that the experience had changed his life. The disappointment at failing to sink the entire High Seas Fleet was profound after the years of hopeful expectation. If they had known the reality, the disappointment would have been more intense. The tally of three British battle-cruisers and four armoured cruisers, against one German battle-cruiser, one German battleship and no armoured cruisers (there were none present), does suggest that there was 'something wrong with our bloody ships', to which Beatty later added 'and with our system, too'.

When the battle report appeared in the newspapers, the public, too, were disappointed. But there was another side to the story, which the Admiralty stupidly failed to define. Within forty-eight hours of Jellicoe's return to base, he could report that the fleet was ready — fully armed, fully refuelled and at full strength as far as the battle squadrons were concerned. It was many months before Scheer could make the same statement. Of Hipper's Scouting Fleet, the *Lützow* was at the bottom of the North Sea, the *Seydlitz* only just made it home, and none of the surviving battle-cruisers was fit to go to sea.

What conclusions can be reached about this one and only battle between dreadnought fleets? On quality of *matériel*, it has to be said that Germany scored, but not by a wide margin. The German Navy had virtually no history, which gave it advantages and disadvantages. In the nineteenth century, the British Royal Navy had descended into a mélange of traditionalism, apathy and self-satisfaction. It was living on the glories of the past, which would have shocked Horatio Nelson. From the turn of the century, Admiral 'Jacky' Fisher began to break up all this traditionalism. As a firebrand, revolutionary and genius, he brought about basic reforms in every branch of the service, tearing down class distinctions, scrapping the old ships that 'could neither fight nor run away'. He inspired the dreadnought, encouraged submarine development and, latterly, even flying. He may have been late on the scene, but not too late.

The German Kriegsmarine was an astonishing creation, built in two decades, as had the Japanese Navy been in the equivalent period of time by Admiral Togo. Germany turned to Britain and the United States for formulas and principles, examined them closely, adapted and in many cases improved on them. Germany was very much an industrious and industrial nation, with long experience of war. Alfred von Tirpitz and his staff, strongly backed by Kaiser Wilhelm II, applied themselves to the problems, created new shipyards, docks and bases. Alfred Krupp was already making guns: the 4.1-inch, 8.2-inch, eleven-inch and then the twelve-inch naval guns were superb weapons with a high muzzle velocity. The armour-piercing (AP) shells were first-rate, with great penetrating power, and only a few duds were found on the British ships after Jutland.

There were no major faults in British guns, and the fifteen-inch gun, fitted to six of the British battleships, was a superb weapon which was greatly feared by the enemy. But the quality of the shells was greatly inferior to the Germans', tending to break up on impact with the protective armour instead of penetrating it before exploding. A high proportion failed to explode at all, and it was with relish that some German crews piled up these duds on the upper deck to be photographed after the battle.

As for the men who manned these ships, German ratings were all conscripts who tended to live ashore in barracks when not at sea. Their quarters when at sea were very confined, partly due to the tight compartmenting which, in turn, controlled the flooding when hit below the waterline. By contrast, British ratings were all volunteers, many of them third- or fourth-generation seamen. Their accommodation was much more open and comfortable than that of their German counterparts, which was just as well because they might be expected to steam to far-distant parts of the Empire, as the crews of the three battle-cruisers searching for Admiral von Spee experienced.

The spirit and zeal of the British rating remained amazingly high considering the long, inclement weather conditions at Scapa Flow, where the wind was ferocious and the sun set at about 3 p.m. in winter.

As to the senior officers and captains of the British ships, they were discouraged from using their initiative by the GFBOs. These covered every imaginable situation and contingency, and totalled 200 pages by the time of Jutland. Jellicoe's predecessor, Admiral Sir George Callaghan, confined his GFBOs to two pages. Jellicoe was a pernickety, tireless C.-in-C. who failed to understand how his ever-increasing GFBOs were sapping the initiative of his commanders. Nelson and his 'band of brothers' was a stark contrast to Jellicoe and his GFBOs. Nelson consulted his captains at every turn; Jellicoe rarely.

The appalling signalling blunders and failure to inform Jellicoe were among the reasons — failing light was another — why Jellicoe did not crush Scheer.

Jellicoe had failed to consult his own staff, even over the crucial decision about deploying to port or starboard when close to the German Fleet.

Although the Royal Navy lost more men and ships at Jutland than the Kriegsmarine, the Battle of Jutland was a considerable British strategic victory. German propaganda loudly claimed a victory for the High Seas Fleet. But the incontrovertible fact was that Scheer had come out with the intention of cutting off and destroying part of the Grand Fleet. Instead, he had fallen into a trap from which he escaped by the skin of his teeth, and during the hours that followed had been preoccupied with making his way home safely. When he did so with his scouting forces *hors de combat*, he left the North Sea in British control as if nothing had changed. Nor had it: the blockade continued without relaxing its grip. Germany suffered shortages of food and material goods. The morale of the Kriegsmarine deteriorated, leading finally to mutiny.

With Beatty now C.-in-C., the German Navy surrendered on 21 November 1918.

But between Jutland and that surrender, the German U-boats, which had played a negligible part in the battle, came close to bringing Britain to her knees by unrestricted trade war: an omen of future fighting at sea.

5

·······················

THE BATTLE OF THE
RIVER PLATE,
13 DECEMBER 1939

The subtle and opportunistic expansion of Nazi Germany by the annexation of adjacent sovereign European territories during the 1930s, led to a crisis which, in 1938, ended with the Munich Agreement and its false promise of peace. However, to match German re-armament, Britain and France increased their own production of arms, the former stepping up the building of convoy escorts in particular. In the autumn of 1939, Hitler's invasion of Poland destroyed the flimsy peace of 1938 and a state of war existed in Europe once again. Although little occurred on the Western Front for some months, the war at sea began immediately. The British liner, Athenia, *was torpedoed on the first day of the war, September 3. One hundred and twelve people died, twenty-eight of them Americans.*

There was a curious similarity in the opening rounds of the naval war of 1939 to those of 1914. But the principal difference was that German rearmament under the Nazi regime had the experience of the First World War to call upon, and they knew the devastating effect which submarine warfare would have upon Great Britain, its principal maritime foe. Nevertheless, both German and British naval orthodoxy still set great store by the employment of the "Big Gun," so much so that the Germans had constructed their

Panzerschiffen. Though known to the British as "pocket-battle-ships," these men-of-war were in fact very heavy cruisers and were intended to act as armoured commerce raiders. Two of them were sent to sea in the late summer of 1939 in anticipation of an out-break of hostilities. One of these, named Graf Spee after the admiral who had inflicted the crushing defeat at Coronel, embarked on a very successful campaign against British merchant ships in the southern Indian Ocean and in the South Atlantic. Such was Graf Spee's success that she set in train a pursuit by British cruisers centred again on the Falkland Islands, but reaching its climax off the Rio de la Plata, a focus point of British trade routes, and known familiarly to them as the "River Plate."

Thus, the first major naval engagement in the Second World War was, like that of the First, fought within a few months of its outbreak, in the southern hemisphere, and consisted of a chase and action between cruisers.

· ·

THE RE-EMERGENCE OF a German Navy was instituted by Adolf Hitler soon after he came to power in 1933. Judging that air power would be more important in a future war, he made no attempt to build a battle fleet, but recognized the importance of commerce warfare, particularly by using submarines. The U-boat branch was therefore given priority, and when war broke out in September 1939, the Nazis had at sea some seventy U-boats of the most modern kind.

The Treaty of Versailles prohibited Germany from building heavy cruisers above 10,000 tons, and there were numerous other restrictions which the Nazi government increasingly ignored. But even before Hitler came to power, Germany laid down a new class of armoured cruiser commonly referred to as 'pocket battleships'. They were nominally of 10,000 tons, but they turned out to be over 12,000 tons. These pocket battleships were diesel-powered and carried enough fuel to give them a range of over 10,000 miles. Their maximum speed was twenty-six knots. They were named the *Admiral Scheer, Admiral von Spee* (after First World War heroic admirals) and *Deutschland* (later changed to *Lützow*, after the only battle-cruiser Germany lost at Jutland).

These ships were clearly designed for commerce raiding and were the source of much speculation, and some anxiety, in the British Admiralty. As anticipated, two of them were at sea when war broke out. They had six eleven-inch guns. These were of a new Krupp type with a high muzzle velocity, and could hurl a 670-pound projectile to a range of 30,000 yards, some 50 per cent farther than Germany's earlier eleven-inch. The only ships that could match them in speed and gunfire were First World War battle-cruisers, and both Britain and the Germans knew how frail these were.

The *Deutschland* had been ordered to harass Allied trade in the North Atlantic. In this role she mercifully showed a lack of enterprise and a fear of interception by British forces. The spirit of the *Emden* in 1914 was not matched by her modern counterpart. After a few weeks she made her way back to Germany by Arctic and Norwegian waters.

The *Spee*, however, showed more of the spirit of the admiral after whom she was named. After operating in the Indian Ocean, her route could be followed by the SOS calls put out by radio by her victims. But she doubled the Cape, far to the south, without being observed, and then found two victims in the area of St Helena in the South Atlantic. Counter-measures had long before been taken by Winston Churchill, back at the Admiralty as First Lord as he had been in 1914. The events that followed reminded him of 'the anxious weeks before the actions at Coronel and later at the Falklands'.

One of the groups searching for the *Spee* consisted of the modern aircraft carrier *Ark Royal*, accompanied by the battle-cruiser *Renown*. Another Anglo-French group which boasted an aircraft carrier and two heavy cruisers was based on Dakar on the western coast of Africa.

A third, commanded by Commodore Henry Harwood, consisted of two eight-inch-gun cruisers and two six-inch-gun cruisers. Harwood cannily anticipated that the *Spee* would next head for the River Plate estuary, where British merchant-men normally abounded. Harwood therefore ordered his four ships to rendezvous off the Plate by 12 December. Unfortunately, his most powerful ship was obliged to refuel and refit at the Falkland Islands, an uncanny parallel with Admiral Cradock's situation before Coronel. If Harwood inter-cepted the *Spee* he could muster only six eight-inch guns of the *Exeter*, and the twelve six-inch guns of his light cruisers against the heavily armoured *Spee* with her six eleven-inch guns.

Harwood had done his arithmetic well: in the dawn light of 13 December, the *Graf Spee* loomed up to the north-west. Mistaking the enemy ships ahead for one light cruiser and two destroyers, Captain Hermann Langsdorff, her captain, ordered his ship to steam full speed for the enemy.

Langsdorff trained his forward eleven-inch guns on the *Exeter*, and, as at Coronel, immediately straddled her. Ineptly he continued to close the range instead of bombarding the British cruiser beyond the range of her smaller guns. But with-in minutes the *Exeter* had her forward eight-inch guns knocked out, while a hit on the bridge killed most of her personnel. Harwood, flying his flag in the *Ajax*, divided his force, the two light cruisers attacking the *Spee* on her starboard, while *Exeter*, using her two surviving guns, hammered away on the German's port side, making several hits.

To have to fight to port and starboard seemed to upset Langsdorff, who retired under a smoke-screen and, to the astonishment of the British commander, appeared to seek refuge in the estuary of the River Plate 300 miles distant.

Captain Parry of the *Achilles* later reported:

> My own feelings were that the enemy could do anything that he wanted to. He showed no signs of being damaged; his main armament was still firing accurately, the *Exeter* was obviously out of it, and so he had only two small cruisers to prevent his attacking the very valuable River Plate trade. It was therefore rather astonishing to find the enemy steaming off at a fairly high speed to the westward.

This was all very different from the conduct of the admiral after whom Langsdorff's ship was named in the battle off the Falklands twenty-five years earlier, almost to the day.

As night fell and the *Graf Spee* had slunk into Montevideo harbour, *Achilles* and *Ajax* hovered just outside the three-mile limit, prepared to use what was left of their 'peashooters' and their torpedoes should the pocket battleship re-emerge. The *Exeter* hove to more distantly, burying her seventy or so dead, tending to the wounded and patching up her damage. But also during the night Harwood's other eight-inch-gun cruiser, the *Cumberland*, which had hastened at full speed from the Falklands, arrived, with her eight guns, as a reinforcement.

The night of 13/14 December was a busy one for all parties. Langsdorff worked on the Uruguay authorities to get an extension on the international limit in a neutral harbour for ships at war, but had less success than Admiral von Spee had earlier at Valparaiso. Permission was given, however, for the wounded to be brought ashore, as well as the crews of the Allied merchantmen whose ships had been sunk over the past weeks.

Busiest of all were the British undercover authorities, who were spreading the word that a carrier and a battle-cruiser were closing on Montevideo in time for the emergence of the *Spee*: the two ships, the *Renown* and *Ark Royal*, were hurrying south but were still 2,500 miles away.

As the time limit approached, Langsdorff telegraphed Berlin:

> Strategic position off Montevideo: Besides the cruisers and destroyers, *Ark Royal* and *Renown*. Close blockade at night; escape into open sea and breakthrough to home waters hopeless ... Request decision on whether the ship should be scuttled in spite of insufficient depth in the estuary of the Plate, or whether internment is to be preferred.

Hitler replied:

> Attempt by all means to extend the time in neutral waters ... Fight your way through to Buenos Aires if possible. No internment in Uruguay.

All the further pleas of Langsdorff and the German envoy in Montevideo were fruitless. On the afternoon of 17 December, a seaplane catapulted from the *Ajax* on a reconnaissance mission reported that the *Graf Spee* was putting to sea. The two British light cruisers and the *Cumberland* prepared for action with growing excitement. Then, as the armoured ship reached the three-mile neutrality limit, a boat was seen to put off. A few moments later the seaplane reported that the *Spee* had been rent asunder by a tremendous explosion which caused her to break apart and settle on the sea bed, her masts projecting into the smoke-filled sky. A second plane, commissioned by a photographer from *Life* magazine, flew over the wreck, and the picture that appeared in his magazine revealed for the first time that the German Navy possessed ship-borne radar, a singular blessing for commerce raiding.

Langsdorff was heartbroken at the loss of his ship, and two days later wrote a memorandum, which began:

> I can only prove by my death that the Fighting Services of the Third Reich are ready to die for the honour of the Flag. I alone bear responsibility for scuttling the pocket battleship *Admiral Graf Spee*. I am happy to pay with my life for any possible reflection on the honour of the flag.

Then he put a pistol to his head and shot himself.

This British victory in the middle of the 'phoney war' provided a great fillip to the Allies, and it had a postscript that was also morale-boosting. Some of the crew of the *Graf Spee* and 300 prisoners who had manned the *Spee*'s victims boarded the German tanker *Altmark* (14,367 tons) which headed for Germany. The only hope of reaching a German port was to steam far into Arctic waters and creep down the Norwegian coast within territorial waters. The Royal Navy at the same time used every endeavour to intercept the *Altmark*. A destroyer flotilla led by the *Cossack* (1,870 tons), commanded by Captain Philip Vian, located the *Altmark* in Norwegian waters; she had fled into a deep fjord, where she was guarded by two Norwegian gunboats. The Norwegians then reassured Vian that they had twice searched the merchantman and found nothing suspicious. Winston Churchill, on his own initiative but with the support of the Foreign Office, instructed Vian to go ahead and board the *Altmark*, regardless of Norwegian protest.

On the night of 16 February 1940, Vian took the *Cossack* up into the fjord, all her searchlights playing on the German ship, which immediately got under way and attempted to ram the *Cossack*. In doing so, she ran aground. In a Valkyrian scene, set against the backdrop of the snow-clad mountains above, the *Cossack* grappled the *Altmark*, and an armed party sprang across. A hand-to-hand contest then ensued, the result of which was the death of four of the German crew and the wounding of five more. There were no British casualties.

The German crew surrendered, though some escaped ashore. The search of the ship then took place, at first without success, and then deep down in the hold the 300 British prisoners were discovered by breaking through some locked doors.

In a melodramatic finale, the prisoners rushed out and climbed on deck shouting, 'The Navy's here!', a cry that echoed all over the world, outside Germany.

Vian also revealed that they had discovered light armament of pom-poms and machine-guns, which if the Norwegians had thoroughly searched the ship twice could scarcely have escaped their eye. But in exculpation of the Norwegian stance, they were very vulnerable to Nazi attack, as was shown weeks later when the German Army invaded and occupied the whole country.

It was no longer a 'phoney war'* but the real thing, and Allied shipping became ever more vulnerable with the German occupation of bases along the whole long coastline of Norway.

6

The Battle with the Bismarck, May 1941

The period between May 1940 and the summer of 1941 marked the nadir of British fortunes. The Anglo-French invasion of Norway had failed to stop the German occupation of that country, while the German Blitzkrieg into northern France by way of The Netherlands and Belgium had forced the French to surrender to partial German occupation and the establishment of a puppet Fascist regime in the southern third of France. The British Expeditionary Force had been extricated with great difficulty from the beaches of Dunkirk in northern France, but had lost its equipment. Britain now stood alone; her cities were being bombed and invasion seemed imminent. Fascist Italy came into the war alongside Germany. In no mood to treat with Hitler, Prime Minister Churchill defiantly dug in. His most important asset was the convoy route across the North Atlantic to the United States which President Roosevelt had declared to be "The Arsenal of Democracy." Preservation and exploitation of this "Atlantic Bridge" became the primary war-aim, a bleak matter of survival for Britain.

For Germany this supply route was a glorious target: strangle it and Britain would starve and be compelled to capitulate, leaving Germany the dominant power in Europe. In addition to her U-boats, the Kriegsmarine of Nazi Germany possessed her capital ships. While these were never comparable in numbers with the

Kaiser's High Seas Fleet, nevertheless in the Tirpitz *and* Bismarck, *the* Scharnhorst *and* Gneisenau, *as well as the* Panzerschiffen *remaining after the destruction of* Graf Spee, *it possessed major warships of such awesome power that the mere possibility of their appearance athwart a British trade route required the retention of overwhelming forces able to contain and counter-attack them. Thus, with a small fleet, the Germans were once again able to tie down British capital ships and their attending destroyer screens, depriving convoys in the Atlantic of much-needed escorts.*

What was worse, however, was for one of these heavy vessels to evade apprehension and embark upon a marauding cruise, such as Graf Spee *had done before her nemesis off the* Plate *Estuary. The consequence of heavy enemy ships at loose in the North Atlantic had already been felt with telling effect by the British when, in November 1939 the* Scharnhorst *and* Gneisenau *had sunk the patrolling British armed merchant cruiser* Rawalpindi; *in June 1940 when the same German battle-cruisers sank the aircraft carrier* Glorious *and her destroyer screen during the evacuation of Norway; and in the following November when the pocket battle-ship* Admiral Scheer *fell upon a convoy gallantly defended to her death by the armed merchant cruiser* Jervis Bay.

The break out of Admiral Lütjens in Bismarck, *in company with the heavy cruiser* Prince Eugen, *was therefore viewed with alarm at the British Admiralty in London. The subsequent location, chase and destruction of* Bismarck *in May 1941 was prosecuted with a tenacity typical of the Royal Navy, but was to cost it dear.*

· ·

COMMERCE WARFARE — the *guerre de course* — came close to strangling Britain in the First World War, and Britain's blockade of Germany in that same war was one of the chief causes of Germany's downfall. The German High Command and Adolf

Hitler fully appreciated the importance in a new European war of closing off Britain's food and war supplies. In addition to a modern and highly effective U-boat fleet, Germany possessed three pocket battleships reduced to two after the Battle of the River Plate — four Hipper-class heavy eight-inch-gun cruisers, and two battle-cruisers, *Scharnhorst* and *Gneisenau*, of 26,000 tons armed with nine eleven-inch guns.

Then in 1935 word reached the British Admiralty that Germany was laying down two giant battleships, to be called *Bismarck* and *Tirpitz*, which were clearly intended for commerce raiding. These two ships, with eight fifteen-inch guns, wide in the beam and with thick armour-plated deck and sides, were the ultimate commerce raiders. The Royal Navy possessed only two battleships that could out-gun these new German battleships, and their design was twenty years old and their speed no match. But at the outbreak of war in September 1939, Britain was completing five new battleships, with a good turn of speed, satisfactory protection and ten fourteen-inch guns.

British Intelligence watched keenly and anxiously the progress of these two ships, and by the spring of 1941, the first, the *Bismarck*, was believed to be on her trials in the Baltic. Admiral Sir Dudley Pound, First Sea Lord, and Winston Churchill, now Prime Minister, discussed dispositions to meet this threat. The Royal Navy was at full stretch, with commitments in the Mediterranean to meet the threat of the powerful Italian Navy, the *Scharnhorst* and *Gneisenau* and a heavy cruiser lurking at Brest on France's Atlantic seaboard.

As a precaution, important Atlantic convoys, one of them with thousands of Canadian troops on board, were additionally protected by old 'R'-class battleships dating from the last war, and certainly no match for the *Bismarck*.

On the other hand, commerce raiding carried with it certain risks. A damaged raider had to seek a friendly port to carry out repairs, and as Admiral von Spee had been forced to recognize a generation earlier, the replenishment of ammunition after battle posed further problems.

British dispositions to counter these threats consisted of four cruisers to patrol the Arctic passages between Greenland and Iceland; two more patrolled the channel between Iceland and the Faroes. Admiral of the Fleet Sir John Tovey, a gallant destroyer commander at Jutland and now commander-in-chief, Home Fleet, had at Scapa Flow two new fourteen-inch-gunned battleships, *King George V* and *Prince of Wales*, and the battle-cruiser *Hood*, laid down in 1917 and, between the wars, the largest warship in the world. She could match the *Bismarck* in speed and armament, but not in her protection. Tovey could also draw on two more fifteen-inch-gunned battle-cruisers, the *Renown* and *Repulse*, which were very fast but even more flimsily protected; more useful perhaps was the modern carrier *Ark Royal*, at Gibraltar. Also available were the *Renown*'s sister ship *Repulse* and another new carrier, *Victorious*, which were about to embark as escort to a troop convoy destined for the Middle East via the Cape.

The *Bismarck*, flying the flag of Admiral Gunther Lütjens, and his accompanying heavy eight-inch-gunned cruiser, *Prinz Eugen*, having completed their working up in the Baltic, rashly left the Baltic via the Kattegat instead of returning through the Kiel Canal and then unobtrusively working their way north up the Danish and Norwegian coasts. As it was, a well-positioned British agent assigned to watch the activities of German warships from the southern tip of Sweden could not fail to see this giant German battleship and her satellite steaming through the Kattegat and north close to the Norwegian coast. He at once dispatched a coded signal to the British Admiralty.

The next step was taken by RAF Coastal Command. At Wick in north Scotland there was based a newly formed PRU (Photographic Reconnaissance Unit). The Spitfires they flew were stripped of all armament and armour plate, which were replaced by long-range drop tanks and cameras of the finest quality for their task.

On 21 May two of these machines took off, one heading for the Oslo area, the second north-east towards Bergen.

The Bergen-destined machine had the luck and produced the result that was so sorely needed. In brilliantly clear weather, and just as he crossed the Norwegian coast, the pilot saw the two German ships hove to in a fjord near the town of Bergen. Uninterrupted by defending fighters who should have been warned by radar of his approach, the pilot calmly took his pictures, reversed course and hastened back to Scotland, releasing his empty drop tanks *en route.*

To complete the RAF's contribution to this hunt, another PRU plane made the same journey the following day. But conditions were very different; the cloud was down to 200 feet and the pilot had to nose his way into the fjord where he was met by a barrage of flak, and with the danger of flying into the high mountains surrounding it. The pilot made a hasty exit but was able to inform his base that the ships were no longer there.

Now that it was clear to Admiral Tovey that the two hostile warships would attempt to break out into the Atlantic, where they could cause havoc among the vital convoys, he made his dispositions accordingly. To the north he dispatched

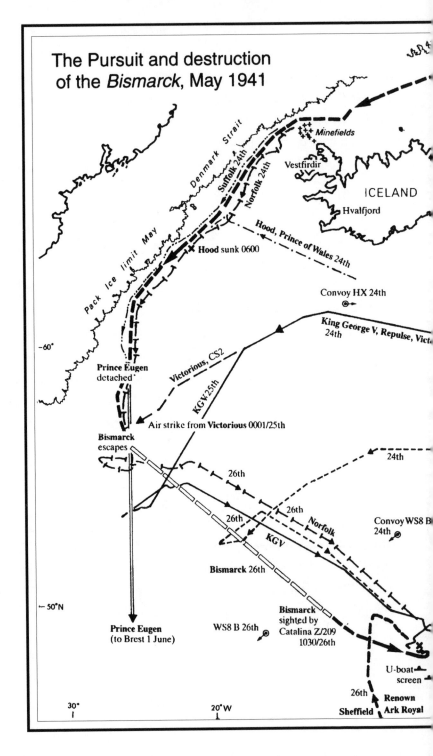

The Pursuit and destruction of the *Bismarck*, May 1941

Weissenburg (tanker)

Bismarck & Prince Eugen

Narvik

NORWAY

Bismarck's destroyers to Trondheim

Trondheim

GERMAN OCCUPIED

Faeroe Is.

22nd

Wollin (tanker)

Shetland Is.

Air reconnaissance

Bergen

Orkney Is.

23rd

Scapa Flow

23rd

60

Kristiansand

Marstrand

21st

Skagerrak

Kattegat

20th

19th

Gdynia (Gotenhafen)

Bismarck, Prince Eugen sailed 2130, 18 May

Kiel

ITISH ISLES

Hamburg

GERMANY AND

GERMAN OCCUPIED EUROPE

50°N

Brest

U-boat bases

Lorient

St Nazaire

ubmarine patrol

La Rochelle

0°

0   100   200   300

Nautical miles

10°E

his fastest ship, *Hood*, bearing the flag of Vice-Admiral Lancelot Holland, and the newly commissioned twenty-eight-knot *Prince of Wales*, captained by John Leach, whose ship had been experiencing trouble with several of her fourteen-inch guns; in fact, there were still workmen on board when she slipped out of Scapa Flow. These two heavy units were ordered to travel towards Iceland at best speed in support of the patrolling cruisers.

Tovey, with the *King George V*, took the *Repulse* and the new carrier *Victorious* with escorting destroyers on a more westerly heading, hoping to cut off the enemy ships if they escaped unscathed through the Arctic corridors. Tovey's carrier was as recently commissioned as the *Prince of Wales*. Her air crews were fresh from training school and many had not even had experience of taking off and landing on a carrier's flight deck. Their Swordfish torpedo bombers, later affectionately known as 'Stringbags', looked like some left-over from the First World War, being biplanes with a maximum speed of less than 100 knots — even slower when carrying their fourteen-inch torpedoes.

Admiral Holland and his force departed from Scapa at midnight on 21/22 May with destroyer escort and with full fuel tanks. Tovey followed later with his mixed but powerful force, still without knowledge of the German ships' position, or even if they were at sea.

Admiral Lütjens with the *Bismarck* and *Prinz Eugen* left the fjord in darkness during the night of 21/22 May on what was code-named Exercise Rhine. The sea was calm, and even the smaller *Prinz Eugen* had no difficulty in maintaining the ordered speed of twenty-four knots. At dawn on 23 May, as they approached the eastern entrance of the Denmark Strait, the weather turned foggy with much rain, ideal conditions for slipping through to the Atlantic. The forecast from home was equally reassuring, promising overcast skies with rain and moderate-to-poor visibility. The white mountains of Greenland were seen intermittently to starboard, and more rarely the northern coastline of Iceland. As at the Battle of Jutland, the visibility was wildly variable, and at times the cruiser and the battleship were out of sight of one another.

Then, at 7.15 that evening, a new sight hove into view at a range of no more than seven miles: a three-funnel heavy cruiser, immediately identified as of the British 'County' class, 10,000 tons with eight-inch guns and a good turn of speed — a most unwelcome sight. It disappeared almost at once into a bank of thick cloud. Lütjens knew that its disappearance by no means signified the end of it; and as if in confirmation a Catalina flying boat was glimpsed briefly, but it, too, disappeared almost at once.

As if to taunt and tease the German ships, a second cruiser of the same class as the first suddenly emerged from a fog bank at an even closer range. This time Lütjens ordered fire to be opened. This was done with a speed spurred on by anger and fear. But it was no swifter than the speed with which the helm was put over on the cruiser, which disappeared into the fog bank from which it had emerged. When last seen it was surrounded by water spouts from bursting fifteen-inch and eight-inch shells.

Now that he had been spotted by two scouting cruisers, Admiral Lütjens prepared himself and his ship for meeting a more formidable foe.

The *Suffolk*, captained by Robert Ellis, had been unable to transmit the important message of his sighting because ice had frozen the spume on his radio aerials, and it was the *Norfolk*, captained by J. R. L. Phillips, and Admiral Wake-Walker's flagship, which continued contact with the *Hood* and *Prince of Wales*.

On the other hand it was the *Suffolk* which kept the German ships in radar touch, owing to the fact that she, unlike the *Norfolk*, had been fitted with the latest improved radar. Admiral Tovey in the *King George V* received the *Norfolk*'s message, and so did Admiral Lütjens in the *Bismarck*, whose cryptographers could read the British code and were quick to do so.

The *Hood* and *Prince of Wales* were still 300 miles away. They immediately increased speed to twenty-seven knots, but their heading did not have to be altered. Admiral Holland's navigating officer calculated that they would be within range of the German ships by dawn on 24 May. The wind and seas got up when it became dark, which did not bother the big ships too much but made life miserable for the escorting destroyers. Regular reports came in from the *Norfolk* and *Suffolk* — her W/T back in action — one on each side of the German ships and dodging in and out of mist and fog banks.

In the British big ships battle flags were hoisted at 3 a.m. and officers and men went to battle stations. The *Suffolk*'s radar reports indicated that the *Bismarck* was no more than thirty miles distant. Admiral Holland ordered his ships on to a south-westerly heading, which should bring the enemy within range at around 6 a.m. But it was earlier than this when, in a clear sky, first the masts and then rapidly the hulls of the German ships became visible. At once Admiral Holland ordered a change of course of forty degrees to starboard. He seemed intent on closing the range swiftly, but the move puzzled John Leach, the captain of the *Prince of Wales*, because they had the whole day before them and the turn masked half the *Hood*'s fifteen-inch guns.

The moment they were on their new heading, the *Hood* fired her first four-gun salvo at 25,000 yards range. Almost immediately the *Prince of Wales* emulated her flagship. Fourteen miles distant, flashes from both German ships told of the opening of return fire. At this range it was difficult to distinguish the *Prinz Eugen* from the flagship; it had been German policy to give their heavy cruisers a similar silhouette to their battleships in order to confuse the enemy, and so it did.

British gunnery from the *Hood* and the *Prince of Wales* was first class and shell splashes soared up close to the battleship and the smaller ship. But the German gunnery was equally good, and an early hit on the *Hood* started a fire amidships. Admiral Holland at once ordered a turn to port, to Captain Leach's relief, allowing his ship's aft battery of four guns to train on the enemy.

Some authorities later defended Admiral Holland's effort to close the enemy because he was fully aware that his light deck armour could not protect him from long-range plunging shellfire. As it so happened, before the *Hood* had completed her turn a forest of tall shell spouts emerged from the sea about the after part of the battle-cruiser. It looked like a full broadside of fifteen-inch shells, and one of them struck the deck between the after turrets. It penetrated the three-inch armour as if it did not exist and plunged down towards the main and secondary magazines, which exploded with devastating results. The destruction of the 42,000-ton *Hood* took place in three almost simultaneous phases: first, flames rose into the air, twice as high as the mainmast, had it still existed, then pieces of the ship — whole turrets and guns, the fore superstructure, great chunks of twisted armour plate, complete funnels and a mass of other detritus — followed the flames into the air, to be followed in turn by a mass of smoke, black as a dark night, which reached as high as the clouds and blended in with them.

Only those who had seen the end of the *Queen Mary* at Jutland — and there were few of those present — had witnessed anything so appalling.

The *Hood* had been laid down after Jutland and was supposed to have incorporated the lessons of that battle. There were to have been four of her class, to match new German battle-cruisers, but when work halted on the German ships in 1917, all but the *Hood* were scrapped on the stocks. The *Hood* had been completed in 1920. During the years between the world wars, she remained not only the biggest warship in the world; many also thought she was the most handsome. And now she was gone, and with her her admiral, captain and more than 1,400 of her officers and men. The men of the destroyer *Electra*, which hastened to the spot within minutes, found nothing but floating wreckage and a sea of oil. They were consternated, and at first could not believe the truth. Then they spotted three figures, two clinging to wreckage, and one swimming. And that was all.

Now it was the turn of the *Prince of Wales* to occupy the full attention of both enemy ships. The range was short enough for the *Bismarck*'s secondary guns to join in the thunder of the fifteen-inch main battery. The British battleship was hit time and again, one heavy shell striking the bridge and killing almost all the personnel on it, though Captain Leach and his yeoman of signals somehow escaped. All four guns in the turret aft were out of action. But she was a strong ship. She was not going to succumb like her cohort, and the forward guns were firing steadily and making hits, though no one recorded them, and few of the men in the *Bismarck* felt them. Then Captain Leach ordered his ship to head away from this intense gunfire, under cover of smoke.

In spite of the loss of almost half her guns, and the inexperience of her gun crews, the hits she had made were to introduce a new scenario to the battle. The first hit was the most serious, striking the *Bismarck* forward, which led to the flooding of the forecastle with some 2,000 tons of water. This caused a nine-degree list to port, reducing her speed by four knots, and led to a serious oil leak. At first 'none of us grasped the gravity of the damage we had sustained', wrote the senior surviving officer of the *Bismarck*.

The first British report of the oil leak, which was like the scent of a fox to hounds during a hunt, was from the captain of a reconnoitring Sunderland flying boat. He signalled his base laconically, 'Losing oil — returning', which was read as the *plane* was losing oil.

With the loss of the *Hood*, Admiral Wake-Walker in the *Norfolk* was now the commanding officer, and his first order was to Captain Leach to join him in shadowing the two German ships. A few minutes later, he signalled Admiral Tovey, his C.-in-C., that the *Bismarck* was turning on to a southerly heading. His signal was received with relief because it suggested that she was heading for a French port, as if she had called off her intended attacks on convoys and had suffered damage. This view was reinforced when it was observed that the *Prinz Eugen* had been detached and was continuing south-west. The situation on that grey, rain-swept afternoon of 24 May was that the *Bismarck* was heading for the western coast of conquered France; Admiral Tovey, flying his flag in the *King George V*, with the battle-cruiser *Repulse*, the carrier *Victorious* and five cruisers, was 350 miles to the south-east of the German battleship, while the sixteen-inch-gunned battleship *Rodney*, the battle-cruiser *Renown* and the seasoned carrier *Ark Royal* were more distant but proceeding at best speed north in an attempt to concentrate an overwhelming force to confront and sink the *Bismarck*.

There was one other warship present, and she was the closest to the battleship, a bizarre intruder. She was the neutral American coastguard cutter *Modoc*, twenty years old, under 2,000 tons and armed with two five-inch guns. Her present mission was to seek any survivors from a convoy that had been badly mauled by U-boats. Instead, her skipper observed, a mile or two away, a huge battleship emerging from the mist, and racing past.

Half an hour earlier, Tovey, who had no knowledge of the *Bismarck*'s damage, and desperate at least to slow her down, took a gamble and ordered off his carrier's torpedo planes, most of the crews having only recently completed their training. In the last stage of their flight, the planes flew close to the American *Modoc*, whose crew were treated to another strange sight. The skipper had no idea that the Royal Navy flew such primitive-looking machines — biplanes with fixed undercarriage flying at about eighty knots, each with a torpedo under its belly. 'If ever there was a death ride...' the skipper pondered. Almost at once the dusk sky was lit up by a firework display of sparks as the battleship opened fire with its multitude of anti-aircraft guns — sixteen 4.1-inch and sixty of smaller calibre.

The Swordfish squadron commander ordered his pilots to split and attack from different directions simultaneously.

'The enemy tactics were such,' wrote a surviving German

officer later, 'that torpedoes were coming in at us from several directions at the same time and, in trying to avoid one, we were liable to run into another.'

The other problem for the German gun crews was that they found difficulty in assessing the planes' speed, even the towed drogues used in training being twice as fast as these lumbering biplanes; nor were their guns calibrated down to such a low target speed. The *Bismarck* resorted to using her larger-calibre guns, even the fifteen-inch, to fire into the sea ahead of the planes. That a modern battleship of 48,000 tons should have to defend itself against wood-and-fabric biplanes with its main armament was a salutary reminder of the changing face of sea warfare.

Through this curtain of fire and water the flimsy Swordfish flew and survived, but made only one hit. It was amidships, where the Krupp armour was at its thickest. It scarcely dented the ship, though the concussion killed or wounded several crew members. But the real damage of this attack was self-inflicted. The *Bismarck*'s helmsman, in swinging the battleship to and fro to avoid the torpedoes, caused the sketchy repairs to the damage inflicted by the earlier gunfire to be destroyed, thus increasing the rate of the water entering the ship.

But in this tit-for-tat pursuit, the next piece of luck fell to the *Bismarck*. During all the zigzagging followed by a 360-degree turn and a new heading, the *Suffolk* lost radar contact. For thirty-one hours the cruiser's radar controllers had been concentrating their eyes on the rotating beam and the blip it recorded with every circulation. And now it had gone! Captain Ellis at once signalled the dire news to Admiral Wake-Walker, and unknowingly to Admiral Lütjens. The dismay of one admiral was matched by the elation of his German counterpart — and throughout his ship. 'Contact had been broken!' exclaimed one survivor. '...It was the best possible news, a real boost to confidence and morale ... Content with the momentary respite, we kept expressing to one another the hope that we would not catch sight of the enemy again before we got to St Nazaire.'

When the news of the loss of contact reached London, Churchill speculated anxiously about Admiral Lütjens's intentions. 'Had he turned west or doubled back to the north and east? This caused the utmost anxiety and rendered all concentration futile.'

At about this time, the Swordfish, only two of them slightly damaged, made their way through the dark and rain, fifty miles to their carrier. The flight deck of the *Victorious* was soaking wet and the big ship was rolling and pitching in the heavy seas. Only the squadron commander had landed on a carrier at night before, but one by one they all touched down safely. It was a remarkable tribute to their training and their courage.

All through the night of 24/25 May the *Bismarck* remained lost and speculation was inconclusive. But, because she might suddenly reappear, the crews could not be stood down. Mugs of hot cocoa and bully-beef sandwiches were distributed among the gun crews, but there was no sleep for anyone in the cruisers and battleships. In spite of the early summer season, temperatures were low and grey clouds scudded in from the west in the wake of a cold front.

It was an uneventful morning, the peace being broken shortly before midday when Admiral Lütjens transmitted a long radio message back to Germany, describing the action the previous day, the sinking of the *Hood* and grave damage to what he incorrectly named the *King George V*.

There could have been two reasons for this astonishing

indiscretion. Lütjens could have thought that it was now safe enough for him to reach St Nazaire unlocated by the enemy; or it was a precautionary move to pass on all his intelligence before he was located and sunk. This message was immediately picked up by British radio director finders (RDF), which 'fixed' the position of the German ship. Its accuracy, however, was distorted by the strong cold front coming in across the Atlantic. It was made more inaccurate by poor chart-work on board the *King George V*, which strongly suggested that their prey was heading north for the Arctic passages from which she had emerged. Admiral Tovey then ordered all his ships on to a northerly heading, away from the course of the *Bismarck*.

Now the most likely force to intercept the German ship were the battleship *Rodney* and carrier *Ark Royal*, making best speed from Gibraltar. The *Rodney* had been deviated from her passage to the USA, where she was to undergo a complete refit. She had on board about 500 soldiers and many American naval officers and diplomatic staff, and a top deck piled high with stores and spare parts. But her magazines were full of shells for her nine sixteen-inch guns.

The *Rodney*, like her sister ship *Nelson*, was laid down in 1922, using some of the material intended for the *Hood*'s aborted sister ships. She was built under the restrictions of the Washington Naval Treaty, which limited tonnage to 35,000 tons. She was very strongly built with fourteen-inch side armour, had a maximum speed of twenty-three knots, and until the advent of the *Bismarck* was considered, with the *Nelson*, the most powerful battleship afloat. In a slogging gunnery duel, she was a match for the *Bismarck*.

The *Rodney*'s captain, the large, formidable Frederick Dalrymple-Hamilton, and his chief engineer officer coaxed what speed they could out of the battleship's old engines, which were the first item on the refit programme, but the 35,000-ton battleship could make only twenty knots. There was no sign of the *Bismarck* when night fell on 26 May. The location and destruction of the *Bismarck* now became a national crusade. Churchill spoke about it in Parliament and the national newspapers took up the cause with (censored) stories and speculation.

Air Marshal Sir Frederick Bowhill, the C.-in-C. of Coastal Command, RAF, had been following the chase with the greatest interest from the beginning. But it was now necessary to increase the intensity of the hunt. The machine best suited to conduct the search at extreme range was the Catalina, one of which had earlier been spotted by the German battleship. The Catalina, or as her American designers and builders called her more prosaically, the PBY, was a remarkable machine, only recently obtained from the USA. It was a twin-engined flying boat/amphibian with a range of some 4,000 miles and a crew of three. She could be armed with depth charges or bombs, and was already proving her worth in the battle against U-boats. One of these Catalinas took off from its base at Lough Erne in Ulster, with orders to sweep out far into the Atlantic, then south to the 50th Parallel. Among her crew of three was a US Navy officer, one of several who quite unofficially had been sent from the US to instruct the RAF in the machine's use.

It was a terrible morning far out in the Atlantic with high winds and low clouds. The crew had already been airborne six hours, and, thankfully, they would soon reverse course for home.

It was one more irony in this enterprise that the American at the controls was about to make an 180-degree turn when they all spotted through the murk the outline of a large ship. The pilot took the 'Cat' up into the safety of cloud, headed in the direction of the vessels. When they dropped down again out of the clouds, there, directly beneath them, was the biggest ship any of them had ever seen, down by the bows but still travelling at a great speed. Moreover, it could still use its guns, as they quickly discovered when the sky about them was filled with the grey puffs of heavy anti-aircraft fire, and tracer lines from the lighter guns. The Catalina was thrown about like a bird in a typhoon, and it was a struggle for the W/T operator to transmit his signal. But he managed to get off the preliminary report: 'One battleship bearing 240 degrees five miles, course 150 degrees, my position 49 degrees 33' North, 21 degrees 47' West. Time of origin 10.30/26.'

The Catalina's message was intercepted by one of the German listening stations and retransmitted to the *Bismarck*. Lütjens considered launching one of his Arado seaplanes to attempt to intercept and shoot down the Catalina. But there would be no benefit except the satisfaction of revenge. The Arado was well armed and would have had little trouble in destroying the amphibian. A second, and deciding, reason for not catapulting the Arado was the state of the sea, which was very rough, making her recovery highly dangerous.

But to Lütjens's consternation, scarcely an hour and a half later a lone Swordfish was briefly sighted, indisputable confirmation that there was a carrier within range. The Swordfish remained for some minutes, just out of gun range. Lütjens drew two conclusions from this. First, that his position was now confirmed and that heavy ships must soon be within range. Second, that they were also inevitably to be the target of another torpedo bomber attack.

The *Ark Royal* was the first of her class of carriers, laid down when, belatedly, the Royal Navy had to recognize that air power had become an integral part of sea power. The newer *Victorious* was one of her sister ships. But *Ark Royal* was already a veteran of the war, operating in the Mediterranean and elsewhere, always in the thick of things, and her air crews were hardened campaigners.

But even the most experienced veterans looked askance at the prospect of taking off in a Swordfish with a heavy torpedo. There was a forty-knot wind blowing, and the rise and fall of the flight deck exceeded fifty feet. It was difficult enough simply to prevent the lined-up aircraft from slipping from the wet deck. When the first crews climbed aboard, the *Ark Royal* had to slow to under ten knots to allow the aircraft to fly forward instead of blowing backwards, their stalling speed being fifty-five knots. But somehow all fifteen of the squadron's Swordfish became airborne, though they found it impossible to maintain any close formation. The first ship they found was the cruiser *Sheffield*, which was keeping close radar cover on the *Bismarck*. The captain on the bridge of the heavy cruiser was on the point of cheering on the Swordfish when they dropped low over the sea and headed for his ship from different bearings.

In these terrible conditions, and unwarned of the *Sheffield*'s presence, the Swordfish commander misidentified her for the *Bismarck*, and attacked. By the skipper's clever handling, the *Sheffield* combed the tracks of all fifteen torpedoes, and then transmitted an admonitory message.

The squadron returned to the *Ark Royal*, and all the Swordfish landed safely. The squadron commander reported bluntly, 'Right height, right range, right speed, right cloud cover, and the wrong f——-ing ship!'

With the wind still blowing a full gale, the carrier's commander ordered a second squadron to be brought up from the hangar, emphasizing to the squadron and flight commanders the vital importance of hitting and at least slowing down the battleship.

They set off in conditions as severe as those suffered by their fellow fliers earlier. The plan was to find the *Sheffield*, climb to 5,000 feet above her, then divide into subsections of three aircraft. Then they would go into cloud to approach as close as possible to the *Bismarck*. In the event they emerged from their cloud cover at about 1,000 feet.

One of the pilots wrote later:

The minute or so which followed will be forever engraved on my memory. There she was, a thousand yards away, big, black, cowled funnel, menacing with every close-range weapon stabbing flame as we steadied on our approach, 100 knots, 1,000 yards, just as the textbook says ... as we dropped our 'tinfish' we almost leapt into the air, and as we turned away aft tightly, we were suspended motionless for a split second that felt like an eternity as every gun seemed to concentrate on us...

An officer survivor of the *Bismarck* wrote:

Once more the *Bismarck* became a fire-spitting mountain. The racket of her anti-aircraft guns was joined by the roar from her main and secondary turrets as they fired into the bubbling paths of oncoming torpedoes, creating splashes ahead of the attackers ... the antique-looking Swordfish, fifteen of them, seemed to hang in the air, near enough to touch ... They flew low, the spray of the heaving seas masking their landing gear. Nearer, and still nearer they came into the midst of our fire. It was as though their orders were, 'Get hits or don't come back.'

To and fro the *Bismarck* swung, altering speed as quickly as if she were a torpedo boat. She took several hits amidships but she brushed these aside as if they were thrown stones. Then an anti-aircraft gun crew aft 'saw two planes approach on the port beam and turn to the right. In no time they were only twenty metres off our stern, coming in too low for any guns to bear on them. Two torpedoes splashed into the water and ran towards our stern just as we were making an evasive turn to port.'

One of the Swordfish's torpedoes exploded right aft, in the ships most vulnerable quarter. It not only damaged her propellers but, even worse, damaged her steering engine. There was no response when they attempted to reverse course. The *Bismarck* was locked on at twelve degrees port helm.

Every effort was made to repair the damage but, having forced entry into the compartment, the men were nearly drowned as oil-soaked water gushed in with every lurch of the ship. As darkness fell, other efforts were made. Even the rigging of a collision mat outside the punctured hull failed to hold back the heavy seas.

As for the Swordfish, they all managed to locate the *Ark Royal* and, one by one, land safely in the twilight and in a rising gale. Not one of them was undamaged, their canvas fuselages and wings peppered with shrapnel holes. One or two of the crew were superficially wounded, and that was all. Several of the pilots claimed hits and one thought he had made a hit on the stern.

The *Sheffield* was too distant to observe this Swordfish attack, and she took evasive action when the *Bismarck* defiantly

Battle of Tsu-Shima, May 1905
Imiral Tozo directing naval operations from the bridge of his flagship the *Mikosa*

Battle of Tsu-Shima. Artist's impression

Battle of Jutland 1916
The final stage – a German ship sinki

Vice-Admiral Sir David Beatty
commanding the first battle-
cruiser squadron

Battle of the River Plate, December 1939
A broadside view of the *Graf Spee* showing smoke and flames
issuing from the scuttled battleship

Battle of the River Plate
HMS *Ajax*, one of the three British cruisers which smashed the *Graf Spee*

Battle with the *Bismarck*, May 1941
Last photograph of HMS *Hood* as she went into action against
the German battleship *Bismarck*, taken from HMS *Prince of Wales*

Admiral Sir Andrew Cunningham, May 1942
at the time of the Battle of Cape Matapan

Battle for the Pacific
Japanese sailors carrying out manoeuvres in the Pacific
in December 1941

Battle of Midway, September 1942
A wounded sailor from the USS *Yorktown* being carried by comrades

Yorktown receives a direct hit from a Japanese plane during the Battle of Midway

Beach landing at Guadalcanal Island in the Solomons, 1943

The Japanese ship *Kinugawa Maru* lies beached at Guadalcanal

opened fire on her, but her radar was firmly locked on the battleship, and to the puzzlement of her captain she was observed
to be on a northerly heading — towards her pursuers, though at
a very slow speed.

The next chapter in this long saga was the arrival on the
scene of five British destroyers, led by Captain Philip Vian,
who had achieved earlier fame by releasing the prisoners
locked below decks in the *Altmark*.* Vian was escorting a convoy but had picked up the Catalina's message and without
orders sped to the scene, arriving as darkness fell. He knew
nothing about the mortal damage the *Bismarck* had suffered
at the hands of the Swordfish, but he recognized that his
job was to harry the battleship. This his flotilla did, darting in
from every side, firing star shells and real shells from his
4.7-inch guns, and, occasionally, a torpedo. He later claimed
several hits with twenty-one-inch torpedoes, but his main
concern was to unsettle the battleship's company and deprive
them of sleep.

Someone else was suffering from lack of sleep, too.
Captain Phillips of the *Norfolk* had kept himself awake with
doses of adrenalin provided by the ship's doctor. At 8.20 a.m. on
this twenty-seventh day of May, and standing on the cruiser's
bridge beside his Admiral — Wake-Walker — he spotted through
the uncertain visibility the great bulk of the *Bismarck*. They
could even discern that she was down by the bows and was
scarcely moving through the water. At once the signal went out
by W/T: 'Enemy bears 130 degrees, 16 miles.'

Captain Dalrymple-Hamilton's *Rodney* picked up the signal and hastened to the spot, and Phillips noted, 'The dear old

---

*These were the crews of merchant ships sunk by the *Graf Spee* to which the
Altmark had acted as a supply ship.

Rodney made off in the right direction, and about half an hour later we heard her guns.'

It was a turbulent night on board the *Bismarck* — turbulent emotionally, with no one getting any sleep, spirits rising when the loudspeakers announced that a strong force of German Ju88 bombers would take off from western France to attack the British ships. But there was no sign of them in the early dawn light. Then the ship was told that a U-boat was approaching, but there was no sign of her either, though the report was accurate.

This emotional turbulence was matched by the sea, and it was made worse by the inability of the battleship to turn into the wind. One of the engines broke down, too, so that they were scarcely moving through the water.

There was a good deal of defeatist talk among the 2,000 officers and men, and one rating was heard to say, 'My wife doesn't know that she will be a widow by tonight.' It was important that they should have some hot food before facing the inevitable battle, and this was provided by the galleys.

The *Norfolk* was the first ship to get a visual on the *Bismarck*, the distance about nine miles, the time 7.53 a.m. At first Phillips misidentified her as the *Rodney*, though their silhouettes were very different, the British ship having all her guns forward on the long forecastle. Phillips ordered recognition signals to be made, but even as this was being done he realized his mistake, and that he was making twenty knots towards the biggest battleship in the world. He made a sharp 180-degree turn and as he did so he saw the real *Rodney* on the horizon to the north. She had the *King George V* with her, line abreast: nine sixteen-inch guns and ten fourteen-inch guns against the *Bismarck*'s eight fifteen-inch. The *Norfolk* signalled Admiral Tovey in the *King George V*, 'Bismarck bearing 130 degrees, range 16 nautical miles.'

Another sister ship of the *Norfolk*, the *Dorsetshire*, appeared out of the mist and rain from the west; she had been escorting a convoy, but when she heard the Catalina's sighting she left her charges and sped north in the hope of intercepting the battleship before she could make port in France. Captain Martin succeeded in doing so, but was misidentified by Admiral Tovey's battleships as the *Prinz Eugen*, which had long since disappeared into the wastes of the Atlantic, refuelled at sea and then headed for France. Tovey's ships were about to open fire when the three funnels of the *Dorsetshire* proved she was friendly.

At a range of 20,000 yards, the *Rodney* opened fire with her sixteen-inch guns at 8.47 a.m. A minute later the *King George V* fired from her forward fourteen-inch guns. Almost simultaneously, *Bismarck* replied with a salvo from her forward guns, the rear turrets being unable to bear.

An observer on the *Bismarck*, an officer survivor, recounted:

I spent the first few minutes of the battle wondering why no enemy shells were landing on us, but that soon changed and there were more than enough of them. At 8.54 a.m. the *Norfolk* which was off the starboard bow began firing her 8-inch battery at a range of 20,000 metres. A few minutes later, the *Rodney* opened up with her secondary battery and around 9.02 a.m. she obtained a spectacular hit on the forward part of the *Bismarck*. At

9.04 a.m. the *Dorsetshire* began firing on us at a range of 18,000 metres. The *Bismarck* was under fire from all directions, and the British were having what amounted to undisturbed target practice.

It was not quite undisturbed; the German ship was keeping up a steady fire, but it was neither as rapid nor as accurate as it had been during the earlier gunnery duel. It was almost as if the range-finders and gun-layers, exhausted from lack of sleep and knowing that they soon must die, had lost their fighting spirit against these impossible odds.

Earlier Admiral Lütjens had sent the ringing message home, 'We shall fight to the last shell. Long live the Führer!'

The *Rodney*'s shooting from the outset was admirably accurate, and her sixteen-inch shells created appalling destruction as the hits multiplied. Her captain remarked after the battle, 'I can't say I enjoyed this part of the business much, but didn't see what else I could do.'

The *King George V* shortened the range, and soon it seemed that every shell was a hit. One by one the German battleship's guns were silenced. Lütjens was suffering the same fate as Admiral von Spee in 1914. But here in this North Atlantic engagement, by contrast with the South Atlantic battle, there was another dimension: air power, the threat of German bombers and the presence of torpedo bombers. The *Ark Royal* had launched fifteen Swordfish, but when they arrived on the scene they saw from above that they were not needed. All they could observe was a giant, battered corpse, heavily ablaze and stationary on the water. They hovered about for a few minutes, awestruck at the destruction inflicted on the enemy. They saw the *Rodney* cruising along one side of the battered wreck with her sixteen-inch guns at flat elevation pouring in point-blank-range salvoes.

Admiral Tovey was anxious to get away and be finished with the combat. Indeed, there was cause for urgency. There was the problem of fuel, and the threat from U-boats and bombers.

Tovey ordered the *Dorsetshire* to commit the *coup de grâce*. She did so, pumping two twenty-one-inch torpedoes into the *Bismarck*'s port beam, then doubling around the bow and launching two more on her starboard side. Their explosions coincided with Lütjens's orders to scuttle his ship, and soon the *Bismarck* heeled over ever steeper to port and sank by the stern.

Back home in Britain, the pursuit of the *Bismarck* was followed with deep anxiety, especially after the loss of the *Hood*. The government was not, of course privy to the details, but at 11 a.m., on 27 May, Churchill reported to the House of Commons in these terms:

> This morning, shortly after daylight the *Bismarck*, virtually at a standstill, far from help, was attacked by the pursuing battleships. I do not know what were the results of the bombardment. It appears, however, that the *Bismarck* was not sunk by gunfire, and she will now be despatched by torpedo. It is also thought that there cannot be any lengthy delay in disposing of this vessel. Great as is our loss in the *Hood*, the *Bismarck* must be regarded as the most powerful, as she is the newest, battleship in the world.

Churchill wrote later, 'I had just sat down when a slip of paper was passed to me which led me to rise again. I asked the indulgence of the House and said, ''I have just received news that the *Bismarck* is sunk.'' They seemed content.'

The members were more than 'content', and in London, when the evening newspapers reached the streets, it was like another Mafeking* night. The war was not going well. Russia had not yet been attacked. And it was another six months before the USA became an ally.

The *Dorsetshire*, the nearest ship to the sinking, picked out of the cold, oily and turbulent water 110 survivors. A number of British ratings climbed down the ropes to assist the Germans, who were sullen and defiant to the end.

The *Dorsetshire*, warned of the presence of a U-boat, was forced to cease this work of mercy, leaving many sailors to drown. Later this U-boat, its torpedos exhausted, picked up five more half-drowned men. The U-boat was assisted by a weather-reporting vessel which happened to be in the vicinity. And that was all.

*The celebrations were widespead in Britain when this besieged South African town was relieved during the Boer War at the turn of the century.

7

···

THE BATTLE OF
CAPE MATAPAN,
28–29 MARCH 1941

The Fall of France in the spring of 1940 compelled the British to neutralise the French navy which, until then had been responsible under the joint strategy of London and Paris, for the defence of the Western Mediterranean. Operating from Gibraltar, Admiral Somerville was charged with this unpleasant task in French North and West Africa. Admiral Cunningham, Commander-in-Chief of Britain's Mediterranean Fleet was based at Alexandria and had with him a French squadron which he skillfully persuaded not to take any action and which remained inactive until the liberation of France enabled it to resume the offensive.

But further misfortunes fell upon the British in their attempt to retain control of the Mediterranean. Fascist Italy declared war, attacking Egypt from Libya. It was critical that Britain maintain the island of Malta – lying in the path of the Italian supply route to Libya – from which attacks on Italian communications were mounted; it was of equal importance for the Italians to subdue Malta, and they possessed numerous airfields nearby, those in Sicily being only 60 miles away. Supplying Malta became a matter of priority for both Somerville and Cunningham, as did the neutralization of Italian air and sea-power. Raids were made on enemy airfields from British carriers, while a successful attack was made on the Italian fleet in November 1940 at its base at Taranto.

The Italian invasion of Albania and Greece in the spring of 1941 faltered and was partially countered by the British switching troops from Egypt to Greece where the Italians had been all but routed. However Rommel and the Afrika Korps were being sent to Libya, while German forces were sent to take over from the Italians in the Balkans. German aircraft had meanwhile succeeded in disabling Cunningham's only aircraft-carrier, Illustrious, and placing Malta under siege from the air. As the fighting in Greece intensified, Berlin pressured Rome to stir the Italian navy to act in support of the German offensive.

Cunningham had been seeking an action with the Italian navy for months and by March had a replacement carrier, the Formidable. He quickly learned of the Italian fleet's movement towards the Aegean, and sailed to intercept Admiral Iachino. The resulting clash consisted of a complex series of movements, a day and a night action to the south of Cape Matapan in southern Greece. Cunningham's victory was to destroy the spirit of the Italian fleet, but was not to prevent the defeat and partial evacuation of British and Commonwealth forces from Greece and Crete. Now dominating the Balkans, France and most of Europe, in that summer of 1941 Hitler invaded Soviet Russia.

....

AT THE OUTBREAK OF war in 1939, the Anglo-French allies divided their responsibilities in the Mediterranean, France taking the western end, with her bases in Toulon, Mers-el-Kebir and Oran. The British Mediterranean Fleet had as its main bases Alexandria in Egypt and Malta, plumb in the centre of the 'Middle Sea', as the Romans termed it. As in the First World

War, France relied heavily on her colonial troops in Morocco and Algeria to reinforce her regular troops on the western front against Germany.

In the early months of the war, Britain could feel secure in the Mediterranean. The fall of France in May 1940, and the subsequent entry of Italy on the German side on 10 June, altered the position entirely. Since the opening of the Suez Canal in 1869, the Mediterranean had been the lifeline to British India and her Far Eastern possessions and Australasia. Britain's later dependence on the oil-fields of the Middle East increased even further the importance of controlling this sea route.

The first anxiety for the British Fleet was the fate of the fleet of defeated France. A few isolated units sailed to British ports voluntarily. But the main body of what was the fourth-largest fleet in the world tucked itself away in its French bases, posing a potential threat to the British Navy. At one of these bases, Mers-el-Kebir, in Algiers, there lay at anchor two powerful new battle-cruisers, two older battleships and six large destroyers.

The British Admiralty created a new squadron, Force H, under the command of Admiral James Somerville. He was instructed to open negotiations with the French Commander, offering him alternative actions, all of which would render the squadron immune from future German possession.

The French admiral remained obdurate, refusing to agree to the ultimatum that he scuttle his ships within six hours or else they would be bombarded and sunk at anchor. With the utmost regret, Somerville withdrew from the discussions and put into effect the distasteful operation of destroying his recent ally's ships. At 5.54 p.m. on 3 July 1940, Somerville's ships opened a withering fire on the French squadron, blowing up one battleship, sinking a number of others and damaging one of the modern battle-cruisers, which was later crippled by torpedo attack. The other battle-cruiser slipped away and escaped in the confusion.

The C.in-C. of the British Mediterranean Fleet, Admiral Andrew ('ABC') Cunningham, now had to face up to the threat of the powerful Italian Fleet. Italy's Navy had been built by the dictator Benito Mussolini for operations in the Mediterranean, and only that sea. Unlike Hitler's new German Navy, it was not intended for commerce raiding. It was designed for home defence against the French Navy, which was no longer in the reckoning by the middle of 1940.

The first notable characteristic of the Italian Navy was the speed of its ships, which were at least five and sometimes ten knots faster than their foreign counterparts. The second feature, purely aesthetic though it might be, was their grace. It was almost as if Michelangelo had been reborn to design them. Its new battleships could exceed thirty knots and were the most beautiful big warships in the world. The Italian Navy had no aircraft carriers, relying on land-based aircraft for its protection and offensive powers.

It had numerous bases around the mainland, and also in Sicily. But its main base was at Taranto, on the northern side of the Gulf of Taranto on the Ionian Sea. Like the German Navy in the First World War, the Italian Navy's chief priority was to remain 'a fleet in being', a constant threat. Risk-taking was not on the agenda, any more than offensive action. Units of the Italian Navy ventured forth only to ensure the safety of convoys to support the Italian Army in North Africa. This led to several brushes with British units. But even though they out-gunned their attackers, they were intent only on escape.

Admiral Cunningham was determined to bring about a resolution to this state of affairs. He was greatly assisted in his planning by the arrival in Malta, first of long-range American photo-reconnaissance aircraft, and, in answer to his pleas to the Admiralty, via the Suez Canal, of a new, fast, armoured aircraft carrier. She was the *Illustrious*, and she had on board a number of the obsolescent but proven Swordfish torpedo bombing planes.

The Italian battle fleet was known to be at its anchorage in Taranto harbour, and this was confirmed by photographs taken from high up by an American-built Maryland aircraft which took off from Malta. This photograph showed five of six Italian battleships at anchor in the outer harbour, and a sixth one heading for that destination.

Cunningham put to sea from Alexandria, flying his flag in the battleship *Warspite* with the *Illustrious* and a protecting screen of destroyers. At 6 p.m. on 11 November, he detached the carrier towards the Ionian Sea. As darkness fell and the carrier was 180 miles from Taranto, she launched twenty-one 'Stringbags', some carrying bombs but the majority fitted with fourteen-inch torpedoes.

The air crews were conscious of the odds against them. Taranto was defended by countless heavy and light anti-aircraft guns; there were barrage balloons, the cables of which they would have to avoid; and there were anti-torpedo nets protecting the battleships. But in their favour was the full moon and the knowledge that some of the balloons had been blown away in a gale. Their torpedoes had been fitted with a new device which would allow the projectile to dive deep under the nets and rise against the hull of the target.

Lacking radar, the Italians were taken by surprise.

Suddenly the skies above their harbour were illuminated by flares dropped from the leading aircraft, turning night into day. It was easy for the pilots to pick out their targets, but the chances of reaching them seemed dim. But, jinking and swerving, they lost height and, in turn, dropped their 'tin fish' and bombs. Two of the Stringbags were shot down, one losing its crew of two; the second crew survived but were taken prisoner. All the canvas-covered aircraft were peppered with shot and shell, but there were no further losses, and, setting their compasses on the bearing for their carrier, they flew home through the night.

Photographs taken the following day showed that the new battleship *Littorio* and two older battleships had been sunk at their moorings. In this action, lasting less than ten minutes and at a cost of two aircraft and two lives, the balance of naval power in the Mediterranean had been reversed.

For a while after this exercise, things went well in the eastern Mediterranean, and on land in North Africa, where the Italian armies were hurled back with the loss of thousands of prisoners. In an attempt to reassert herself, Italy invaded and conquered without too much trouble the small state of Albania. Then, on 28 October 1940, using Albania as a springboard, Italian troops invaded Greece. Germany was not informed, and was not pleased. She was even less pleased when the campaign fared badly. The Italians, fighting as they were on difficult terrain against a determined enemy who knew every inch of the mountainous ground, could make no progress.

Meanwhile, Nazi Germany was secretly preparing for the most massive and momentous of all its military operations —

the invasion and conquest, no less, of the Soviet Union. In order to secure Germany's right wing, Hitler embarked on a great Balkan offensive in April 1941. This included Greece, where the Italian armies were floundering.

It was like calling in the professionals. Hitler's panzers swept through Greece, burning, pillaging and massacring on the way. To counter this the British dispatched an expeditionary force from Egypt. This they could ill afford to do, but it did demonstrate to the neutral world, and especially the United States, where the passage of the Lend-Lease Bill was at a critical stage in Congress, that Britain and the Commonwealth were still hard at war with Germany and Italy.

Admiral Cunningham now had to face up to new responsibilities: the brief honeymoon following Taranto was over. Not only would troops and supplies have to be transported from Egypt to Greece but, having learned that the Luftwaffe was going to support this new German offensive, Cunningham was threatened from the air in a much more serious manner than ever by bombers. Fliegerkorps X had already made its mark far to the north in the Norwegian campaign. The air crews were veterans, their planes, including the feared Stuka Ju87 dive-bomber and its larger brother, the Ju88, formidable.

The German planes soon made their presence felt, bombing convoys from Gibraltar to Malta and from Malta east to Alexandria. They also bombed from high level and dive-bombed the convoys from Egypt to Greece. The consequences for Admiral Cunningham were profound. His pricelessly valuable carrier, *Illustrious*, was bombed and bombed again when in Malta harbour until she was no longer capable of fulfilling her function. If she had not had an armoured deck, which limited the damage to some extent, she would have been sunk at her moorings. She crept away under cover of darkness, reached Alexandria safely, progressed thence through the Suez Canal and eventually to Norfolk, Virginia, USA, for repair.

Without a carrier, Cunningham was for a time blind. However, the British Admiralty was fully aware of his vital need and hurried out, via the Cape, a new modern armoured carrier, the *Formidable*. She arrived on 10 March 1941, equipped with some Fulmar eight-gun fighters in addition to torpedo bombers, including the Swordfish and the slightly less ungainly Albacore torpedo bomber.

The *Formidable*'s arrival coincided with a move by the Germans to press for positive action from the Italian Navy in order to cut off British convoys with essential supplies destined for Greece.

Early in March 1941, the C.-in-C. of the Italian Fleet, Admiral Angelo Iachino, received orders to take his fleet to sea and conduct a sweep through the Aegean as a show of strength and in the expectation of intercepting and destroying one of these convoys. His fleet consisted of the battleship *Vittorio Veneto*, which was so new that she had not been a victim of the Taranto raid. She was a formidable vessel armed with nine fifteen-inch guns, adequately armoured and capable of thirty knots. To accompany and protect him, Iachino had six heavy cruisers armed with eight-inch guns, two light cruisers and thirteen destroyers. All he lacked was air reconnaissance and air cover, but this was promised by the Luftwaffe.

Iachino sailed from Naples at 9 a.m. on 26 March, rendezvousing with his cruisers the next day. The only air reconnaissance he received, however, was the enemy's. An RAF Sunderland flying boat spotted part of his fleet almost at once, so Iachino had already lost the advantage of surprise. Only one hour later the leading Italian heavy cruisers sighted smoke on the horizon and, a few minutes later, identified British light cruisers. The Italian cruisers opened fire with their eight-inch guns at 24,000 yards, far beyond the range of the British light cruisers, which were seen to turn through 180 degrees and speed away behind a smoke-screen.

The British light cruisers, scouting for Admiral Cunningham's main force, were commanded by Vice-Admiral H. D. Pridham-Wippel, searching ahead of Admiral Cunningham's main force. The situation was, in miniature, similar to that of Admiral Beatty at the Battle of Jutland. Pridham-Wippell hoped to draw the Italian Fleet within range of Cunningham's battleships. These consisted of the *Warspite* (flag), *Barham* and *Valiant*. All three had been under Beatty's flag at the battle forty-five years earlier. The first and last, however, had been radically modified, and were equipped with radar and many more anti-aircraft guns. These two could also steam at twenty-five knots, a knot or two faster than the unmodernized *Barham*. But none of them could approach the speed of the Italian flagship. Besides one and a half flotillas of destroyers, Cunningham had with him the newly arrived and pricelessly valuable carrier *Formidable*.

When the reports arrived from his scouting cruisers, Cunningham ordered off scouting planes from his carrier.

In his turn, Pridham-Wippell emerged from his smoke-screen, found the sea apparently empty, and returned to a westerly heading, hoping to sight and feed back to the *Warspite* more intelligence about the Italians. He did not have to wait for long. Suddenly from out of the blue there fell about his light cruisers a salvo of heavy shells. The guns were evidently at their maximum range, but the shooting was also disturbingly accurate. Once again in a naval battle events assumed an Homeric quality.

The Albacore planes from the *Formidable*, armed with torpedoes, were witness from several thousand feet above to this dangerous gunfire on the unarmoured light cruisers. These pilots could also see some fifteen miles distant the *Vittorio Veneto*, its forward heavy guns flashing as she fired salvo after salvo — ninety-four heavy shells in all. Cunningham's battleships were still too distant (and too slow) to intervene, but he ordered off more Albacores, one attack in the middle of the afternoon and another in the evening. No hits were made in the face of dense fire from the battleship and the heavy cruisers escorting her. But almost at the end of the evening strike, the Flight Commander held his machine within point-blank range of the *Vittorio Veneto*'s stern, and at the cost of his life and his observer's scored a hit, which resulted in the battleship losing some fifteen knots of speed.

But the more important strike was made by a pilot who, temporarily outmanoeuvred by the twisting and turning of the main target, aimed his tin fish at one of the heavy cruisers. The *Pola* was brought to a halt like a braking car, and she was left at a complete standstill while her cohorts sped north-west for Taranto, the flagship having now repaired the worst of her damage.

Admiral Iachino then took pity on the thousand or so officers and men of the *Pola* and unwisely dispatched two more heavy cruisers with destroyer escort back to her to take off her crew.

The Italian admiral should have remembered the lesson of the First World War when three patrolling British armoured cruisers were picked off by one U-boat which sank first one then a second when she returned to pick up survivors, and then the third on the same mission, drowning in total nearly 1,500 sailors.

Night closed in but that did not not affect the radars of Cunningham's flagship and the *Valiant*, which picked up, at short range, the two cruisers and escorting destroyers as they sped south-east on their mission of mercy. But there was to be no mercy from the British battleships, nor from the C.-in-C., though he did not relish the destruction that he wrought. Admiral Cunningham's account of the battle includes this passage:

> The enemy was at a range of no more than 3,800 yards — point blank ... The Fleet Gunnery Officer gave the final order to open fire. One heard the ting-ting-ting of the firing gongs. Then came the flash and the violent shudder as the six big guns bearing were fired simultaneously. At the very same instant the destroyer *Greyhound* switched her searchlight on to one of the enemy cruisers, showing her momentarily up as a silvery-blue shape in the darkness. Our searchlights shone out with the first salvo, and provided illumination for what was a ghastly sight. Full in the beam I saw our great projectiles flying through the air. Five out of the six hit a few feet below the cruiser's upper deck and burst with splashes of brilliant flame. The Italians were quite unprepared. Their guns were trained fore and aft. They were hopelessly shattered before they could put up any resistance...
>
> The plight of the Italian cruisers was indescribable. One saw whole turrets and masses of other heavy debris whirling through the air and splashing into the sea, and in a short time the ships themselves were nothing but glow-

ing torches and on fire from stem to stern. The whole action lasted no more than a few minutes.

That left the *Pola*, the cause of all this mayhem, to be dealt with. She had been a distant witness to the destruction of her would-be saviours. Cunningham left her to his destroyers, and they found her in a sorry state, not from damage but from the depredations of her own crew. By searchlight the destroyers observed that the crew were quite out of hand, drunk, some hurling themselves into the water. The quarter-deck was littered with clothing, empty bottles and carousing sailors. The destroyers took off as many of the crew as they could, then sank the helpless heavy cruiser with torpedoes.

Admiral Cunningham returned to the scene of the engagement at dawn and 'found the calm sea covered with a film of oil, and strewn with boats, rafts and wreckage, with many floating corpses'. Destroyers were detached to save any of the living. Including those from the *Pola*, some 900 survivors were picked up. There could have been more but German bombers put in an appearance. Cunningham hastily withdrew, but dispatched a signal to the Italian Admiralty giving the position of the remaining survivors. An Italian hospital ship later appeared on the scene and saved another 160.

The Battle of Cape Matapan off the southern tip of Greece was the bloodiest as well as the most decisive engagement between surface ships of the Mediterranean war. Although the *Vittorio Veneto* escaped, that night massacre dissolved the last remnants of Italian Navy morale and any surviving desire to get to grips with the enemy. At the cost of one aircraft and its crew of two, three of the finest and most powerful modern heavy cruisers had been sent to the bottom.

8

....

THE BATTLE IN THE
SOUTH CHINA SEA,
10 DECEMBER 1941

Despite being the world leader in naval aviation in 1918, in the interval of peace between the wars the hidebound British Admiralty had neglected naval aviation to such an extent that until shortly before the outbreak of war in 1939, aircraft operating from carriers were provided and controlled by the Royal Air Force. Although the Fleet Air Arm was quickly established, British aircraft operating from the Royal Navy's carriers were woefully inadequate; senior admirals remained wedded in thought to the merits of the "Big Gun."

The Japanese nurtured no such misconceptions. Imperial Japanese naval observers attached to the Royal Navy during the final years of the Anglo-Japanese alliance returned home to preach the new gospel, and by 1941 Japanese carriers were the most formidable in the world, while their carrier-borne aircraft were superior to anything in the United States or Europe. Their attack on Pearl Harbor in December 1941 was a defining moment in history, the most incontrovertible evidence of Japan's mastery of the weapons of modern warfare.

The imperial expansion that had caused war with Russia in 1904 had not waned. Successive Japanese governments were increasingly militaristic, and long before 1939 the Japanese had taken over Manchuria and invaded China, acquiring an empire by occupation and dominance of their sphere of interest. This concerned the United States, which had large investments in China, and more immediately Britain, with her own Far East imperial possessions of Hong Kong, North Borneo, Burma and Malaya. Less vulnerable but requiring protection, were India and the Dominions of Australia and New Zealand. Malaya and Singapore were particularly vulnerable and in an attempt to deter any meditated Japanese aggression in that direction, the British sent a powerful naval squadron of two capital ships known as Force Z, to the South China Sea.

As the Japanese began their offensive, attacking the United States at Pearl Harbor and the British in Hong Kong, they also landed on the eastern coast of Malaya. In response to this, Force Z sailed north from Singapore. Its aircraft carrier, the Indomitable, *had failed to materialize, having been damaged by running aground. Moreover its commander, Admiral Phillips, was a blinkered believer in the "Big Gun" and contemptuous of the Japanese and their aircraft.*

• • • • • • • • • • • • • • • • • • • •

SINCE THE BATTLE OF Tsu-Shima, the Imperial Japanese Navy had been through many vicissitudes and learned many lessons. Although it was regarded by many as a 'copycat' service, the Japanese did much more than copy from others' lessons — they improved on them in many cases. For example, during an exchange visit to British navy ports in the 1920s, the Japanese representatives observed that Britain's new battleships, the *Nelson* and *Rodney*, were fitted with twenty-four-inch torpedo tubes rather than the standard eighteen-inch and twenty-one-inch. Of even more interest to them, they learned that the British were experimenting with a new fuel, oxygen, offering far greater power and range than the normal fuel. The only drawback was that it was highly volatile and so dangerous to handle that the Royal Navy had ceased further experiments and development.

This did not deter the Imperial Japanese Navy, which at considerable loss of life introduced the oxygen-powered Japanese Type 93 or 'long lance' torpedo. This had the phenomenal range of 22,000 yards and a speed of fifty knots.

The Japanese naval authorities also observed the interest taken in naval flying by the Americans and the British. The IJN bought a number of naval planes from the British and, again like the US and Royal Navies, converted two of the giant battle-cruisers they had under construction to aircraft carriers. The conversion conveniently created the core of the Japanese Air Arm, and demonstrated that they were conforming to the recently signed Washington Naval Treaty which limited the construction of major capital ships, and their size to 35,000 tons.

Besides these big carriers with their capacity of sixty or more planes, by the outbreak of the war Japan had a number of purpose-built modern carriers. Although the IJN had battleships under construction at the beginning of the Pacific war (and they were to be the biggest battleships in the world, dwarfing the *Bismarck* and *Tirpitz*), it was clear to the outside world that Japan was laying the emphasis of its sea power on the carrier and carrier-built aircraft.

What was not clear was the advanced specifications of the aircraft intended for carrier operations. The Mitsubishi A6M Zero fighter was brilliantly designed and built. At 300 mph it was much superior in speed to any Western carrier-born fighter. It was very light and manoeuvrable and was in every respect superior to any carrier-borne American or British fighter. The backbone of the land-based IJN's bomber and torpedo bomber force was the Mitsubishi G4M, code-named 'Betty' by the British and Americans, which was capable of over 250 mph and had a range of more than 300 miles. The IJN's dive-bombers were equally formidable.

The quality of all these aircraft was seriously underestimated by both American and British authorities; nor had the number of machines Japan possessed been appreciated. There were approximately 1,750 front-line fighters, bombers and torpedo bombers in all, in addition to 350 reconnaissance flying boats and seaplanes.

The Japanese were full of confidence in their ships, their weapons and their personnel, whose spirit was as high as that of Admiral Togo's officers and men in 1905. But their one abiding anxiety was fuel. In 1905 their ships had been coal-fired, and there was plenty of domestic coal available. But modern naval ships were nearly all oil-fired. The Japanese government had stockpiled enough oil for its estimated needs for two years of war. Most of this had come from the United States, the rest from Dutch-owned oil-fields in Sumatra.

In the 1930s the world watched with increasing anxiety Japan's aggressive expansionist policy. Her first target was Manchuria, which would provide a stepping-stone for her planned campaign against the rest of China. This province was rapidly overcome; Japan did not even bother to listen to the protests from the League of Nations.

On the Japanese political front, a moderate government was replaced by the militarist Hirota government. In 1936 it took the nation, as a third member, into the Italo-German Axis pact.

On 7 July 1937, an 'incident' in Peking served as the justification for a full-scale invasion of China. In reply, two years later, against cries of anguish from major American business interests in oil, iron and steel, the US administration under President Franklin D. Roosevelt gave notice of the termination of the Japanese-American Commercial Treaty, which had been signed as long before as 1911. Although this did not apply immediately, the political effect in the Japanese capital led to the establishment of an even more militarist government and the appointment of General Tojo as Army minister. The tension between the two countries increased further when the United States shut off all oil supplies to Japan.

Three European nations now became involved. Pressure was applied on the Dutch to increase their oil exports to Japan; on the French for the lease of airfields in Indo-China; and on the British to close the Burma Road through which supplies had been pouring to the Chinese forces. In 1940 France and Holland were conquered by Japan's ally Germany. Only Britain and her Commonwealth survived to fight the tyranny of fascism. And Britain was already overstretched in the Mediterranean and in the protection of North Atlantic convoys.

As for the Americans, although they had not suffered the horrific casualties of the French and British in the First World War, there was a strong element of pacifism and isolationism among the people. In spite of this, Roosevelt succeeded in mounting a rearmament programme as well as a propaganda campaign against Japan.

As the year 1941 drew towards its close, so did the inevitability of war in the Far East. For Britain, in the eye of the storm, if it broke, were Malaya and Singapore and the two Commonwealth nations of Australia and New Zealand.

Churchill informed the Russian leader Joseph Stalin, now an ally of Britain against Germany, 'With the object of keeping Japan quiet we are sending our latest battleship, *Prince of Wales*, which can catch and kill any Japanese ship, into the Indian Ocean.' That was on 4 November 1941.

Churchill wrote later in his memoirs, 'It was decided to send as a first instalment of our Far Eastern Fleet both the *Prince of Wales* and the *Repulse*, with four destroyers, and as an essential element the modern armoured aircraft carrier *Indomitable*.' He also sent reassuring messages to the Prime Ministers of Australia and New Zealand.

Japan's overall strategic plan had been complete ever since the extreme military government had taken command in Tokyo. Speed was of the essence to this plan. It was to be a swift, crushing attack on both Britain and the United States to gain total control of the Pacific, including the Dutch East Indies, Burma, Indo-China (where the Japanese had leased air bases from the French), Malaya, Siam, and finally India. Later, Australia and New Zealand would fall like ripe fruit into Japanese hands. No invasion of the United States mainland was envisaged, but with her fleet destroyed, Japan then intended to negotiate a peace settlement on her own terms, making her the most powerful nation in the world.

The first stroke, the 'deadly stroke', was to destroy the American fleet at its base in Pearl Harbor in the Hawaiian Islands. This was planned and rehearsed in great secrecy weeks before the assault. On 2 December 1941, under the overall command of Admiral Isoroku Yamamoto, the greatest force of carriers the world had seen set sail from their base in the remote Kurile Islands. They carried 360 bombers, torpedo bombers and fighters, and this armada was escorted by battleships, heavy cruisers and a swarm of destroyers. They planned to attack at dawn on Sunday, 7 December, when, intelligence told Yamamoto, many of those manning the land-based defences and the battleships themselves would be slow to register the arrival of the attacking planes. The weather was fair as this armada headed south-east across the Pacific.

Back in Britain, the First Sea Lord, Admiral Sir Dudley Pound, argued vehemently against the dispatch of one of the Royal Navy's newest battleships together with an old but modernized battle cruiser to Singapore. He regarded as essential the presence of the *Prince of Wales* in home waters to guard Atlantic convoys against attack by German heavy surface warships.

Churchill was adamant, and Pound was persuaded to form what was code-named Force Z and dispatch it halfway round the world as a deterrent to Japanese attack.

However, Pound took some advantage from his setback by appointing as C.-in-C. of Force Z his Vice-Chief of Naval Staff at the Admiralty, Admiral Sir Tom Phillips, with whom he had not got on very well. Tom ('Tiny Tom') Phillips was, as his nickname implies, of diminutive height but was considered 'brainy' in the Service. He had been the Director of Plans at the Admiralty for three years. He was approaching fifty-three years of age at the time of his appointment. But he had little experience of battleship work, and his last sea appointment was commanding Home Fleet destroyer flotillas before he had been sent to the Admiralty as Vice-Chief of Naval Staff. His flag-captain was to be Captain John Leach, forty-seven years of age, a sound gunnery man.

Since her repair after the extensive damage suffered at the hands of the *Bismarck*, the *Prince of Wales* had carried the Prime Minister across the Atlantic for the Atlantic Alliance conference with President Roosevelt in Newfoundland in August 1941.

The *Repulse* was one of the 'large light cruisers' laid down in the First World War under the regime of Jacky Fisher at the Admiralty. They had a heavy armament of fifteen-inch guns, light protection and shallow draught, and were intended for shore bombardment of the Pomeranian coast during Fisher's pet scheme of landing there 'and marching to Berlin'. One of this class carried eighteen-inch guns, the biggest in the world at the time, but like two of her sister battle-cruisers, she had been converted into an aircraft carrier.

The *Repulse*, like her sister ship *Renown*, had been subjected to extensive modification costing over £3 million, a great deal of money in the late 1930s. Without any loss of speed (thirty-one knots), she had had her armour increased and anti-aircraft capacity augmented.

Repulse's captain was William Tennant, who survived the war. This author stayed with him when he was an old man but able to recall vividly his experiences as captain of the *Repulse*.

The *Repulse* was in the last stage of escorting a large convoy round the Cape to the Suez Canal when she received orders to form the second big ship of Force Z. For this reason, the *Prince of Wales* sailed without her for the first part of her voyage to the Far East. As for the *Indomitable*, she had run aground and damaged herself in the West Indies and was unable to join

Admiral Phillips, depriving him of what Churchill described as 'an essential element' in Force Z. Phillips carried on nonetheless. He was an officer who had a higher regard for the big gun and the power of anti-aircraft guns than for air power.

On the way out down the west coast of Africa, with two escorting destroyers, Phillips exchanged signals with the Admiralty, suggesting that he should rendezvous with Tennant at Ceylon before proceeding to Singapore. Churchill recommended that the *Prince of Wales* spend several days at Cape Town 'to show the flag'. He also suggested that Phillips should confer with Field Marshal Smuts, the South African Prime Minister, whose opinion Churchill always respected.

When the battleship came alongside in Cape Town harbour, a car whisked Phillips away to the airport, where a plane awaited to fly him to Pretoria. The Admiral and the Field Marshal held several conversations. Smuts was not reassured by Phillips's confidence in his big guns and his small regard for the Japanese ships and aircraft he might have to face.

In his signal to Churchill describing his talks with Phillips, Smuts sounded a warning note, which included the fateful summary 'If the Japanese are really nippy, there is here an opening for a first-class disaster'.

The *Prince of Wales* and her two destroyers left Cape Town on 18 November. Ten days later she dropped anchor at Colombo. The *Repulse* awaited her, but not the two additional destroyers from the Mediterranean which Phillips had been promised. At the same time, the Admiralty was impatient for him to be off, as the political situation with regard to Japan was worsening daily. On his own initiative, Phillips made the journey to Singapore by flying boat, leaving Force Z in the hands of Tennant. He therefore had several days to consult with the authorities in Singapore and bring himself up to date with the latest news, which was threatening.

The two big ships with their escorting destroyers arrived at Singapore on 2 December, bringing a sense of relief to the garrison and the native people, and also to the governments and people of Australia and New Zealand.

But among those cheering at the dockyard gates, the newsreel cameramen, the reporters from newspapers in Australia and America, there was little consideration for the fact that Force Z had no carrier and that the few shore-based aircraft were obsolescent short-range Buffalo fighters manned by inexperienced Australian pilots.

By contrast, the Japanese had assembled on the one-time French airfields in Indo-China over one hundred bombers, which could also carry torpedoes of the latest type. There were also squadrons of Zero fighters. The air crews had enjoyed much successful fighting over China, and had just completed an intensified training course on attacking ships at sea. Reconnaissance planes reported the two big ships in Singapore harbour. On 8 December the admiral commanding the Japanese air force in Indo-China called all his squadron commanders to a conference. They were told that two great convoys of troop-carriers were about to cross the South China Sea and land on certain points of the north Malaysian coast. If they were intercepted by the two British capital ships there would be dreadful carnage in spite of their naval escort. A plan was drawn up to attack these ships in Singapore harbour, as the British themselves had attacked the Italian Fleet at Taranto. The bombing force was about to take off for an evening strike when a signal arrived from Japanese Intelligence saying that both big ships were no longer there. It was a false report.

Four days earlier, Admiral Phillips judged it essential to consult with his future allies in the event of a Japanese attack. He therefore flew to Manila, where the American Admiral Thomas Hart commanded the Philippines naval forces. There he had a meeting with Hart, General Douglas MacArthur, commanding the land forces, and the Dutch naval representative. The agenda of these conversations was based on the assumption that all three powers would be attacked. MacArthur unsuccessfully attempted to persuade Phillips to bring Force Z to the Philippines. Phillips insisted that his big ships would be used as a striking force against an attack on Malaya, but he agreed this might be extended to the Dutch East Indies.

None of this was satisfactory in terms of a united front, but all the parties agreed that the danger was imminent. Phillips wasted no more time and flew back to Singapore.

Meanwhile, in Phillips's absence, Captain Tennant, after consultations with the authorities in Singapore, steamed off to Darwin in north Australia as a gesture of assurance to the Commonwealth nation that Britain meant business.

Tennant's stay was a short one. It was learned in Singapore that an invasion fleet had departed from its bases in Indo-China on 6 December. A signal was at once sent ordering Tennant to return 'with all dispatch'. This the *Repulse* did, testing her old engines severely. She secured herself in her old berth behind the *Prince of Wales*; and twenty-four hours later, Phillips returned by air from Manila.

On the evening of 7 December, two Catalina flying boats had been dispatched from Singapore to reconnoitre and report on the Japanese invasion fleet. One delivered its report; the other was shot down.

Admiral Phillips, looking gaunt and tired, assembled a

conference of Captain Tennant and other senior officers of Force Z. He told them that the landings on the coasts of Siam and northern Malaya had all succeeded but they would need constant reinforcements, and although these would be escorted by warships he proposed that they should immediately mount a raiding operation up the east coast.

When Phillips turned to Captain Tennnant for his views, the latter replied, 'We've come to secure our communications. That was our real purpose. Now that we're here, I don't see what possible alternative we have but to do as you have proposed.'

Phillips signalled his plan to the Admiralty, and also signalled to the commander of the RAF, requesting air cover over his destination, Signora, where a landing had taken place.

There were mixed feelings among those on shore, and in the ships themselves, when the two big ships with their four destroyers steamed out of Singapore at 5.35 p.m. The civilians who saw them steam away, heading north-east, were full of apprehension; news had filtered through of a massive attack on the American fleet at Pearl Harbor, which suggested very strongly that the Japanese were serious in their bid for domination of the Pacific and its bordering nations. These Singaporese felt naked without even a destroyer to protect them. The battery of fifteen-inch guns that had been installed some years earlier gave little comfort, as it was widely known that they could fire only out to sea, when it was more likely that Singapore would be attacked by land.

There were mixed feelings among the officers of the *Repulse* and *Prince of Wales*. Among the senior officers and the two captains, John Leach and William Tennant, there was a certain unspoken anxious awareness.

None of this, however, had penetrated to the lower deck, where there was a great eagerness for action. In order to encourage this, Leach and Tennant addressed their men. Tennant told them, 'For two months past the ship has felt that she has been deprived of her fair share of hitting the enemy. Although we have been constantly at sea and steamed 53,000 miles, we have seen practically nothing. There is every possibility that things are going to change completely. We are off to look for trouble. I expect we shall find it.'

After this exhortation, Tennant outlined their plan, and completed his speech, 'I know the old ship will give a good account of herself. May each one of us, without exception, keep calm when action comes.'

The tropical sun was setting behind them when the two ships and their destroyers headed for the Anambas Islands far out in the South China Sea. For a short time the *Repulse* led the way, then slowed to allow her flagship to pass her. The men on deck on the starboard and port sides respectively waved and gave a cheer. On the bridges of the two ships, Captains Tennant and Leach saluted each other and took off their hats in a more muted demonstration. Even Tom Phillips briefly waved as a gesture of encouragement.

Darkness fell with its usual tropical speed, and the blacked-out ships of Force Z kept on at a steady twenty-seven knots, only their bow waves and stern wash visible.

The first news Admiral Phillips received that night of 7/8 December was not good. It was a signal from Singapore. 'Fighter protection on Wednesday 20th [the planned day of the raid] will not, repeat not, be available.' To match the sombre nature of this signal, the weather rapidly deteriorated. The barometer was plummeting and tropical storms must soon break out.

On the other hand, the poor weather might be on their side, reckoned Phillips. If they could get through the next day, 9 December, without being spotted, then turn west for the Malay coast, the raid could well be worthwhile, especially if they met up with enemy escorting cruisers and destroyers. There was also an intelligence report to the effect that the old battleship *Kongo* was helping with the escort work. She had been built in Britain before the First World War and they could comfortably deal with her, too.

Admiral Phillips issued a signal to all ships' companies at dawn. It contained the explanation 'We have made a wide circuit to avoid air reconnaissance', and concluded, 'Whatever we meet I want to finish it quickly and so get well clear to the eastward before the enemy can amass too formidable a scale of attack against us. So shoot to kill.'

At almost the same time as these words were heard over the ships' loudspeaker systems, the destroyer *Vampire* signalled that a look-out had sighted an unidentified aircraft before it was swallowed up by the swirling rain clouds. It was not seen again or by any other look-out, and Phillips decided to ignore the report. His decision seemed justified when, soon after noon, a large aircraft broke through the mist to reveal herself as a Catalina, the survivor of the two dispatched from Singapore. The pilot flew low over the flagship, flashing by lamp the information that the Japanese were landing at Singora, the very destination Phillips had planned to raid.

At 5 p.m., and ninety minutes before their planned alteration of course towards the Malay coast and Singora, the weather began to clear. The light anti-aircraft gun crews, who for hours had been sodden by the sweeping rain, were relieved to see and feel the late afternoon sun. But they were the only personnel pleased. To the look-outs and those on the bridge of the battle-ships and destroyers, the clear, sunny weather revealed far to the north a flight of three aircraft, far out of range. Nor were these RAF machines, and their radio operators must be flashing the news back to base. Force Z had been discovered.

Admiral Phillips had complete confidence in Force Z's ability to fight off any air attack the Japanese might mount. Not only was his flagship heavily armoured but so up to date were its massed anti-aircraft armaments that they were as numerous as that of any other ship in the Royal Navy, with sixteen 5.25-inch heavy guns, four multiple two-pounder pom-poms (nicknamed 'Chicago pianos') and a great number of light machine-guns to deal with close-range attack. What concerned Phillips were the anxieties of any surface raider, from the *Admiral Graf Spee* to the *Bismarck*: that of being damaged and being obliged to reduce maximum speed. Speed was the very essence of this raid, as he had emphasized to his staff and senior officers.

As the light began to fail, the three aircraft still hovered in the northern sky like threatening ghosts. Suddenly, or so it seemed, Phillips decided he must take his force back to its base. While there was still light in the sky, Force Z continued on its northerly heading, then under the cover of darkness, at 7 p.m., swung on to a north-westerly heading as if continuing the raid on Singora. But at 8.15 p.m., Phillips swung Force Z on a reverse heading for Singapore.

Admiral Phillips's intention of deceiving the enemy paid off, at least for the present. Following the report from the Japanese shadowing aircraft, a powerful force of bombers was dispatched to find and then to destroy the big ships. Their task was not easy. The weather closed in again when they left behind the Indo-China coast. The bombers found it difficult to fly in their usual formation, and they were fearful of misidentifying any warship they did find. It was just this event which caused the Admiral to abort the operation. One Japanese bomber crew radioed that they had located a large warship and were dropping a flare. This flare revealed a Japanese heavy cruiser. By now Force Z was far to the south, steaming at twenty-four knots. Phillips had earlier detached one of his destroyers, the *Tenedos*, because of its shortage of fuel, but the other three remained with him.

In spite of the deteriorating weather, a keen look-out was kept for scouting aircraft. But it was not an aircraft, it was a submarine which first identified them, far from the assumed search area. The submarine was dead in the track of Force Z's course, and crash-dived to avoid being rammed. She just had time to fire five torpedoes at the great shapes in the darkness, none of which hit. Then, when they had passed, she resurfaced and radioed her position and the heading of the enemy ships.

Force Z had kept strict radio silence on its course south. But this silence did not interfere with incoming calls, and one of these, from base at Singapore, put a fresh complexion on the operation.

'Enemy reported landing Kuantan, latitude 03 degrees 50 north.' That was all, but it was enough. A successful landing further south, intended to cut off any defending force at Singora, made good sense tactically.

Once more on that night of varying fortunes, Phillips decided to try to rescue something from this so-far abortive raid. He altered Force Z's heading to south-west for the coast, without signalling base but assuming that they would know what he was doing and provide air cover. By 8 a.m. in full daylight he was off Kuantan and sent the destroyer *Express* into the harbour. A few minutes later, the *Express* re-emerged, signalling to the flagship, 'All's as quiet as a wet Sunday afternoon.'

A further complication to their fortunes was the sighting of a barge towing a number of small boats. Captain Tennant signalled to Phillips, suggesting that they might be the spearhead of an invasion and that Singapore had got the timing of the landing wrong. So, once again, Force Z reversed course on its heading for Singapore and put out from the coast to the northeast. At the same time Phillips catapulted one of his scouting aircraft to search ahead. It found nothing.

A few minutes later, however, Admiral Phillips received an alarming report from the destroyer *Tenedos*, which was now far to the south. The radio message ran succinctly, 'Am being bombed.' In the event, all the bombs missed, but if the Japanese area of search had reached this far south in the South China Sea, it suddenly seemed inevitable that they would be found. Visibility had increased during the morning and was now almost limitless.

Sure enough, soon after Force Z altered course to the south and increased speed, a 'blip' on the *Repulse*'s radar turned out to be a Japanese scouting machine poised high in the sky as if secured to a fragment of cumulonimbus cloud.

The next radar sighting was more of a smear than a 'blip'. Three minutes later, at 11.13 a.m., radar was no longer needed. Phillips and his staff on the compass platform of the *Prince of Wales*, and Tennant on the *Repulse*'s bridge, and everybody above deck, could make out a squadron of nine twin-engine machines, high up in tight line-abreast formation. Only the heavy anti-aircraft guns could reach them, and they opened up, breaking the silence of the morning with their staccato c-r-a-c-k. Seconds later the shells exploded, dotting the clear sky. It was accurate firing.

They seemed to be concentrating on the *Repulse*, and the bombs were released simultaneously. Captain Tennant ordered the helmsman to alter course sharply in an effort to evade them. But it was too late; everyone on deck, as well as the captain, could see the ever-growing black globules. One fell close to the starboard side, another close to the port side, then, like a good straddle from heavy guns, the third hit the ship amidships. It first struck the hangar beside the catapult, tilting the plane on its side. It did not explode until it struck the armoured deck below, destroying the Royal Marines' mess. It killed and injured a number of officers and men, and first-aid parties were rushed to the spot. Fire parties were needed equally urgently, for the black smoke that rose was followed by flames.

The pilot of the plane called for help to hurl it into the sea before the flames reached the fuel tanks. The fighting power of the battle-cruiser had not been affected, nor its speed, and the *Repulse* assumed station in loose line abreast with the flagship.

They were not left in peace for long. The planes came in from the north-east, a bigger formation this time — fifteen or twenty of them, all twin-engine machines, flying as high as the earlier formation but losing height quickly as they approached the ships. Was it going to be dive-bombing this time? The gunners opened fire — first the heavy guns, then the two-pounder pom-poms and finally the multiple machine-guns.

The bombers came in at great speed, levelling off at about 500 feet, and then, to everyone's astonishment, they began dropping torpedoes. Recovering from his near-disbelief,

Tennant ordered forty-five degrees to starboard in the hope of 'combing' the tracks of these super-torpedoes. Because the ship was farther away from the direction of the attack, Tennant completed his sharp turn before the bombers arrived and the *Repulse* offered only her stern to the torpedoes. All passed by on the port or starboard side of the ship.

As the planes passed low overhead, the rear gunners hosed the *Repulse's* deck, aiming at the gun crews, some of whom were hit. These machines were as far removed from the stately 100-knot Swordfish and its eighteen-inch torpedo as the Wright brothers' machine was from a Blenheim light bomber. Clearly, they must be land-based, as no carrier could launch and land these big twin-engine planes.

The *Prince of Wales* had not had time to turn to comb the tracks of the torpedoes aimed at her, one of which struck her far aft. Tennant saw the confirmation of this, and the strike of a second torpedo almost simultaneously in the same area. A great cloud of black smoke rose in the air, and, through his binoculars, he could see that his flagship had assumed a steep list to port. Within moments the *Prince of Wales* was almost stationary on the ocean, and had hoisted her 'not under command' balls.

It was not surprising that this mournful message had appeared. Like the torpedo attack on the *Bismarck* months earlier, the explosion of the two big torpedoes had severed the port propeller shaft and opened up a gaping hole, allowing the sea to pour in. The loss of the port propeller shaft had led to the ruination of half the ship's turbines.

The flagship was little more than a floating corpse, without half her light and without the power to operate her aft anti-aircraft guns. Tennant realised that his admiral might also have lost the means to communicate by radio. This seemed to be confirmed when the *Prince of Wales* used lamp Morse code to send messages to her junior partner.

In the brief lull after the last torpedo attack, Tennant learned to his horror that Admiral Phillips had made no signals to Singapore reporting the attacks, so he immediately sent, on his own initiative, an emergency signal saying that they were being bombed and giving their position. If fighters made an emergency take-off, he reasoned, they might arrive in time to interfere with further attacks, giving at least the *Repulse* the chance of steaming south flat out for Singapore.

The chance of doing so slimmed to nothing when, just before midday, more formations of aircraft were sighted, coming in from the south this time. It quickly became clear that this was to be a simultaneous attack by high-level bombers and torpedo planes, thus dividing and confusing the gun crews.

The bombers concentrated on the *Repulse*, recognizing her as the least damaged ship which might slip away south, leaving her flagship to look after herself. The bombs exploded in the sea, to port and starboard, very close and soaking everyone on deck. But none made a direct hit and, bearing a charmed life, the *Repulse* steamed out of the trap, still heeling hard over from her last evasive action.

The close-following torpedo bombers seemed to be concentrating on the *Prince of Wales* before, suddenly, three of them turned sharply to port in a steep bank and headed for the *Repulse*. This attack gave Tennant no time to starboard the helm to comb the torpedoes' tracks.

One of them, Tennant saw, was going to hit the *Repulse*. The torpedo came in shallow and fast, leaving a white stream in its wake. It was 12.23 p.m. when it struck amidships, and the ship shook like a whipped mare and began to list. But that was only the beginning. Suddenly the big planes were coming in from port and starboard like jackals about a wounded prey. Some of them were hit at close range, and three were counted exploding in the air or just dropping with a white splash into the sea. One of the torpedoes struck the ship right aft, and, like the *Prince of Wales* before her, the *Repulse* was no longer able to answer to the helm, because the rudder was no longer there. Water was pouring in from at least five more hits, and clearly the end was near.

A voice came over the loudspeaker system, steady and clear: 'Everybody on deck. Prepare to abandon ship. Clear away Carley floats.' It was amazing that the loudspeaker system still worked, and it saved many lives. 'Come up from below.' Climbing up ladders and down again to avoid the worst of the rising water, the men clambered up on to the listing decks. Most wore blown-up lifebelts; others from the sick quarters were helped along by their mates. There was no time to launch the boats. The forecastle was packed with men, milling about like commuters in a crowded train. But there was no train; just the rising sea, already blackened with oil.

A voice was heard from above them. It was the voice of their captain, speaking through a megaphone. Tennnant did not call out the cliché 'Every man for himself'. He called, 'You've put up a good show. Now look after yourselves and God bless you all.'

There were several ways of reaching the sea. The wisest men waited until the list was about seventy degrees and then walked uneasily down her oily, barnacle-ridden side, letting the sea engulf them, and then swam, literally, for their lives. Several, who were still in the air defence positions high up on the masts, dived towards the sea, some prematurely, and were killed when they hit steel instead of water.

At 12.33 p.m., the ship went down, stern first, with little fuss.

Captain Tennant and his Assistant Navigator and Signal Officer both survived and had similar experiences: the latter, John Hayes, said later:

> My movements were dictated by gravity, like one of those balls on a bagatelle table which bounce off pins — the funnel red hot from steaming, then against the port flag-lockers, by which time, normally some fifty feet above the waterline, they were almost awash, and so overboard helplessly and down for what seemed a long time.
>
> When I bobbed up, the great iron structure of the main top, normally some one hundred feet above the waterline, skidded just above my head as the ship plunged on and down with the screws still turning.

Captain Tennant recalled:

> I had moved down to B gun deck which was a better place to enter the water, then the sea came up rapidly to meet me. I let it come; there was nothing else I could do. My ship turned right over on me, and I was at once drawn into the blackness of her death and taken far down on her turbulent descent to the bottom. I wondered whether I should take one deep swallow in an effort to hasten my end. But I held on and saw the black change to dark green, then to light green as I swiftly rose again above my ship that had so miraculously allowed me to live.

When he surfaced he heard a voice calling, 'Here you are, sir.' Men who had at once recognized him were leaning from the edge of a Carley float and dragged him on board.

Admiral Tom Phillips was not too preoccupied with his own ship's precarious condition to fail to see the sinking of the *Repulse*, and he signalled two of the destroyers, which had been shocked spectators of the carnage, to the *Repulse* to pick up survivors.

It seemed that the Japanese had calculated that torpedoes had done all that they could and decided that bombs might finish off the flagship sooner. The bombing was a replica of the first attack, which seemed like hours ago. It was equally accurate, too, from nine twin-engine bombers in line-abreast formation.

Most of the heavy bombs fell aft, tearing the heart out of the ship, while one struck amidships, instantly starting a fire. By 1 p.m. John Leach had to accept that they were not going to survive, and called up the last destroyer, the *Express*, to come alongside and take off the wounded. She hurried to the starboard side, against the steep list that must soon cause the battleship to capsize. The sick and wounded were quickly transferred, but behind them were hundreds who had answered the call to abandon ship. Ropes and nets were rigged between the two ships and the men slid or climbed down in their life-jackets to be pulled on deck by the destroyers' men. Others jumped into the sea between the two vessels. Yet others decided that they would never make it, blew up their lifebelts and jumped into the sea, hoping to reach one of the Carley floats that had been thrown in before them.

There was a limit to the number the seven-year-old, 1,300-ton destroyer could accommodate without herself capsizing. The danger was relieved when the battleship's list became so acute that her keel threatened to take the destroyer down with her. But, just as the keel and hull made contact, the commander of the *Express* ordered full astern and she just escaped. The sound of her turbines blotted out the sound emerging from the *Prince of Wales*'s ventilator shafts of trapped men below screaming and shouting. But many in the water heard it and were thankful to be swimming or crouching in a Carley raft. The captain and the admiral, who had remained on the compass platform throughout, must have heard it, too. But no one could do anything to save them now.

At 1.20 p.m. the battleship shuddered, as if fearful of her fate, rolled over and turned turtle. The only merciful occurrence was the extinguishing of the fires that had spread to many parts of the ship.

The *Express* headed south for Singapore. It was impossible to lie down on the hot steel deck, so the men stood all the way back to base; while the stench of oil and chloroform below decks was almost suffocating. She left behind the other two destroyers, which continued to pick up survivors, mostly from the *Repulse*, until 4 p.m.

The *Express* finally moored alongside at Singapore at 11.55 p.m., in the berth previously occupied by the *Prince of Wales*. It was pitch dark, with the blackout strictly enforced, and a tropical rain was falling. The wounded were carried off first and taken straight to hospital. Captain Tennant and the other officers were transported to the officers' mess, where they cleaned up and had stiff drinks and then bacon and eggs. The petty officers and ratings were directed to a large shed where tea was brewing.

When the other two destroyers moored alongside the *Express*, the casualties could be counted. It emerged that forty-two officers and 1,195 petty officers and ratings were missing. They had either gone down in their ship, had died in battle or had drowned or choked to death in the oil-saturated sea.

Back in London, the Prime Minister was awoken by the telephone ringing at his bedside. It was the First Sea Lord, Admiral Sir Dudley Pound, who had so strongly opposed the dispatch of Force Z. But there was only distress in his voice when he told Churchill: 'I have to report to you that the *Prince of Wales* and the *Repulse* have both been sunk by aircraft. There is no doubt about the truth of the report.'

Churchill, and he alone, was responsible for insisting on sending the big ships to Singapore as a deterrent. Churchill wrote later: 'As I turned over and twisted in bed the full horror of the news sank in on me. So I put the telephone down. I was thankful to be alone. In all the war I never received a more direct shock.' The whole nation was shocked when the news was known. Harold Nicolson, the statesman and author, wrote in his diary for 19 December 1941:

> Go up to Leicester. I find them all rather depressed. The sinking of the *Prince of Wales* has made an impression out of all proportion. They ignore the Russian victories, the

Libyan advance and the entry of America. They are faced with the fact that two of our greatest battleships have been sunk within a few minutes by the monkey men, and that we and the Americans have between us lost command of the Pacific.

9

···

THE BATTLE FOR THE PACIFIC: OPENING ROUNDS, 7 DECEMBER 1941– 8 MAY 1942

The near simultaneous Japanese attacks on Pearl Harbor, Malaya, the Philippines and Hong Kong in December 1941, were the prelude to a rapid and aggressive expansion of the Japanese Empire into Burma, the north-west Pacific and, after Malaya, the extensive archipelago of the Dutch East Indies (Indonesia).

At the end of 1941, there now began the battle for the Pacific and the war against Japan. The American people could now no longer distance themselves from a purely European conflict, an outcome that Roosevelt had long known and for which he had prepared. The United States reeled from the speed and effectiveness of the Japanese advances in the Pacific but, though brilliant in concept and execution, they were to draw down a mounting, merciless and overwhelming reprisal in the following four years. Had not Roosevelt begun the prodigious build-up of U.S. industrial output in late 1940, the outcome may well have been less certain.

On February 15, 1942, British-held Singapore fell to the Japanese. Not long after, U.S. forces in the Philippines and Dutch forces in the East Indies proved inadequate to stem the Japanese advance. The Dutch surrendered on March 9, 1942, leaving exten-

sive oil fields in Japanese hands, an important asset which, in Burma, the British had denied them by the destruction of the oil fields. The United States lost its last toehold in the Philippines on May 8, and this collapse enabled the Japanese to land successively on the islands of New Britain, New Ireland, New Guinea and the Solomon Islands. To hold this southern outwork of their Empire, the Japanese required combined sea and air control over the region. On New Guinea they had encountered the stiff resistance of Australian troops and they were not entirely uncontested at sea. In the coming months of 1942, the United States Navy was to fight fire with fire: they too had learned the painful lesson that naval aviation was no longer a matter for contempt, it was the naval weapon.

In those first uncertain months of the war in the Pacific, the Allies joined forces as far as their limited resources enabled them. A combined squadron of U.S., Australian, British and Dutch ships was placed under the command of a Dutch flag officer. Admiral Karel Doorman's ad hoc squadron was defeated by the Japanese at the end of February 1942 in the Java Sea.

But both the British and U.S. fleets were in the throes of reorganization. The British Far East fleet was now based on Ceylon (Sri Lanka) with a secret base at Addu Atoll and while it sustained further losses, it avoided annihilation. By now the tide was turning. A bold U.S. counter-attack, a bombing-raid designed to damage national morale, was mounted on Tokyo and Yokohama from the carrier Hornet. The Japanese were taught that those who sow the wind will reap the whirlwind.

Meanwhile Japanese forces reached ever eastwards, towards Hawaii, whose possession would allow them to dominate the Pacific. First, they had to seize the United States base at Midway. The two fleets locked horns for two days in early May 1942, contesting mastery of the Coral Sea.

....

THE SINKING OF THE two capital ships of Force Z was no more than an overture to Japan's conquest of the Pacific and its surrounding territory. The planning and timing had been meticulous. Although the attack on Pearl Harbor appeared to be the opening round, owing to the time difference it coincided precisely with the invasion of Malaya and other offensive operations. Although the Japanese government, the Imperial Japanese Navy's High Command and Admiral Chuichi Nagumo, who led the attack, believed they had scored a decisive victory, the truth was otherwise.

When the news came through to the mainland of the United States, the shock was prodigious. This writer was at Santa Monica, about the nearest point to the Hawaiian Islands, when the news was announced on the radio and there was near-panic in Los Angeles; but within hours, not days, the panic had turned to anger and determination. Shifts were increased at defence plants, the production of war planes soon began multiplying, women volunteered to work in defence plants, new shipyards were opened. Motor-car tyres became difficult to find; many consumer goods like razor blades were soon in short supply.

President Roosevelt called the Pearl Harbor attack 'The day of Infamy', as indeed it was, but it did wonders for the spirit of the biggest industrial state in the world.

Almost the entire American battleship fleet was anchored in Pearl Harbor when the Japanese attacked with the biggest carrier fleet ever seen. Of the eight battleships moored in 'Battleship Row' only one, the *Arizona*, was deemed unsalvageable, and her upturned hull, with many of her crew still entombed in her, remains today as a monument to all who lost their lives in the attack. One other battleship was considered unsuitable for repair; the rest were salvaged and rebuilt to modern specifications and greatly increased anti-aircraft capability.

The Japanese fliers also claimed that they had sunk one of America's few aircraft carriers, but this was false, for the two carriers that were based there were at sea on other business; this Pacific war was to be a carrier war, the first ever, and the battleship was seconded to the roles of support to the carrier and shore bombardment.

With the sinking of Force Z, it took the Japanese land forces only a few weeks to overwhelm Malaya and, later, Singapore itself. It also opened up the inevitable invasion of the Philippines and the Dutch East Indies, with all their priceless riches of oil, tin, rubber and other essentials for the Japanese war effort. The only obstruction was a mixed force divided among four nations — the United States, Britain, the Netherlands and Australia. This force varied in its contribution, as in its variety of ships, language, signalling and almost everything else. Admiral Thomas Hart, whom Phillips had consulted briefly before returning to Singapore, was soon due to retire, and the only ship he had to offer was the already damaged heavy cruiser *Houston*; the British the heavy cruiser *Exeter*, now repaired after the damage sustained at the Battle of the River Plate; the Australians the light cruiser *Perth*; the Dutch the light cruisers *Tromp* and *De Ruyter*, which were fine ships and only a few years old. The Dutch Rear-Admiral Karel Doorman was appointed to command this mixed bag of ships, which also included nine destroyers of varying age and quality.

This, then, was all that the Japanese had to face before continuing their westward drive across the southern Indian Ocean. Admiral Doorman selected Sourabaya on the north coast of Java as his base. On 27 February 1942, smoke was sighted on the horizon. It turned out to be a powerful landing force escorted by two heavy cruisers, the *Noti* and *Haguro*, armed with ten eight-inch guns, and two light cruisers together with a strong force of destroyers but no carrier, as far as could be seen.

Doorman was the first to open fire at the maximum range of his eight-inch guns. The Japanese heavy cruisers immediately returned the fire. It was as accurate as the German fire at the Battle of the River Plate, at which the *Exeter* had received her baptism. The *Exeter* soon received a direct hit in her engine room, knocking out one of her boilers and reducing her speed to about fifteen knots; she was ordered back to Sourabaya under the cover of a smoke-screen laid by two destroyers. In the style of a First World War battle, the Japanese counter-attacked, but their weapons were not of that vintage. For the first time the Japanese made use of their twenty-four-inch liquid-oxygen-powered 'Long Lance' torpedoes. The *Electra*, a recent component of Force Z, was hit and brought to a standstill, and a Dutch destroyer was blown to pieces. The eight-year-old *Electra*, which had earlier rescued survivors of the *Repulse*, was then surrounded by the entire Japanese destroyer force, which opened fire at point-blank range. The British destroyer fought back with her 4.7-inch guns, but she was torn to pieces and turned over and sank with all her crew.

Doorman, meanwhile, with his much-reduced force, attempted to get round behind the Japanese heavy cruisers under the protection of darkness to attack the transports carrying the invading troops. He probably thought he had a chance.

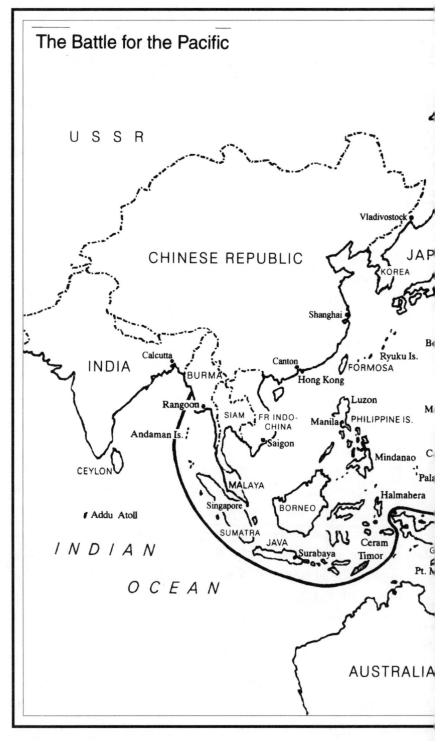

The Battle for the Pacific

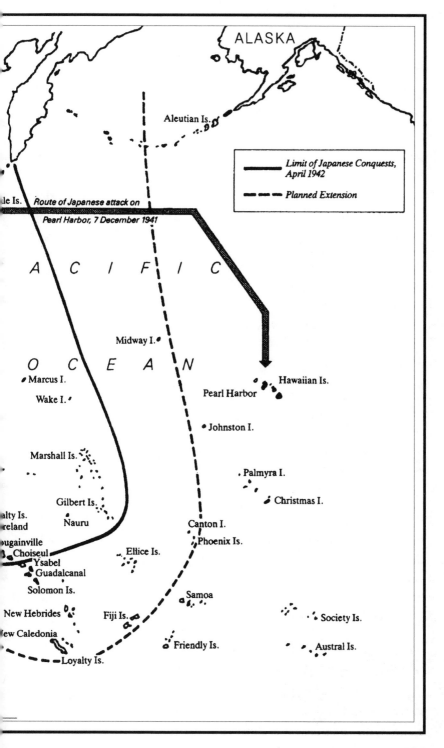

ALASKA

Aleutian Is.

*Limit of Japanese Conquests,
April 1942*

- - - *Planned Extension*

le Is.   *Route of Japanese attack on*
Pearl Harbor, 7 December 1941

P   A   C   I   F   I   C

Midway I.

O   C   E   A   N

Marcus I.

Wake I.

Hawaiian Is.

Pearl Harbor

Johnston I.

Marshall Is.

Palmyra I.

Gilbert Is.

Christmas I.

alty Is.
reland

Nauru

Canton I.

ugainville
Choiseul
Ysabel
Guadalcanal

Solomon Is.

Phoenix Is.

Ellice Is.

New Hebrides

Samoa

ew Caledonia

Fiji Is.

Society Is.

Friendly Is.

Austral Is.

Loyalty Is.

But he was mistaken. Another force was protecting the transports. Suddenly star shells turned the darkness into day. 'Long Lance' torpedoes struck his ships. No gunfire was required.

Doorman was as brave as the seventeenth-century Dutch admiral after whom his ship was named; but he did not have his luck.

Under orders from Doorman, before he was sunk, the *Exeter*, the *Houston* and the surviving destroyers headed for the Sunda Strait in a final endeavour to survive. At dawn they spotted a scouting seaplane.* Shortly after they were confronted by the Japanese heavy cruisers and were all sunk by the deadly eight-inch gunfire.

A year earlier the ship's company of the *Exeter* had marched through cheering crowds in the City of London. Now they were all at the bottom of the Java Sea in their battered heavy cruiser.

The Battle of the Java Sea was as decisive and overwhelming a defeat as Force Z had suffered the previous December.

After the Pearl Harbor operation, Admiral Nagumo and his men received a hero's welcome when they returned to their base in mainland Japan. But their stay was brief. They may have wiped out the American battleship fleet, but to claim total control of the Pacific they must now secure its frontiers. First Nagumo was ordered south, where landings were taking place at Rabaul and other points in New Guinea. The Australian government had been aghast at the sinking of Force Z and now, as a consequence, all Australia was under threat. To underline this threat,

*At this stage of the Pacific war, the Japanese, having no radar, used catapulted seaplanes to great effect in finding and shadowing enemy ships.

Australia's northernmost town, Darwin, was attacked by Nagumo's bombs, escorted by fighters. The shanty-town buildings were wrecked. A few fighters took off but they were soon wiped out by the Zeros.

The Japanese High Command next turned its attention to the western frontiers of the ocean Japan now dominated. Their intelligence department told them that, following the disaster in the South China Sea and the loss of Singapore, the British Royal Navy had dispatched a force that included battleships, two carriers and supporting cruisers and smaller craft to Colombo, the capital city of Ceylon. Intelligence also informed them that this fleet was under the command of Admiral James Somerville, a very experienced commander who had for many months commanded Force H at Gibraltar.

All this was true, and Somerville had brought with him two armoured fleet carriers, including the *Indomitable*. Apart from his other big ships, the battleship *Warspite* arrived in support. She came direct from the American shipyard that had been repairing the damage she had suffered in the Mediterranean. The British Admiralty was taking a calculated risk in denuding the Mediterranean and home waters of so much of their strength. But these were desperate times, and if these marauding Japanese ships cut off the Cape route to Suez, and with it the oil supplies of the Middle East and Arabia, then it would be a mortal blow to the Allied cause. The Americans helped by sending several powerful ships to support the British Home Fleet.

The British had had the foresight to build a reserve base some 600 miles south of Ceylon. This base was no more than a ring of coral islands surrounding a deep-water anchorage called Addu Atoll, but it had the necessary facilities, and its greatest advantage was that the Japanese knew nothing about it.

As Admiral Nagumo with his powerful carrier force sped across the Bay of Bengal, Admiral Somerville took his ships out of his base at Colombo to Addu Atoll. It was not his business to risk himself against this all-conquering carrier force. It was his business to remain a threat, a 'fleet in being'.

Nagumo, with his five carriers, including the giants *Akagi* and *Kaga*, sighted the east coast of Ceylon at dawn on 5 April, Easter Sunday. It was like a repeat of Pearl Harbor. The air crews were as boundlessly self-confident as they had been back on 7 December 1941. The carriers launched their Zero fighters, their 'Val' dive-bombers and their high-level bombers with the same *bravura* as before.

Over the mountains of this island they roared, the protecting Zeros on high. When they were over Colombo, and the 'Vals' were preparing to tip over, all the pilots observed with deep dismay that 'the cupboard was bare'. They had been ordered to concentrate on the carriers, and after dealing with them the battleships and any heavy cruisers they could see. But they saw nothing except a few fishing boats. Undeterred, the group leader ordered the dive-bombers to attack the harbour installations and the adjoining airfield. If there were no big ships neatly moored in lines, as there had been at Pearl Harbor, they could make the harbour unusable when the British returned. They were halfway down in their dive when the pilots and rear gunners became aware of two unpleasant facts: first the anti-aircraft fire, which was heavy and accurate; then, even more disturbing, there were fighters mixing in with them. They were modern fighters, too, with pointed noses (owing to their in-line Merlin engines; the Japanese Zeros had radial engines).

Two Hurricane fighter squadrons had been hurried out to Colombo in anticipation of an attack by air. One had arrived on the carrier *Indomitable*; 258 Squadron had been formed just after the Battle of Britain but had experienced some action before being sent out to Singapore, arriving in late January. They fought manfully to repel Japanese bomber raids, but it was too late. They retreated to the Dutch islands only days before the city surrendered. But they were hounded out of their Dutch airfields there, and on 1 March the squadron withdrew to Colombo.

Number 30 Hurricane Fighter Squadron had been operating thousands of miles distant from Singapore. Led by Squadron Leader G. F. Chate, DFC, it, too, had been on the retreat, first from Greece, thence to the island of Crete, and finally to Egypt. From there, they and their machines were packed on board a carrier in which they sailed through the Suez Canal and east to Ceylon, where they arrived on 24 March 1942, under a new commander, Squadron Leader R. A. Milward.

Anticipating that Admiral Nagumo's armada of carriers would next attack India or Ceylon, a flight of nine Catalinas was kept busy on reconnaissance patrol from Colombo. On Easter Saturday, 4 April, one of these Catalinas was flying far to the east of Ceylon when at 4 p.m. the crew sighted at the limit of visibility five 'flat tops' and a dense mass of escorting vessels. The captain, Squadron Leader L. J. Birchall, approached closer to confirm his sighting. It was not a wise thing to do. A few minutes later a flight of Zero fighters closed in and shot his

flying boat to pieces, but not before the Catalina's wireless operator had transmitted an urgent signal to his base at Colombo.

Shortly after dawn broke on Easter Sunday morning, there
were further sightings of ships and planes approaching; 258
and 30 Hurricane Squadrons scrambled and, climbing at full
boost, were there to meet the first 'Val' dive-bombers a few seconds and no more before they tipped over into their dive.

But this was no repeat of Pearl Harbor. Not only were there
no ships, but they were 'jumped' by modern eight-gun fighters.
In the dog-fight that followed, the Hurricanes had no trouble
shooting down the fixed-undercarriage dive-bombers, which
disintegrated with one three-second burst. It was a different
story with the Zeros, which were quite as fast as the Hurricanes
and carried cannon-fired explosive shells.

As this deluge of twisting and turning planes fell towards
Colombo docks and the airfield, Chater's squadron shot down
eleven of the enemy, and another eleven were so badly damaged that it was unlikely they would get back to their carrier.
The price paid by Chater's squadron was the loss of five pilots.

Not quite so fortunate was 258 Squadron, which lost nine
aircraft, though some of the pilots escaped by parachute, after
shooting down or disabling five of the enemy. Statistically,
these losses were not important to the Japanese. But finding an
enemy prepared and with material as good as theirs, and missing the fleet they were sent to destroy, had a baleful influence
on their spirits. But these spirits were lifted marginally when a
report came in from one of the fleet's reconnaissance planes
that two big ships had been sighted well south of Ceylon. The
surviving Vals refuelled and rearmed, took off again, and made
their way south-west.

The ships were two 'County'-class, 10,000-ton British

cruisers, which had been the last to leave Colombo and were now hastening to rejoin Admiral Somerville's force. The dive-bombers came down out of the sun, making counter-fire difficult for the gunners. But with twice their number of anti-aircraft guns they could not have escaped their fate. The *Dorsetshire* took six direct hits from 800-pound bombs; she capsized and went down a few minutes later. The *Cornwall* soon followed her. Surprisingly, there were more than 1,100 survivors, although they could not be picked up until the following morning.

Admiral Nagumo, no doubt frustrated and angry at the small rewards of the great effort he had made, now returned to Ceylon in the hope of finding the elusive British fleet at the island's second base in the north, Trincolamee. The reception and absence of targets were the same as at Colombo. Modern fighters were defending the base, and there were dog-fights, and losses, on both sides. But again there was a consolation prize. As Nagumo's armada was flying along the north coast of the island, he sighted an aircraft carrier skirting the shore, as if hoping not to be seen.

She was the *Hermes*, laid down in the First World War as the first-ever purpose-built carrier. She was also almost the smallest carrier, being of only 11,000 tons. The Val pilots did not know nor care about her size; they just wanted to dispatch her to the bottom, and this was what they did with consummate ease.

The sinking of this carrier and the two heavy cruisers provided Nagumo with some consolation for failing to find and destroy Britain's Eastern Fleet, for the Japanese commander had decided to quit Ceylon and seek prizes elsewhere.

Winston Churchill wrote later of this critical period of the eastern war:

The stubborn resistance encountered at Colombo convinced the Japanese that further prizes would be dearly bought. The losses they had suffered in aircraft convinced them that they had come in contact with bone ... Apart from isolated activities by a few U-boats and disguised raiders, the Japanese Navy never appeared again in Indian waters. It vanished as suddenly as it had come, leaving behind a vacuum from which both antagonists had now withdrawn.

When Admiral Nagumo returned home he was again treated as a hero. The negative aspects of his raid were not considered, nor even known to the public. But they were soon to receive a jolt that would succeed in denting their pride and war spirit.

Soon after the humiliation of Pearl Harbor, American military and naval leaders conferred to consider a counter-attack. The suggestion was made that a bombing attack on Tokyo might raise morale in America and damage it in Japan. But if a carrier approached the Japanese capital close enough for naval bombers to take off, they would surely be shot down and the carrier treated equally roughly.

Equally out of the question was a long-distance land-based bomber raid. Both the American mainland and the Hawaiian Islands were too distant for the double journey. Moreover, it was known that the Japanese had organized a standing patrol of picket boats off the Japanese east coast, and their warning would allow plenty of time for fighters to take off and intercept the bombers.

The plan finally agreed was a daring one that was not without risks, but it was calculated that the effect on Japan would be so great that the risks were worth taking. A carrier would transport twin-engine, long-range bombers, release them outside the line of picket boats, and they would then fly to Tokyo and other cities at low level and release their bombs, both incendiary and high-explosive weapons. Then — and this was the ingenious part — they would not attempt to return but instead overfly the country and the Sea of Japan, and crash-land or bail out over friendly Chinese territory.

The ship chosen for this daring raid was the *Hornet*, which had just completed its acceptance trials, at which she had shown the ability to steam at thirty-three knots. The bomber selected was the equally new North American B25 Mitchell which, at her trials, had notched up over 300 mph, had a good bomb-carrying capacity, and was to become the best medium bomber of the war.

Trials were carried out in early February 1942. In secrecy, after passing through the Panama Canal, the *Hornet* embarked sixteen Mitchells on the west coast of America. She then sailed for Midway Island, where she rendezvoused with another carrier, the *Enterprise*, which was to provide fighter cover on the long Pacific voyage. Until this point none of the air crew, who were to be led by the veteran Colonel James Doolittle, knew their destination. When they were told there was predictable excitement among the fliers.

Escorted by cruisers, the task force set sail in turbulent weather that threatened the safety of the bombers, lined up on deck, even before they set off on their raid. Winds of over forty knots and high seas accompanied it on most of its voyage. This was an unpleasant overture to the operation; but worse was the sighting of a Japanese picket boat much farther from the Japanese coast than had been calculated. One of the cruiser's guns swung on to it and with a few salvoes blew it to pieces.

This was quick destruction, but not quick enough. The wireless operator in the picket boat managed to transmit a warning signal before his vessel's destruction. This was intercepted by the Americans and presented the commander of the task force, Captain Mark A. Mitscher, with a dilemma. He decided that the chance had to be taken, even if surprise had been lost and all his Mitchells might be shot down.

Early in the morning of 18 April, the air crews climbed in and Doolittle opened the throttles of his twin-engined machine. The *Hornet* was pitching and rolling and the wind was howling, but the Mitchell lifted off safely before the end of the flight deck, giving more space for the pilots behind him. A few minutes later all the sixteen bombers were airborne, heading for the Japanese mainland 600 miles distant.

The message from the picket boat had reached the Japanese High Command, and preparations were made accordingly. But they were made on the assumption that the American carriers would approach to within one hundred miles or so before launching their single-engine bombers. This, they calculated, would take approximately seven hours. Instead, it took little over two hours for the fast, low-flying bombers to cover the distance. At 10.30 a.m. Colonel Doolittle saw the buildings of Tokyo loom up ahead. His navigator was spot-on.

At first, there was no sign of any defences, and Doolittle found his target, a munitions factory, without difficulty and unloaded his incendiaries. One of the bombers had the naval shipyard at Yokohama as a target, and made a direct hit on a carrier with a high-explosive 500-pounder. All the bombers found and hit their targets and raced west for the South China Sea. One or two were pursued by fighters, but most of the scrambled aircraft assumed that the bombers were going to steer east to return to their carrier. All the American bombers survived the journey to China. Several found airfields; other crews bailed out or crash-landed when their fuel was exhausted.

As anticipated, the bombing of Japanese cities acted as a tonic for the American people. The enthusiasm was greatest among the citizens of the Hawaiian islands.

For the Japanese High Command, coming after the failure to destroy the British Eastern Fleet, the setback demanded a complete reappraisal of their plans and brought about, more than ever, the realization that they must act quickly. The Commander-in-Chief, Admiral Yamamoto, who had been to America before the war and had observed the might of American industry, recognized that a long war would be Japan's undoing.

The first anxiety concerned the number of trained air crews. There was plenty of oil now, as well as rubber and other resources needed to run a great war machine, but a pilot took at least nine months to train. Already the naval air arm had suffered considerable losses, and there were certain to be many battles ahead. The same had been true for the British RAF in the crucial Battle of Britain.

The next priority for the Japanese High Command was to consolidate their position in the south of their new empire. Their first target was Port Moresby on the south coast of New Guinea. With its capture, the next targets were the islands surrounding the Coral Sea. In the longer term, this would lead to the capture of the advanced American base at Midway Island, from which the carriers for the attack on mainland Japan had originated. With Midway in their hands, there would be a final lunge towards the Hawaiian islands, the loss of which would finally surrender to Japan total control of the Pacific.

The Americans received advance warning of the New

Guinea enterprise, although it was 'top secret' to the Japanese. Not only did the Americans have radar, but their code-breaking capacity was infinitely superior to Japan's. For this reason, the Americans had early warning of Japanese intentions. They made their dispositions accordingly, concentrating two carrier groups in the Coral Sea by 1 May 1942.

These American carriers consisted of the *Lexington* and *Yorktown*, supported by cruisers and destroyers. The *Lexington*, nicknamed 'Lady Luck' by her crew, was bigger than the largest Japanese carriers. Like them she had been converted during construction from a battle-cruiser. Commissioned in 1927, the *Lexington* displaced 41,000 tons, had a speed of thirty-one knots, and a capacity for sixty aircraft: a valuable ship indeed. She had been delivering aircraft to the American base at Midway when Pearl Harbor was bombed. The second carrier, the *Yorktown*, was much newer and was a sister ship of the *Hornet*.

The Japanese force consisted of two groups, one covering a convoy for the landing on New Guinea. This comprised the light carrier *Shoho* and four heavy cruisers and a destroyer. The second and more formidable force consisted of the sister carriers *Shokaku* and *Zuikaku*, modern carriers of 25,000 tons, each carrying eighty-four aircraft and with a speed of thirty-four knots. These were escorted by two heavy cruisers and six destroyers. The allied task forces, under the command of Rear-Admiral Frank Fletcher, assembled 400 miles south of the island of Guadalcanal on 5 May and left there with the intention of intercepting the Japanese invading force and any Japanese escorting ships.

Admiral Fletcher sent ahead the mixed force of Australian and American cruisers to locate and then attack the invasion force. Fletcher, with his two carriers, followed close behind to back them up, then turned north. Soon they found the light carrier *Shoho* and accompanying cruisers. They quickly disposed of her with the loss of just three aircraft. The triumphant phrase 'Scratch one flat-top' went out *en clair* from the commander of the attack; it was to become one of the most exhilarating and best-remembered phrases of the Pacific war.

The battle now entered what can only be called its confusion stage. The weather was foul; conditions resembled those round Iceland during the *Bismarck* chase: dark clouds and strands of mist and patches of tropical rain. Groping around like two blind men, both Admiral Tukagi, the Japanese commander, and Admiral Fletcher received false reports of the enemy's position. At this stage of the war American radar, though pricelessly valuable, had only a restricted range. It was not until late in the afternoon that Fletcher learned that the main Japanese carrier force was behind him and not ahead as falsely reported.

The next morning, 8 May, each side soon accurately located the other. Conditions were more favourable than on the previous day, and the Japanese dive-bombers, torpedo bombers and escorting Zero fighters were soon thundering down the decks of the two carriers — more than 120 in all. The Americans were also scrambling everything that could fly — nearly eighty Dauntless dive-bombers and Devastator torpedo bombers with a dozen or more Wildcat fighters. They went on their way, disturbed only by the intermittent rain clouds at varying heights.

They located the *Shokaku* first, some distance away from her sister ship, whose anti-aircraft guns were out of range. But enough black spots dotted the sky around the Dauntlesses at 17,000 feet to toss them about before they turned over into their sixty-five-degree dives. Further down, light tracer flak crisscrossed about them, ceasing only when the Zeros joined in the frantic rush. The dive-bombers' rear gunners added their contribution, and one or two of the Zeros were shot down into the distant sea below. But none of the first wave of dive-bombers made a hit. The second wave experienced more favourable conditions. Not only were the gunners preoccupied with the simultaneous torpedo attack, but the Zeros had not had time to climb high enough after the first attack to be a similar menace. The leading Dauntless, while on fire from many flak strikes, pulled out low over the carrier and dropped its bomb smack in the middle of the flight deck before crashing into the sea. It was enough to put the big carrier out of the battle, but two more hits followed and the *Shokaku* became a blazing wreck.

The Devastator torpedo planes had a rougher and less successful time. They jinked and twisted and turned, but the light flak forced some pilots to drop their 'tin fish' too far from their target, and other torpedoes, through a fault in their steering mechanism, simply swung round in circles. (This was the first occasion when torpedoes of the US Navy revealed their faults. Many more followed before the failure was diagnosed.)

Not a hit was made, but though many were damaged the slow Devastators managed to limp away.

While the Americans were 'deleting one flat-top', the same number of Japanese planes were heading for the *Lexington* and *Yorktown*. They concentrated first on the bigger carrier, the *Lexington*. She launched what few Wildcat fighters were held in reserve, and put up dense anti-aircraft fire, but neither prevented the Val dive-bombers from finding their target. But it was the Japanese torpedo bombers which inflicted the greater damage, coming in fast and low while the gunners were distracted by the Vals. They scored two strikes on the port side, and the big ship at once assumed a list. Boiler rooms had been damaged, too, causing the speed to drop.

The *Yorktown* was the next to suffer as a second wave of dive- and torpedo bombers came in. She took an 800-pound bomb which exploded deep inside, affecting only partially her flight deck. But, being nippier than the *Lexington*, she succeeded in combing the tracks of all the torpedoes aimed at her. For the first time, the Japanese aircraft paid a heavy price for their success. Twenty-six fell to the guns of the defending American aircraft and anti-aircraft guns, including the group leader of the attack.

Many more, returning to their carriers, found one of them unable to take them, while the *Zuikaku*, though undamaged, found herself overwhelmed by the number of planes, many short on fuel, that sought her flight deck. Nor could she operate her lifts, and so many planes were stranded on her flight deck that some had to be pushed over the side into the sea. Other planes, their fuel exhausted, splashed into the sea, some of the crew being picked up by destroyers.

The *Shokaku*, meanwhile, limped away from the scene of battle and headed back to her base in Japan. She faced a long and slow journey, but she got there in the end and was taken in hand by the ship repairers.

The Japanese had no means — nor planes — to follow up their earlier attack. The convoy heading for Port Moresby also turned back as it was threatened by American land-based heavy bombers based in Australia.

Admiral Fletcher's two carriers were still fully operational, in spite of *Lexington*'s seven-degree list, and they both headed back for Pearl Harbor, mission accomplished. But then occurred another turn of events in this long-drawn-out battle.

Fumes had been steadily building up in the boiler rooms of the *Lexington*, and it needed only a spark to cause an explosion. A commutator in a motor generator room provided this. Instantly, flames flew high into the air, followed by black smoke. It looked as if 'Lady Luck' was out of it and would soon sink. But the great old carrier seemed to pull herself together. The flames died down and the fire parties took control. Then another two explosions followed the first; the flames took over again, and this time they could not be controlled.

A few minutes after 5 p.m. the order to abandon ship was broadcast. Some 2,700 officers and men were picked up, including the captain, who had been standing on the bridge to the last in accordance with tradition. Then one final huge explosion blew the ship apart. The sound was like a giant volley over the grave of a dead sailor. But she had been a giant ship and was much mourned by those who had served in her. Thirty-six of her planes and 200 of her crew were lost.

The *Yorktown*, flying the flag of Admiral Fletcher, left the scene of battle and made her way to Pearl Harbor to be repaired.

The consequences of what was to be called the Battle of the Coral Sea were greater by far for the Allies, and the New Zealanders and Australians especially, than the loss of one small carrier against a big fleet carrier. This suggested a Japanese tactical victory. But the truth that could not be denied was that the previously unconquerable Japanese fleet had been stopped in its tracks and denied its next target. The loss of trained, experienced air crew and their machines was another blow.

The damage to the *Shokaku* alone was to make a fundamental difference in the next and critical stage of the Pacific war.

10

························

THE BATTLE OF MIDWAY,
4–7 JUNE 1942

The loss of the Lexington *at the Battle of the Coral Sea gave that action the specious appearance of a tactical defeat for the U.S., and the Japanese concentrated on following up what they thought of as their advantage by pressing forward to take Midway Island. On the face of it the Japanese had the upper hand with four fast aircraft carriers,* Kaga, Akagi, Soryu *and* Hiryu *against the United States Navy's two, the* Hornet *and the* Enterprise.

The Japanese attack was complicated but very carefully planned by Admiral Yamamoto, and consisted of no less than eight separate task forces. These were to achieve a wide range of objectives that covered the whole northwest Pacific Ocean, from the Aleutians to Hawaii. The attack on the Aleutians was intended to draw the U.S. fleet north, exposing Midway. To further prevent U.S. interference Yamamoto drew up a patrol line of submarines west of Hawaii intended to prevent penetration of the Midway area. The main Japanese attack on Midway was to be led by Admiral Nagumo's First Carrier Strike Force, supported by Yamamoto and a battle fleet, both coming from Japan. Subsidiary transport, support and minesweeping groups would arrive from the Mariana Islands, Saipan and Guam.

Yamamoto's plan was assiduously countered by his opposite number, Admiral Nimitz of the United States Navy. Thanks to the breaking of Japanese codes, the United States Navy had divined Yamamoto's intentions, in particular his deceptive feint towards the Aleutians. This, combined with the hurried repair of the carrier Yorktown, *enabled Nimitz to dispatch two task forces, under Admirals Spruance and Fletcher. Outnumbered by the Japanese, the United States Navy exploited the weapon of surprise with devastating effect.*

During three days in early June 1942, six months after they had attacked Pearl Harbor, Admiral Nagumo's assault was brilliantly met by the defenders of Midway. The U.S. victory was the high-water mark of Imperial Japanese expansion and was the turning point of the Pacific War.

••••••••••••••••••••

WITH THEIR BRILLIANT intelligence brought about by their ability to read Japanese coded signals, the Americans were well aware of Japan's next move. This was supported by evidence that the enemy had postponed — actually cancelled — any further move into the Coral Sea and Port Moresby. Clearly the target would be Midway, the farthest outpost west the Americans possessed. They therefore used every endeavour to reinforce the tiny island's defences. It had had for a number of years long runways, and the island's fighter force had been strongly reinforced. There was also a squadron of B17 heavy bombers and some eighteen Catalinas for reconnaissance. Strong gun defences — especially anti-aircraft guns — had been installed.

Admiral Chester W. Nimitz, the C.-in-C. of American naval forces in the Pacific, gathered together his last two operational carriers, under the command of Admiral Fletcher. Fletcher had performed credibly in the Coral Sea engagement and was placed in command of a quite inadequate force to face Admiral Nagumo's all-conquering carrier force. Nimitz cast aside his pride and asked the British Navy for the temporary loan of a couple of modern armoured carriers. But the British were too committed in the Mediterranean, the eastern Indian Ocean and in home waters to spare even one carrier.

Fletcher's two carriers were the *Enterprise* and the *Hornet*, with her untested air crews. The damaged *Yorktown* had arrived at Pearl Harbor from the Coral Sea for repairs on the afternoon of 27 May. Could she be made operational by the predicted time of Nagumo's arrival on 4 June, two days and two nights away? It was surely not possible. But an army of repairers of every trade descended upon the damaged vessel. Even the civil population took part — willy-nilly. Such was the demand for electricity down at the shipyard that it had to be cut off from time to time.

The battle of the shipyard was won shortly before noon on 29 May. The *Yorktown* put to sea and took on her complement of fighters and bombers. When the ship rendezvoused with the other two carriers, she became the flagship of Task Force 17, flying the flag of Admiral Fletcher. Task Force 16 was commanded by Admiral Raymond Spruance, who had never served in carriers before but was greatly admired for his decisiveness and authority. Not for nothing was he to be nicknamed 'Electric Brain' Spruance. His flag-captain was Captain Elliott Buckmaster.

Admiral Yamamoto, the C.-in-C. of the Japanese Navy, was seen as the Admiral Togo of the 1940s, and was quite as highly regarded as his predecessor. Yamamoto had devised a complex plan, dispatching a force sufficiently large to impress his enemy to Dutch Harbour, the perversely named American base in the Aleutian Islands. This he hoped would draw what carriers the Americans still possessed far north of Midway, while Nagumo's main force of four carriers, eleven battleships, twenty-three cruisers, sixty-five destroyers and the invasion force of troop carriers fell on Midway. The Japanese believed that they had sunk both carriers at Coral Sea, leaving them possibly with only one to deal with. They were disabused of this notion when radio signals were intercepted between two 'carriers' far to the south. They were in fact two American heavy cruisers simulating the role of carriers, signalling to their 'planes' and each other on a wavelength the Americans knew the Japanese could read.

The Japanese timetable conformed precisely and reassuringly to American predictions. On the morning of 3 June 1942, the Japanese carried out a bombing raid on Dutch Harbour. It was a half-hearted affair, and the weather was terrible. But the Japanese hoped the Americans would fall for their ruse and detach from the Midway area such carriers as they had to seek out the two Japanese carriers involved. But the two American task forces remained where they had rendezvoused earlier at a point code-named optimistically Point Luck, north-west of Midway Island.

For some days now scouting Catalinas had flown from Midway on varying easterly vectors as a precautionary measure. On the same morning and approximately at the same time as the Dutch Harbour attack, a Catalina crew caught sight of two small ships ahead. They could not identify them but received a dose of flak before pressing on. The captain suspected that they might be a precursor to the expected invasion force. His suspicions soon turned out to be correct. Next he identified a fleet of mine-sweepers and then later a fleet of transports. That was enough — which was as well because he was at the extreme limit of his aircraft's range. He identified his position and reported what he had observed.

Back at Midway, the last precautions were taken, the defences alerted, and the B17 heavy bombers took off to attack the van of the advancing fleet. They found the transports in the middle of the afternoon. They bombed from 8,000 feet and failed to score a hit. But it was to be the opening round in one of the most decisive contests in naval history.

Admiral Nagumo began launching his attack on Midway and its satellite island, Sand Island, at dawn on 4 June; 108 planes, fighters and bombers, roared down the deck of the four carriers, up into the early sun, and steered south-east. As a precaution Nagumo retained on board the *Akagi* and *Kaga* a reserve of Kates equipped with torpedoes.

On Midway preparations were as complete and comprehensive as they could be. The radar aerials rotated remorselessly on their towers; every three-inch gun was manned and with plenty of ready ammunition. There was not a defender who did not recognize that they were about to face the worst crisis in their lives. All the Catalinas were ordered off and to make themselves scarce. Four of them, however, had unfamiliar torpedoes slung under their bellies with orders to find and damage some of the oncoming ships. The fighters followed them, but their role was defensive, and they climbed up high into the dawn sky.

It was the radar, of course, that picked up the raiders first, just before 6 a.m. and at a range of over ninety miles. A quarter of an hour later the first whisper of massed aero engines became audible. The decibels increased with hurricane speed, and then the radar became redundant as the human eye took over. The three-inch anti-aircraft guns blasted out before the bombers were over the island, then ceased as the defending fighters dived down from 18,000 feet — stubby Brewster Buffaloes and the more modern Wildcats, tearing apart with their half-inch guns half a dozen or so Kates. But Zeros soon moved in to defend their charges. The ancient Buffaloes were almost wiped out. The gun crews on Midway, who could do nothing to intervene, watched the awesome dog-fights over their island.

Then the bombs began to fall from diving Vals and high-level Kates above them. The noise was outrageous. Surely nothing and nobody could survive this onslaught? The Zeros came in low to strafe with their twenty-millimetre cannon anything they could see and recognize as a useful target. But like a summer thunderstorm, the assault did not last for long, and within minutes a ghostly silence fell over these atolls in the middle of the Pacific, broken only by the crackle of fires and then the more familiar sound of returning fighters, some half of which had been shot into the sea.

The fires were restricted to a dummy fighter, a favourite target for the Zeros, and, more seriously, fuel tanks on Sand Island, which the bomber crews had ignored at Pearl Harbor although they had now learned better.

As so often happens in a raid on a small target, most of the Japanese air crews were confident that they had virtually wiped out their target, such was the dust and the smoke rising from it as they turned back for their carriers. But their leader, Lieutenant Tomonaga, knew better, and he radioed back to Admiral Nagumo, 'There is need for a second attack.' On hearing this, the Admiral ordered the reserve Kates, which were fitted with torpedoes, to change their load to bombs. This was a daunting assignment for the armourers and mechanics. They were all experienced, but it took time, and at 7.30 a.m. the tropical heat was already rising as they worked away in the hangars of the *Kaga* and the *Akagi*.

While this was going on, and the planes from the Midway attack were beginning to land, a signal was received from one of the reconnaissance seaplanes which earlier Nagumo had ordered to be launched from his escorting cruisers. Most had seen nothing and were already returning. But one, far to the north-east, radioed that he had sighted 'what appears to be surface ships' and reported their position and speed.

Admiral Nagumo signalled back, asking the seaplane captain to 'ascertain ship types'. It was some time before the seaplane commander radioed the dread words 'The enemy is accompanied by what appears to be a carrier'.

If that was the case, the reserve bombers would need to be armed with torpedoes after all, and Captain Mitsuo Fuelida gave orders accordingly. Pandemonium reigned down below in the hangars when this counter-order was received. Heavy bombs and long torpedoes littered the steel deck.

One Japanese officer later described the situation in these words:

> I will tell you how bad it was. We had about one hundred Zeros, Vals and Kates in the air, low on fuel, the Zeros out of ammunition, too, some of them damaged. They all had to be recovered and serviced. That would take one hour. And we could not launch an attack meanwhile. The Zeros that had not gone to Midway were out of ammunition and

half out of fuel as a result of defending our carriers. Some of our bombers were armed with bombs, some with torpedoes, some unarmed. It was not a good situation — not good at all.

The situation might have been worse if the truth had been known: that there was not one carrier up there in the north-east, not two, but three. So if carriers were now 'queens of the ocean', as indeed they were, the Japanese, who had judged that there would be no carrier opposition round Midway, now faced odds in their favour of only four to three.

As soon as Admiral Fletcher had located the position of the enemy carriers, he launched, at extreme range, the Devastator torpedo bombers of all three of his carriers. The Devastator was a lumbering, obsolescent machine with a maximum speed when loaded of 115 mph, no more than the British Swordfish. Its range was limited to under 500 miles. By contrast, the Japanese Kate could fly at 220 mph fully loaded with a torpedo heavier than the Devastator's, and enjoyed a range of 1,200 miles. Moreover, the Kate had twice the defensive armament of the American machine.

The Japanese had no idea of the superiority of their bomber over its opposite number. The first hint came when the initial wave of Devastators emerged from the smoke-screen and came in straight at the *Akaqi*, not jinking or swerving or attempting to split up and attack from different bearings. They simply came straight on, sitting targets for the Japanese gunners. Of the first wave of fifteen, all crashed into the sea, some in flames, others just torn apart. The next wave did rather better, four of the planes surviving the holocaust, although none of the survivors scored a hit. The third wave of fifteen bombers was, providentially, escorted by a handful of Wildcat fighters. Zero fighters began their brutal work on the Devastators. The Wildcats jumped them long before the bombers could drop their 'tin fish' (or 'pickles', as the Americans called them). A desperate dog-fight ensued above the advancing Devastators, but the Wildcats were outnumbered two to one, allowing half the Zeros to get on the tails of the American bombers, only two of which escaped.

After this attack Admiral Nagumo and his captains could view the situation with satisfaction. We can imagine the Japanese Admiral pacing his bridge, waiting impatiently for the Kates in the hangars to come up in the lifts, then line up and take off to demonstrate to the enemy the inferiority of their torpedo bombers. Then the silence following the last abortive attack was broken by a look-out's cry: 'Dive-bombers!'

The sharp-eyed look-out was right. High in the morning sky, three specks could be seen, growing in size with every passing second. The resting, triumphant gun crews had no time to swing their weapons up to the required seventy-five degrees. All they saw was three planes pulling out of their near-vertical dives while three black bombs detached themselves as the planes flattened out and screamed away at full throttle, jinking and swerving in their effort to avoid the flak.

The first bomb of this initial flight of three dive-bombers just missed. It struck the water on the port side, rocking the great carrier and deluging everyone on the bridge. The second, in the American jargon of the time, was a humdinger. The 1,000-pound high-explosive bomb landed plumb in the centre of the flight deck, exploding deep in the hangar. The result was catastrophic. There were bombs and torpedoes everywhere; there were high-octane 'avgas' fuel tanks and oil tanks. The multiple explosions tore the heart out of the ship, sending all the contents of the hangar, all the aircraft, high into the air. When the smoke eventually died down, Kates, Vals and Zeros, some broken to pieces, others almost intact, could be seen on the litter-strewn water.

Miraculously the engines were still running, although this corpse of a ship, with rudders jammed twenty degrees to port, could only make circles. Minor explosions continued down in the hangar — perhaps a belt of twenty-millimetre shells — for some time. Up on the bridge, Admiral Nagumo seemed paralysed by what had happened and had to be persuaded to abandon his flagship. He and his captain and staff had to climb down a hastily rigged rope to the hot, sloping deck. Rescue boats were all around, and they were not in the sea for long. The Admiral hoisted his flag in a light cruiser.

The second flight of Dauntlesses went for the *Kaga*. Four 1,000-pound bombs sealed her fate as comprehensively as that of her cohort. The only difference was that two bombs exploded close to the bridge, killing the captain and all his staff.

Inevitably, fire broke out in the hangar. The fire raced along rivulets of gasoline, spreading disaster below decks. Men trapped behind blistering bulkheads were roasted alive. Hoses rolled out in a frantic effort to hold back the flames caught fire. Some officers and men, their uniforms smouldering and their faces blackened by smoke, were driven back to the edge of the flight deck, and from there they leaped into the sea. Then the fire travelled to the bomb storage lockers. Suddenly there was a thunderous detonation, and sheets of glowing steel were ripped like so much tinfoil from the bowels of the ship. The hangar deck was a purgatory within a few minutes, and great clouds of black smoke rose from the *Kaga*, carrying with them the smell of burning gasoline, paint, wood, rubber and human flesh.

Flights of Dauntlesses now dropped down on the last of the carriers in the area, the *Soryu*. It was the same story. Three hits on her flight deck were enough to settle her fate. She went down within twenty minutes, a blazing wreck.

The only survivor was the *Hiryu*, which was too distant for the range of the Dauntlesses. As these American dive-bombers headed back to their carriers, fuel gauges well below the danger mark, they were distantly followed by Kates, Vals and Zeros.

From his new flagship, Admiral Nagumo had ordered his last surviving carrier to make an all-out assault on what he still believed to be the sole American carrier. The *Yorktown* was the nearest American carrier to the advancing Japanese air armada of forty mixed torpedo and dive-bombers and escorting Zeros.

For the radar operators on the *Yorktown*, it was a repeat of the experience of the operators on Midway itself. First a faint smudge as the aerial rotated, then a more clearly defined signal, then the eye could take over from the cathode ray tube. The gun crews were ready, everything was battened down, the fire parties and first-aid parties at the ready. One or two Dauntlesses attempting to land were signalled away, much to their crews' distress and anger. For them there was now no alternative to splashing down in the sea.

The first opposition experienced by the Japanese dive-bombers came not from the multiple anti-aircraft guns but from patrolling Wildcats. They tore into the vulnerable Vals and shot down six of them before they were in range of their target. But there were still seven left, and the Japanese had recently demonstrated what even one could do. The leading Val took the most intense flak, which killed the pilot and tore off the Val's wings. But before he died the pilot proved he had good eyes, for when his bomb detached itself from the wrecked plane it landed plumb on the flight deck alongside the bridge. Two more from those behind followed, one exploding against the funnel uptake, which caused the carrier to lose speed to around ten knots. Smoke rose high into the sky, warning Admiral Fletcher's other two carriers.

On the way back, the Vals were again attacked by Wildcats, whose pilots had got their eye in by now. Only one Val survived to tell the tale. And the tale was: 'One carrier burning'. So when the torpedo-carrying Kates took off they judged their role to be to ensure the elimination of the American carrier. But when, low over the sea, they sighted their target, their first reaction was that they had found another carrier, even though the Americans had only one, or so they thought.

In fact, so efficient and diligent were the *Yorktown*'s fire-fighters and repair crews that the ship was like a new carrier. She was launching Wildcats and steaming into the wind at twenty knots. When the Kates got close they were met by a screen of light flak. One after another they fell into the sea — but two survived to drop their torpedoes. They sealed the fate of the *Yorktown*. She assumed a steep list with her rudder jammed, as the *Bismarck*'s had been jammed all those months ago on the other side of the world.

It was clear now that the *Yorktown* would never fight again. Admiral Fletcher, therefore, handed over command to his deputy, Admiral Spruance. Spruance had already dispatched scouting planes to establish the whereabouts of the last Japanese carrier. Having succeeded in this, he dispatched no fewer than twenty-four Dauntlesses. Three of these never returned, but enough got through the flak and the Zeros and the message soon came through: 'Scratch one flat-top.'

But the *Yorktown* appeared to be indestructible. She lay without movement in the water, her vast flight deck at too acute an angle for any plane to land. But most of her crew remained on board, together with her captain, Elliott Buckmaster. There was talk of a tow. The tough 'old lady' had survived Coral Sea. She would survive again. Back to Pearl Harbor, a patch-up there, then off to the west coast for a real overhaul.

Two nights passed. Then, at 7 a.m. on 7 May, a lookout saw the telltale wash of four torpedoes coming straight for the crippled carrier. One missed, one struck a guarding destroyer, blowing the little ship apart, then two struck the big ship amidships.

A Japanese submarine, the *I-168*, had been stalking the carrier for hours, all through the night, and as dawn broke the commander approached slowly, at no more than five knots, raising his periscope intermittently, then firing a full salvo of torpedoes at point-blank range.

Everyone left on board the *Yorktown* knew that this was the end. The two explosions corrected the tilt, but water was pouring in and the ship was rapidly sinking lower in the water. Two more destroyers came alongside, picking up survivors. There were men in tears as the ship turned over and disappeared, leaving a lake of fuel oil and a mass of debris behind her.

Spruance's scouting plane had also identified two battleships and a strong force of heavy cruisers not too distant from the doomed carrier. Spruance therefore decided that it would be suicide to renew the contest. The Japanese force had lost all its carriers. The Americans had lost one carrier. That was enough. 'I did not feel justified,' Spruance reported later, 'in risking a night encounter with possibly superior enemy forces, but on the other hand I did not want to be too far away from Midway the next morning. I wished to have a position from which either to follow up retreating enemy forces or to break up a landing attack on Midway.'

This was sound judgement. Had Spruance advanced he might well have been confronted in the morning by nine battleships in all, including the *Yamato*, in which Admiral Yamamoto flew his flag. She was the biggest battleship in the world, armed with the largest-calibre guns, 18.1-inch. As well there was a carrier, withdrawn from the Dutch Harbour diversion, and a heavy contribution of heavy cruisers.

It was the wisest decision the wise Admiral Spruance ever made.

Midway was one of the major decisive victories for the Allies in the Second World War, comparable with the Battle of Britain, the battle for Stalingrad and the Battle of Kursk, July—August 1943. Winston Churchill signalled Franklin D. Roosevelt on the evening of 13 June, 'This is the moment to send you my heartiest congratulations on the grand American victories in the Pacific which have very decidedly altered the balance of the naval war.'

Later he wrote in his memoirs:

This memorable victory was of cardinal importance not only to the United States, but to the whole Allied cause. The moral effect was tremendous and instantaneous. At one stroke the dominant position of Japan in the Pacific was reversed. The glaring ascendancy of the enemy, which had frustrated our combined endeavours throughout the Far East for six months, was gone for ever.

In spite of manful efforts, the Japanese Navy never recovered from the loss of carriers, air crew and aircraft. But there was a long struggle ahead for the Americans in the Pacific. Admiral Yamamoto was forced to cancel the attempt to capture Midway Island. He, above all others, recognized that this was going to be a prolonged war, every passing day diminishing the chance of final victory for Japan in the Pacific war. By 1944 Japan was reduced to converting battleships into make-do carriers, while towards the end of that year America was launching a carrier *every week*. Air crew were pouring out of new training schools in America while Japan had to resort to *kamikaze* (or suicide) pilots who were only just able to take off in their 'flying bombs'.

11

....

THE BATTLE FOR
GUADALCANAL,
AUGUST 1942–
FEBRUARY 1943

After Midway, the United States went on the offensive. This was a remarkable transformation, but the initial planning of an offensive operation was torn by internal disagreements between the Joint Chiefs of Staff as to a proper objective.

Then intelligence reports settled the matter. Japanese reinforcements were reported moving to Guadalcanal and the surrounding islands in the Japanese-held Solomon Islands. These were being prepared for a long-planned attack on Australia and plans were quickly made for Vice-Admiral Ghormley to be overall strategic commander, with Rear-Admiral Fletcher in tactical command and Major-General Vandegrift to lead the landing force of marines. These factors, the haste of its preparation and the poor morale of the designated troops, led it to being nicknamed 'Operation Shoestring'.

The 19,000-strong United States Marine force was landed unopposed on August 7, 1942, but the Japanese ferociously counter-attacked, and the control of the waters around Guadalcanal was seized by a cruiser force under Admiral Mikawa. Thereafter, in a series of furiously contested actions that lasted from August to November, the Japanese Navy sought to dislodge the Marines from their beachhead. From their base at Rabaul, the United States reinforced the troops on Guadalcanal by rushing heavily escorted troop convoys through "The Slot," the channel lying between the east and west Solomons. So regular did these convoys become that the Americans nicknamed them "the Tokyo Express." During these long weeks in which the advantage swung back and forth, the United States Navy, supported by a few ships from the Royal Australian Navy, painfully gained the upper hand. The climax came on November 12, when Rear-Admiral Callaghan's cruiser force engaged a battle-group of the Imperial Japanese Navy which were intending to put Henderson Field out of action. Commanded by Vice-Admiral Abe, the Japanese group included two battleships, Hiei *and* Kiri-Shima. *In a bloody and confusing night action the United States Navy lost heavily, and Callaghan was among the killed. But the U.S. cruise force had prevented the reinforcing of Guadalcanal, and the damaged* Hiei *was afterwards sunk by American aircraft. However, this was only the opening round of the three-day naval battle.*

By the following night, when the Japanese, under Admirals Mikawa and Tanaka, made their second attempt to get troops through, the Americans had a battle-group under Admiral Kinkaid in the area. This included the battleships Washington *and* South Dakota, *and the aircraft carrier* Enterprise. *Despite losses, Mikawa bombed Henderson Field and Tanaka succeeded in pushing troops ashore. By daylight on November 14 matters hung in the balance. Then, on the night of November 14-15, Vice-Admiral Kondo with the* Kiri-Shima, *four cruisers and destroyers met the United States for the second and final time. In spite of a power-failure knocking out the* South Dakota's *guns,* Washington's *main salvoes destroyed* Kiri-Shima *in seven terrible minutes and the Japanese were finally compelled to retreat.*

....

BUOYED UP BY their success at the Battle of Midway, the Allies made plans for their first major offensive. They could go north to the Philippine Islands, or south to the Solomon Islands. The American High Command chose the second option.

The Solomon Islands consist of an archipelago of volcanic islands south-east of the Bismarck archipelago. The northern Solomons form part of Papua New Guinea and include the large island of Bougainville. The southern Solomons form a long double archipelago, an extension of the northern Solomons running south-east of Bougainville to San Cristobel. The area between these archipelagos was known as 'the Slot'.

To gain possession of these archipelagos would protect Australia and New Zealand from invasion by the Japanese. It was appropriate, therefore, that there was a significant Australian and British involvement in this combined operation, code-named Watchword. The carrier force consisted of the *Enterprise*, the *Wasp* and the mighty *Saratoga*, sister ship to the *Lexington*. The *Saratoga* had been torpedoed early in the Pacific war but was now repaired. These carriers were supported by the new battleship *North Carolina*, five heavy cruisers, an anti-aircraft cruiser and a large contingent of destroyers.

The plan was to seize the large island of Guadalcanal and surrounding islands. Among these, and the first on the list, were the Santa Cruz islands, together with Tulagi, a small island north of Guadalcanal which had been used as a seaplane base by the Japanese at the time of the Battle of the Coral Sea. D-day was fixed for 1 August 1942.

In overall command of this powerful naval force was Vice-Admiral Richard Ghormley. The three carriers, *Saratoga*,

Enterprise and *Wasp*, were commanded by Rear-Admiral Frank Fletcher, Rear-Admiral Thomas C. Kinkaid and Rear-Admiral L. Noyes. Rear-Admiral Richard Turner commanded the amphibious force, consisting of twenty-two transports for the Marine Corps contingent of 19,000 officers and men, protected by three heavy and a light cruiser; two of the heavy cruisers and the light cruiser were Australian, commanded by a British admiral, Rear-Admiral V. C. Crutchley. There was also a six-boat flotilla of submarines, commanded by Rear-Admiral Charles Lockwood, based in Australia at Brisbane.

Just as Admiral Ghormley was about to put into effect the first phase of Operation Watchword a reconnaissance plane returned from a photographic flight over Guadalcanal.

One of the photographs revealed a nearly completed airfield on the only area of flat land on this mountainous island. It was now evident that the Japanese had stolen a march on them.

Admiral Ghormley reacted swiftly, dispatching Marines in transports direct to Guadalcanal. As they waded ashore they met little resistance. Clearly, the Japanese had not yet landed in force, because all the Marines encountered were workers completing the airfield. They were rapidly overcome and the Marines occupied the field. It was given the pretentious name Henderson Airfield, though it was only a levelled-off area of muddy ground. But Henderson was to figure importantly in the battles that lay ahead.

Uncharacteristically, the Japanese were taken by surprise, too. They had no knowledge of Admiral Ghormley's armada of warships and transports hovering off the Solomon Islands, and it was not until news arrived of the Marines' landing on Guadalcanal that the need for instant counter-attack was recognized.

The Japanese C.-in-C., based at Rabaul in northern New Guinea, was Vice-Admiral Gunichi Mikawa. He had been ordered to occupy the island of Guadalcanal and other Solomon Islands as the next stage in the planned direct attack on Australian targets, and eventually the defeat and occupation of this vast subcontinent.

Mikawa responded rapidly to the Allied threat to his plans, sending off a striking force of Bettys escorted by Zeros with drop tanks for extra range. With early warning of this attack, sixty Wildcats were scrambled from Fletcher's carriers, and they were well placed above the twin-engine Bettys as they came in from the south-east. The Wildcat pilots, many of them veterans of Midway, tore into the attack, which, supported by the heavy flak from the ships, accounted for more than a dozen Bettys and a number of Zeros. No damage was done to Ghormley's ships, much to the Admiral's satisfaction.

Now Admiral Ghormley calculated that the time had come to dispatch his main body of transports loaded with Marines to Guadalcanal. He kept his carriers out of harm's way but dispatched a strong force of cruisers, Australian and American, to cover the landings. These were under the joint command of Admirals Turner and Crutchley. They positioned their ships on two patrol lines on both sides of Savo Island, which is just north of the eastern tip of Guadalcanal. As a further precaution, two radar-equipped destroyers were dispatched to patrol 'the Slot'. The American and British admirals now felt confident that they could protect the transports and the Marines.

As daylight faded on 8 August, officers and men not on watch turned in. Everyone was tired from the exertions of the day, which had been warm and clammy. They looked forward to a long night's sleep, confident that the Japanese were reluctant to fight at night. No one, however, underestimated their skill and ruthlessness in day fighting, especially by their air arm.

But the IJN had learned the value of night fighting capability as long before as their war with Russia in 1904, which opened with a torpedo-boat night attack on the anchored Russian Fleet in Port Arthur, crippling it — just as they were to cripple the American battleship fleet at Pearl Harbor thirty-nine years later. The Japanese had also noted the historical fact that it was the refusal of the British Grand Fleet to continue the fight at Jutland into the night which had enabled the German High Seas Fleet to escape.

Between the wars, the IJN, in the utmost secrecy, developed their night fighting skills to a high degree, albeit at the cost of many lives. The same ruthlessness that had governed the development of the oxygen-powered twenty-four-inch 'Long Lance' torpedo was also applied to the technique of fighting at night.

The United States Navy, on the other hand, had for long underestimated the advantages of night fighting ability. Exercises at night were judged to be too dangerous.

Appraised of the presence of Allied transports landing their troops on the beaches of Guadalcanal, Admiral Mikawa departed from Rabaul with three light cruisers and five heavy cruisers mounting eight-inch guns — a formidable force indeed. During daylight hours on 8 August, Mikawa remained concealed and anchored just east of Bougainville. There he briefed his commanders on the forthcoming night raid on the Allied transports.

At midnight on 8/9 August 1942, Mikawa gave the order to move off. Flying his flag in the light cruiser *Chokai*, the

Admiral led the way, and all his ships raced down 'the Slot' at twenty-four knots. At 12.54 a.m. one of the *Chokai*'s look-outs sighted through his long Zeiss night-glasses a destroyer. It was one of the two radar-equipped destroyers ordered to patrol 'the Slot' in order to give Admiral Fletcher warning of any enemy. Mikawa sped past in the dark, giving no order to open fire: he was after bigger game.

Mikawa sighted another destroyer a few minutes later. That, too, was passed by. Then, at 1.43 a.m., a third destroyer; this time it was with one of the groups of cruisers. This destroyer sighted the Japanese ships and transmitted a warning. At the same time, flares suddenly illuminated the whole scene — the American and Australian cruisers with their accompanying destroyers were all suddenly visible as if night had been turned into day.

Mikawa noted that there were two groups of cruisers, one distant yet still clearly visible. But it was the first one which attracted his attention. They were both big heavy cruisers with their guns trained fore and aft as if their crews were still fast asleep, as indeed they were.

The two heavy cruisers were the HMAS *Canberra* and the USS *Chicago*. The *Canberra* was the pride of the Australian Navy. Of 10,000 tons, she was similar to the British 'County' class and was built in Britain between the wars. She carried a main armament of eight eight-inch guns and could steam at around thirty-one knots. Her accompanying heavy cruiser, the USS *Chicago*, was of about the same vintage as the *Canberra*, with one more eight-inch gun, and with a slightly higher top speed. She featured a large hangar amidships for her complement of four seaplanes, and the catapult to launch them.

Mikawa immediately ordered 'Open fire' on these two

juicy targets, at the same time ordering the 'Long Lance' torpedoes to streak away on their deadly errand. The first salvo of eight-inch shells and the forty-eight-knot Long Lances struck almost simultaneously. The *Canberra* was the first to suffer, a shell killing her Australian captain and everybody on the bridge. Within two minutes the 10,000-ton heavy cruiser was rendered redundant, though she remained afloat for a number of hours.

The *Chicago*'s end was also abrupt. A Long Lance exploded forward, taking away most of her bow. Then a shell hit the foremast and others followed. She drifted away, a giant corpse on the sea.

The captain of the *Chicago* can scarcely be blamed for failing to give warning to the second group of patrolling cruisers. Everything had happened so suddenly and, besides, he had lost all means of communication. The senior officer of the northern group of cruisers was Captain Frederick Riefkohl, and his ship was the heavy cruiser *Vincennes*. He had observed the flash of guns to the south, but this was the first warning he had had. Then, suddenly, as with the southern group, all those above deck were half blinded by exploding flares.

In the course of dealing with the *Chicago* and the *Canberra*, Admiral Mikawa's cruisers had drifted apart into two groups, so that when Mikawa opened fire the American cruisers found themselves attacked from both sides. This added even more to the confusion on board all four of Riefkohl's cruisers. Gunnery officers' orders to open fire were countermanded by their senior officers, who were fearful that the fire might be directed towards friendly ships. Never had the lack of training in night fighting in the US Navy been more evident and costly.

Captain Riefkohl's own ship, the *Vincennes*, took the

worst of the damage, catching fire in a number of places. The worst was the unarmoured hangar in which the four planes' full fuel tanks exploded. There was no possibility of her surviving, and less than an hour later she turned over and sank with more than half her company going down with her.

The fate of the *Astoria*, her sister ship, was less fearful. She was hit time and again by six-inch and eight-inch shells, killing many of her company, but the repair parties did a wonderful job patching her up and she remained under control, although the gunnery officers could not get a 'bead' on any of Mikawa's ships. Searchlights only attracted a concentration of enemy fire, and were soon doused. The *Astoria* survived, but her fighting capacity had been rendered worthless by the end of this engagement.

The *Astoria*'s sister ship, *Quincy*, was less fortunate. At least the *Astoria* could be repaired and perhaps take part in some future operation. The men of the *Quincy* suffered a terrible fate. A shell exploded in her sick-bay, which was full of wounded and dying — then they were all dead. Nor did any of the engine-room crew survive, cut off as they were by fires and battered bulkheads.

The cruiser's second-in-command, Lieutenant-Commander J. D. Andrew, lacking all other forms of communication, climbed up to the bridge to seek orders from his captain. He wrote later,

> When I reached the bridge level, I found it a shambles of dead bodies with only three or four people still standing. On the bridge the only person standing was the signalman at the wheel, who was vainly endeavouring to check the ship's swing to starboard and to bring her to port. On ques-

tioning him I found out that the Captain, who was at that time lying near the wheel, had instructed him to beach the ship and he was trying to head the ship for Savo Island, distant some four miles on the port quarter. I stepped to the port side of the pilothouse, looking out to find the island and noted that the ship was heeling rapidly to port, sinking by the bow. At that instant the Captain straightened up and fell back, apparently dead, without having uttered any sound other than a moan.

The score in the early hours of the morning was five modern heavy cruisers against four hits in all on the Japanese force of Admiral Mikawa, none of which did any serious damage. It was the first sea battle of the Pacific war conducted by surface ships without the intervention of air power. And by any reckoning it was an overwhelming Japanese victory. But those hundreds of American and Australian sailors had not died entirely in vain.

As dawn approached, Admiral Mikawa, fearful for the safety of his ships, withdrew from the Slot and Savo Island itself in the knowledge that the enemy had carriers not far away. He remembered how those American Dauntlesses had screamed out of the sky to destroy the cream of the Japanese carrier force at Midway. Rabaul became his destination on leaving the scene of his success. He did not even pause to attack his main target, the troop-carriers unloading reinforcements for the American Marines on Guadalcanal.

By a piece of good fortune, which had been in short supply for the Allies that night, an American submarine caught sight of Mikawa's speeding cruiser force, sank to periscope depth, and launched a salvo of four torpedoes at the eight-inch-gunned heavy cruiser *Kako.* All of them hit, and the cruiser sank within minutes.

Never before in the history of combined operations had a land battle for an apparently insignificant target depended so heavily on sea-power. Both sides at Guadalcanal relied on reinforcements and supplies. The Japanese had the moral advantage of achieving an outright material victory at the Battle of Savo Island; the Americans had the singular advantage of possessing the now-completed airfield, Henderson, which acted as an unsinkable aircraft carrier.

Japan's High Command decided that drastic action was called for. Guadalcanal was a prime target and must not escape like Midway. Two 'Midways' would be a near-fatal blow to the morale and reputation of the IJN. Reinforcements on an appropriate scale must be sent to deal with the enemy. No lesser a figure than the C.-in-C., Admiral Isoroku Yamomoto, would command. He flew his flag in the giant *Yamato,* the near-indestructible 62,000-ton battleship. This battleship was augmented by the sixteen-inch-gunned *Mutsu,* the fast battleships *Hiei* and *Kirisima,* and the two fleet carriers *Shokaku* and *Zuikaku,* which had taken part in the Coral Sea battle. A strong contingent of heavy and light cruisers, all protected by many flotillas of destroyers, completed this task force. But at the heart of this giant armada were two old destroyers and an old cruiser packed with troops and their equipment and stores destined for the beaches of Guadalcanal.

Awaiting Yamamoto off the South Solomons was Admiral Frank Fletcher's reinforced fleet of the carriers *Saratoga,* *Wasp* and *Enterprise,* and to oppose the *Yamato* and the other

Japanese capital ships the new, powerful *North Carolina* with her nine sixteen-inch guns.

This was to be a critical battle, one side as determined as the other finally to settle possession of these islands.

It might have been a set-piece battle of the eighteenth century, so formal and rigid was Yamamoto's strict formation as he fell upon the Americans. Far in the vanguard was a scouting line of submarines, supplemented several miles back by the heavy cruiser *Atago* (ten eight-inch guns), flying the flag of Admiral Nobutake Kondo, with a seaplane carrier; then two battleships and three more heavy cruisers. These were followed by the veteran Admiral Nagumo with the carriers *Shokaku* and *Zuikaku* with a combined complement of 130 aircraft. After them were the transports, the whole *raison d'être* of the operation, and for this reason closely escorted by a powerful force of destroyers.

The *Yamato*, flying the flag of the C.-in-C., remained like a giant in the wings, ready to bring to bear her 18.1-inch guns should they be needed. But that was not all: in the hope of springing a surprise Yamamoto had, far to the rear, something with which to bait his enemy, a small group consisting of the light carrier *Ryujo*, with her thirty-seven planes, escorted by a cruiser and a pair of destroyers.

On the morning of 23 August 1942 Admiral Fletcher's force, less the carrier *Wasp*, which needed to top up her fuel, was at the eastern approaches to the Coral Sea; Admiral Yamamoto to the north of the Solomon Islands. Fletcher launched reconnaissance aircraft which soon reported the approach of the enemy's submarines, cruising fast on the surface. When he received reports of the next enemy group he launched dive-bombers and a group of his new Avenger torpedo bombers, which were twice as fast as the old Devastators. From his 'fixed' carrier, Henderson Field, a group of dive-bombers took off. Once they knew they had been spotted, the vanguard of Yamamoto's armada reversed course, not from fear of engaging the enemy, but in order to confuse him and choose their own time to strike. For this reason neither of Fletcher's carrier-borne strike aircraft, nor the land-based bombers, found their target — any target. The American aircraft returned to their carriers, or to Henderson.

There was a long lull during which both admirals puzzled and tried to sort out the position of the enemy. It was not easy: visibility was poor to bad, and tropical storms as well as the enemy lurked beyond the horizon.

It was not until the following morning that one of Fletcher's scouting aircraft told him that enemy carriers were heading towards him. This was confirmed when scouting Japanese seaplanes were observed on radar screens. Fletcher hastened north, launching fighters with orders to shoot them down. They were followed by a strong force of dive-bombers and torpedo bombers from the *Enterprise.* They in turn were followed by a second group, this time from the *Saratoga.* They had better luck than the first, finding quite soon a single enemy carrier. There was not a Zero in sight, so the Dauntlesses turned over and went down, each with a 1,000-pound bomb, while the Avengers glided down, timing their torpedo drop with great precision. If ever there was a sitting target, this carrier was it. None of the bombers was hit by the fire of the carrier, which was left a wreck on the bottom.

The Americans had risen to the bait. It was the little *Ryujo* they had battered to death. Earlier, the *Ryujo* had launched her bombers to deal with Henderson Field. This 'carrier' had had plenty of radar warning and had scrambled her Wildcats in time. They had a field day, shooting down twenty-one of the *Ryujo*'s bombers, and those that survived had no carrier to return to.

The position at 3.30 p.m. for Admiral Nagumo was that he had just heard of the sinking of his 'live bait' *Ryujo*, and now took advantage of his situation. Thanks to one of his scouting sea-planes, he knew the position of Fletcher's carriers while Fletcher's planes were still in the air, on the way back after their triumph. Fletcher knew only that his enemy was somewhere to the north. On this occasion, human eyes from a lumbering sea-plane had proved more efficient than newfangled radar. But Fletcher knew he was in dire danger and acted accordingly. Both his carriers battened down, ready for the worst — guns manned, look-outs posted, repair and medical parties on their toes.

Fortunately, Admiral Fletcher had learnt the lesson of denuding himself of all fighter protection. All his remaining Wildcats were scrambled and ordered to climb fast; the big *North Carolina*, with the heaviest anti-aircraft protection in the fleet, stationed herself between the two carriers. With her twenty five-inch, forty-six 1.1-inch and fifty machine-guns, her sixteen-inch-thick side armour and six-inch deck armour, she was not worried about herself: her job was to protect her charges with these massive batteries.

Nagumo's planes came in two waves; the dive-bombing Vals, at 18,000 feet and with camouflaged underwings, were scarcely visible. The Kate torpedo bombers, travelling much faster, came in to their attack at 3,000 feet, dropping lower as they steadied to launch their torpedoes.

A few Wildcats were high enough to jump the Vals and follow them down, mixing in with their escorting Zeros. Vals were easy meat if you could get at them, and one pilot claimed three, as well as two Zeros. But most of the Wildcat pilots concentrated on the Kates. It was like target practice. One after another they 'splashed', the ships' guns taking over when they could. Not one of the torpedo bombers got through this holocaust: it was like the Devastators at Midway.

Once again, it was a different story with the dive-bombers. They came down through the exploding five-inch shells, which spotted the sky about them like a bad case of black acne. Then the tracers set about them, streaking up almost vertically.

A battery officer spotted a single Val and ordered his 20 mm.s to designate the target with a stream of tracer bullets. That thin threat of golden tracers was the baton for a cacophony of 5-inch, 1.1-inch and 20 mm. gunfire, converging on the tiny silhouette of the Japanese plane leader [wrote Admiral Morison]. *Enterprise* put her rudder over in a series of violent turns, weaving and twisting to dodge the enemy bombs. She was in a tough spot.

In the carrier's gun sponsons, and on her island superstructure men watched with indrawn breath ... On and on came the flying Nip. Behind him in a long spiralling column were his fellows, tangling with a few angry American pilots who chanced the anti-aircraft fire in order to destroy one more assailant. The leading dive-bomber filled more and more of the gun-sight field. Val's distinctive landing gear 'pants' and the dark carcass of the bomb tucked under the fuselage were now plainly visible. The plane and bomb separate.

No carrier had fought for her life so hard as the 'Big E'. But when the punches came she could not evade them all. Two bombs, one after the other, struck the same spot, the after flight deck lift, exploding close to the ship's waterline, killing a number of men and allowing the sea to rush in. The third bomb might have been aimed at the Admiral himself. Fletcher was saved by the faulty detonation of this bomb — a rare occurrence. It fell alongside the island superstructure but did little harm.

The *Saratoga* did not become a target for the Japanese dive-bombers. Instead, sixteen Vals concentrated on the massive target of the battleship *North Carolina*. It was not a wise choice. The flak was the most dense and destructive that any of the Japanese pilots had seen. Many of them never saw any more flak anyway. The *North Carolina* shot nearly all of them down and suffered only a few near-misses, which troubled the big battleship not at all.

Back on the *Enterprise* the medical teams and the damage-control parties were working flat out. As evening approached, they got her in some sort of order, and by 6 p.m. Fletcher's flag-ship could steam fast enough to take on board her Wildcats, some of which had given up and landed on a less damaged carrier — Henderson Field.

It was from Henderson that a powerful force of Devastators took off in the evening to search for Admiral Nagumo's two big carriers. Instead, after 120 miles, the dive-bombers found Admiral Tanaka's surviving ships. His carrier had gone hours earlier, but he still had the precious transports and was preparing to land their contents on Guadalcanal. Admiral Tanaka was flying his flag in the cruiser *Jintsu*, which naturally became the centre of attention of the passing Devastators. They turned over and went down, meeting little flak, spotting their target with 1,000-pound bombs. They wrecked the cruiser, killed half her crew and forced Tanaka to shift his flag to a destroyer.

One of the Devastators also scored a direct hit on the 9,000-ton cruiser-transport, causing great loss of life. One of Tanaka's destroyers was dispatched to take off the wounded and came alongside. But luck was not on Tanaka's side that evening. A formation of land-based heavy bombers — B17s — like the Devastators, chanced on the scene. They ignored the wrecked *Jintsu* and selected the cruiser-transport. The B17s hit this but, from their great height, struck the destroyer hove to alongside too, destroying it like a swatted fly.

Admiral Tanaka now thankfully shrank back into the growing darkness.

Later, Admiral Tanaka succeeded in getting his surviving transports to the beaches of Guadalcanal by way of the Tokyo Express route, as it was dubbed by the Americans: the string of islands — the Slot — east of Guadalcanal.

Admiral Frank Fletcher could congratulate himself on a modest victory. But not for long. Where the carrier-borne aircraft had failed, the Japanese submarine force now came into its own.

Some days later, on 31 August, the submarine *I-26* spotted the great bulk of the *Saratoga* cruising along slowly. The submarine commander stalked this juicy target and positioned the *I-26* so that he could deliver a salvo of torpedoes at close range. They all struck, seriously damaging the carrier but not sinking her. The *Saratoga* limped away, heading for Pearl Harbor, where her repair took three months. The carrier *Wasp* was not so 'lucky'. The submarine *I-19* succeeded in hitting her with a salvo of three torpedoes. The American carrier sank a few hours later. Even the 30,000-ton *North Carolina* was severely damaged by submarine torpedoes, and they sank her accompanying destroyer.

When the news reached Admiral Nimitz, C.-in-C. Pacific at Pearl Harbor, he sent an admonishing signal to Fletcher:

> The torpedoing by submarines of four warships, with the loss of two of them, is a serious blow that might possibly have been avoided. Carrier Task Forces are not to remain in submarine waters for long periods. They should shift operating areas frequently and radically, must maintain higher speed and must in other ways improve their tactics against submarine attack.

Admiral Halsey was right in his criticism, but he may not have appreciated the great superiority of Japanese torpedoes — including the 'Long Lance' — over their American counterparts, which at this early stage of the war were highly inefficient, much slower and with a tendency to alter course at will and have a shorter range.

However, the Battle of the Eastern Solomons could be considered by Admiral Fletcher as a victory. He still held air superiority over the islands, and soon his superiority at sea was to be confirmed by the arrival of much-needed reinforcements: the new battleship *Washington*, a sister ship to the *North Carolina*; and, under the flag of Rear-Admiral Norman Scott, a task force of heavy and light cruisers and destroyer flotillas.

With the loss of Tanaka's cruiser-transport and the supplies and troops it contained, the Japanese knew that they must take drastic action to support and reinforce their troops on

Guadalcanal. They were suffering heavy losses at the hands of the American Marines holding Henderson Field. The Japanese attacking troops were getting some supplies from ships racing down the Slot, in darkness but not nearly enough to capture the pricelessly valuable airfield and drive the American Marines off the island altogether.

A new Japanese commander was appointed to organize a major relief operation. He was Rear-Admiral Aritome Goto, flying his flag in the heavy cruiser *Aoka*. He was given command of a veritable armada of packed transports and a strong force of cruisers. His plan was to approach the opening to the Slot in daylight from the east, and then as darkness fell rush flat out down it in the dark, with his cruisers escorting the transports. They would then simply run aground on the Japanese-held beach while Goto raced away south, but not before giving the airfield a thorough 'pasting' with eight-inch shells.

It was over-optimistic of the Japanese admiral to judge that his advance would not be spotted in daylight. American scouting planes found and reported Goto's great armada as it approached the Slot. When Admiral Scott learned the position and clear intentions of his Japanese adversary, he raced at twenty-nine knots, the maximum his cruisers could achieve, from his position just to the north of Guadalcanal. His radar took over from the reporting seaplanes and he made his dispositions accordingly, planning to 'cross the T' of his adversary.

Again the Americans were facing a night battle. Admiral Scott, as well as all the other commanders involved in the battle for Guadalcanal, now recognized the superiority of the enemy's ability to fight at night. The Americans had the inestimable advantage of radar; but they still lacked the experience of the IJN of fighting by night.

In the event, the action turned into a mêlée of misunder-stood signals and the ever-present fear that the Americans might be firing on their own ships. Action was opened when Admiral Goto was taken by surprise as he raced down the Slot, with his guns trained fore and aft. The first he knew of his dan-ger was when shells came out of the night and exploded about his ships. The *Helena* in the van opened fire at 11.30 p.m. The *Salt Lake City*, with her bigger, eight-inch guns, soon joined. Admiral Goto's flagship, *Aoka*, was badly damaged and set on fire in the first few minutes. Casualties were heavy and included the Admiral himself, who died on his bridge.

The next ship to receive a deluge of six-inch and eight-inch shells was the heavy cruiser *Furutaka*. Her fires lit up the sea all around her. Assisted by this light, the American gun crews began hitting the cruiser's accompanying destroyers, sinking one of them and setting two more on fire. Admiral Scott found the situation totally confusing. He was not even sure that they had not been firing on friendly ships and ordered a cease-fire. The captain of the cruiser USS *Boise* (9,700 tons, fifteen six-inch guns) was similarly bewildered, and ordered search-lights to be switched on to confirm a radar sighting. This brought forth the wrath of revenge: six-inch and eight-inch shells tore into her, setting her on fire and killing more than a hundred of her crew. Admiral Scott, whatever his faults, did not lack courage and ordered his flagship to counter-fire and intervene between the Japanese cruisers and the *Boise*.

Admiral Scott did better than that. Perhaps his eyes had accustomed themselves to the dark. Whatever the reason, he pursued the enemy cruisers like a terrier, chasing them whence they had come — up the Slot and so back to their base.

Admiral Scott could claim a famous victory, having lost

just one destroyer and suffered damage to the cruiser *Boise*.

But in reality it was no victory at all. He may have sent the enemy packing and killed their admiral, but he had utterly failed in his first priority. This was to prevent reinforcements and heavy artillery and stores reaching Guadalcanal.

The Marine Corps was fighting for its life on this steamy, malaria-ridden island. But that was by no means the end of their troubles. The Japanese dispatched two battleships to bombard Henderson Field with fourteen-inch shells. Then, on the night of 14/15 October, two days after the Battle of Cape Esperance (as Admiral Scott's engagement came to be known), Henderson was blasted by two bombing raids followed by bombardment from the sea by heavy cruisers firing nearly 1,000 eight-inch shells. By the morning of 15 October; Henderson was non-operational, with the loss of all its parked planes and the blowing up of all its avgas (fuel). This was followed by the unopposed landing of a further 4,500 Japanese infantry.

A new Japanese offensive reached within a mere 100 yards of the perimeter of the wrecked airfield. But the Marines fought back in the true tradition of the Corps.

Back at Pearl Harbor, Admiral Nimitz, C.-in-C. Pacific, reckoned that this vital operation needed to be reinforced, and the Commander South-West Pacific replaced. The reinforcements were hard to find. The new C.-in-C. was less difficult. The most admired and popular American carrier commander was Admiral 'Bull' Halsey. He personified the air arm in the US Navy. He would certainly have led the carriers at Midway, but to his fury had been laid up with an illness that prohibited him from taking up his post. But he had recovered from that, and now he had a second chance to lead his beloved carriers at the head of the fleet in the south-west Pacific.

Halsey's force included the new battleship *Washington*, her sister ship *South Dakota*, five cruisers, two of them heavy cruisers, and eight destroyers, all under the command of Admiral Daniel Callaghan. But there were only two carriers, the *Hornet* and *Enterprise*.

On the Japanese side, Admiral Kondo could muster four battleships, four carriers, fourteen cruisers and a mass of some thirty destroyers.

Kondo's intention was to land an overwhelming force of fighters and bombers on the now-repaired Henderson airfield, once it had been captured by the Japanese ground forces. But still the American Marines fought on, killing thousands of Japanese troops imbued with a near-suicidal spirit.

At sea Bull Halsey was not in the least discouraged by the odds against him. On 24 October the two carriers rendezvoused and prepared to seek out and then attack Admiral Kondo's force, giving special attention to his carriers. Two mornings later the Japanese force was located far to the north-west, and eight Dauntlesses were launched, each with a 500-pound bomb. They were followed by a message from Bull Halsey: 'Attack! Repeat, Attack!'

It was still early dawn when the pilots located a single carrier, the *Zuiho*, her deck lined with Zeros. Before their pilots could think about taking off, two 500-pounders fell on the flight deck near the stern. The Zeros would never take off now. A fire broke out and rapidly ran the length of the carrier. Another Dauntless attack, this time with 1,000-pounders, located and went down on the *Shokaku*, preventing her from taking any further part in the action.

But, unlike the *Zuiho*, the *Shokaku* had launched her planes in time, and they, with many others, were racing towards the two American carriers.

The sky was full of Wildcats when the Vals and Kates arrived. The Japanese pilots could locate only the *Hornet*, the *Enterprise* being concealed by a typical South Pacific rain squall. The Vals came down from their usual height of 18,000 feet. Of the first wave, only three survived the intense flak and the half-inch fire of the Wildcats. One bomb exploded on the carrier's bridge and two on the flight deck, penetrating deep down before exploding. These two ripped the heart out of the ship, while two Kates added to the *Hornet*'s misery with their torpedoes.

In the afternoon of this bloody day of conflict, the *Enterprise*, no longer concealed, was attacked. This time there was no rain squall to conceal her. The 'Big E' took two bombs but remained operational. The big *South Dakota* was bombed, too. She made a massive target, but she scarcely noticed a 500-pounder that struck one of her turrets.

A lurking Japanese submarine might have made more of an impact (literally), but all she got was a destroyer close to the battleship.

As dusk fell, Bull Halsey could not look back on the day with much satisfaction. However, the losses in the air for the Japanese led to the ironical situation that Nagumo's surviving carriers could not even fill their hangars.

October turned to November 1942, and while the land fighting on Guadalcanal continued as fiercely as ever, there was no further sign of Japanese forces attempting to wrest control of the sea from the Americans. Admiral Halsey therefore retired to his base at Nouméa, an island in New Caledonia. He left behind off Guadalcanal Admiral Daniel Callaghan with a force of cruisers and destroyers but no carrier. The *Enterprise* had been patched up and was operational again, but was still at Nouméa with Halsey's sixteen-inch-gun battleships, *Washington* and *South Dakota*.

Then, in the middle of November, Admiral Callaghan received word of a gathering Japanese naval force. This force was under the command of Vice-Admiral Hiroaki Abe, who flew his flag in the battleship *Hiei* (eight fourteen-inch guns), an old but comprehensively modernized ship, British-built before the First World War. He also had his flagship's sister ship *Kirishima*, a cruiser and a strong force of destroyers.

Admiral Abe advanced to meet his puny foe on the night of 12/13 November. Admiral Callaghan, his confidence inspired by the supposed success of Admiral Scott (this time flying his flag in the cruiser *Atlanta*) at the Savo Sea engagement, advanced with his radar-equipped ships. But it was the same story as in that earlier night action.

With their powerful night glasses and with years of training in fighting by night, Admiral Abe's captains knew precisely where the enemy was, while Callaghan's commanders had no idea of the whereabouts of the enemy, in spite of their radar. As before, the Americans fired indiscriminately on friend and foe alike. No one will ever know the origin of the shell that exploded on the *Atlanta*'s bridge, killing Admiral Scott and all his staff. Admiral Callaghan shared the same fate. Fourteen-inch shells from the *Hiei* or *Kirishima* struck his flagship, *San Francisco*, wrecking the heavy cruiser and killing the Admiral and most of the ship's crew. On the other hand, as some sort of compensation for this catastrophe, one of the American heavy cruisers caught sight of the great bulk of the *Hiei* looming out of the dark. Fire was opened and eight-inch shells tore into the upper works of the old battleship, causing her to limp away to safety north of Savo Island.

Help was at hand for the American survivors of this dreadful night of slaughter. Bull Halsey was racing from his base at Nouméa with two battleships, the repaired carrier *Enterprise* and cruisers and destroyers. Ahead of them flew the *Enterprise*'s fighters and bombers, lusting for retribution. This they satisfied by bombing and destroying Admiral Tanaka's latest and largest convoy of transports before they could land their guns, troops and supplies.

Halsey's battleships and cruisers, with their accompanying destroyers, arrived as daylight was fading, and his ships now faced the prospect of a night of action. The *Washington* and *South Dakota* had the latest radar, but this did not prevent the *South Dakota* becoming the target of Japanese battleship and heavy cruiser fire. She could not see to return the fire, her radar being temporarily inoperable. But her sister ship, *Washington*, whose radar remained in good order, came to her rescue, firing sixteen-inch shells with deadly accuracy at a range of five miles at the battleship *Kirisima*, knocking her to pieces, making the *Kirisima* the first battleship to be sunk in this new electronic era of fighting at sea.

The fate of the second Japanese battleship, *Hiei*, was as decisive but more orthodox. She became the target of attack by American dive-bombers and torpedo bombers. These decided her fate. Her crew gave up the fight, opened her sea-cocks, and down she went.

The end was near now. Without reinforcements or supplies, the Japanese soldiers on Guadalcanal began to lose heart. The American Marines took full advantage of this, killing hundreds of the enemy and advancing far beyond the perime-

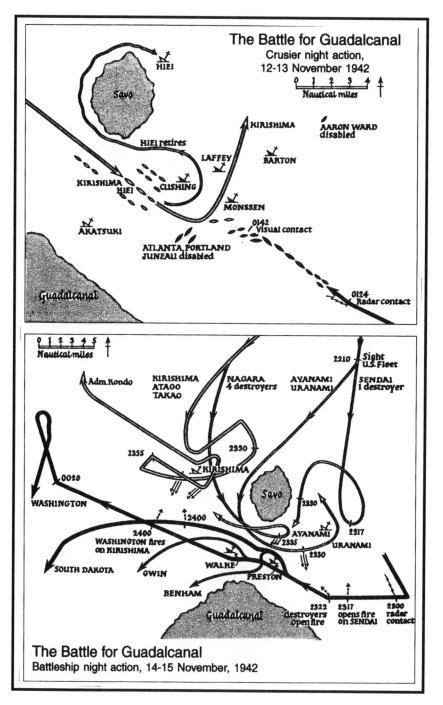

The Battle for Guadalcanal
Crusier night action,
12-13 November 1942

The Battle for Guadalcanal
Battleship night action, 14-15 November, 1942

ter of Henderson Field. The fighting went on, but with the Americans controlling the air and the sea around this stinking, hot, damp but strategically vital island, by January 1943 the outcome was inevitable.

On 9 February the commander of the ground forces on Guadalcanal sent a rousing message to Bull Halsey: 'Total and complete defeat of Japanese forces on Guadalcanal effected at 16.45 today.'

12

···

THE BATTLE OF NORTH CAPE,
26 DECEMBER 1943

As soon as Hitler attacked Russia, Churchill had ensured that
Britain would supply the Soviet forces with tanks, aircraft and
other war matériel by convoy through the Barents Sea to north
Russian ports. This was only a year after the British army was
desperately attempting to re-equip, having lost most of its hard-
ware in its evacuation from Dunkirk in the summer of 1940.

These Arctic convoys had to run the gauntlet of German submarines in the Barents Sea and enemy aircraft based in northern
Norway. They were restricted in their passage by the presence of
ice to the north and, in high summer, by 24-hour daylight.

The presence of German capital ships in the Norwegian
fjords was a constant additional threat to these convoys and while
Hitler kept his heavy units like "chained dogs," their very presence
tied down numerous units of the British Home Fleet. The mere
threat of the departure of the Tirpitz from her anchorage in north
Norwegian waters in June 1942 had caused the scattering and subsequent piecemeal destruction, by U-boats and aircraft, of convoy
PQ17, the worst British convoy disaster of the war.

An attack on the Russia-bound convoy JW51B by the
Panzerschiff Lützow and heavy cruiser Admiral Hipper in
December 1942, was brilliantly warded off by the destroyers of the

convoy escort under Captain Sherbrooke. A British cruiser rein-forcement under Admiral Burnett then arrived with spectacular timing to secure the safe passage of the convoy. Greater resolution by the German admiral, Kummetz, might have accomplished the utter destruction of this convoy, but what was called the Battle of the Barents Sea was a British victory, carried out against consider-able odds.

On the Eastern Front the Red Army began to throw the invad-ing German armies back, increasing the German need to control the Arctic convoy route. By the end of 1943 the formidable Scharnhorst lay in the fjords of the polar coast, ready to pounce. At Christmas she was ordered to sea to intercept convoy JW55B, consisting of nineteen merchantmen.

In addition to their close escort of anti-aircraft and anti-submarine destroyers, frigates and corvettes, Anglo-American convoys bound to Russia were covered by a British cruiser squadron in the vicinity. It also became common practice for the Commander-in-Chief of the Home Fleet to sail from Scapa Flow in the Orkney Islands to provide a heavy battle-squadron within call. It was also usual for a homeward-bound convoy of empty merchant ships, in this case RA55A, to return at the same time, running closer to the enemy-held coast to act as a decoy, for the destruction of the German capital ships was the aim of the Royal Navy. This was the scenario for the battle off the North Cape of Norway.

....

THE BIG SHIPS OF Hitler's navy, built for commerce raiding, provoked anxiety out of all proportion to the damage they caused. Their combined total of tonnage sunk throughout the war was about equal to a week's total by Admiral Karl Dönitz's U-boat fleet. The *Graf Spee* certainly sank a number of mer-chantmen in the Indian and South Atlantic Oceans. But the mighty *Bismarck*, the most feared of all, did not have a single merchantman to her credit when she was sunk in the North Atlantic.

The surface ships best known to the British public and the Royal Navy alike were the battle-cruisers *Scharnhorst* and *Gneisenau*, named after the raiders of the First World War sunk by Admiral Doveton Sturdee's squadron in 1914. This new generation of battle-cruisers were nicknamed 'Salmon and Gluckstein' after the well-known catering firm. It was typical of the British public's style to turn a menace into a joke, like calling the flying bombs of 1944 'Doodlebugs'.

Their first major success was in the Norwegian campaign of 1940 when they sank the carrier *Glorious*. Later, in January 1941, they underwent the same experience as the *Bismarck* — of being spotted by a British agent in southern Sweden — emerging from the Baltic like two gangsters, clearly hell-bent on attacking Allied Atlantic shipping. After sheering away from battleship-escorted convoys and refuelling at sea off Newfoundland, Captain Jürgens (who was to die later in the *Bismarck*) found an unprotected convoy and sank sixteen of its ships. The two battle-cruisers then headed for the French port of Brest.

'Salmon and Gluckstein' remained there for a year, the target of countless bombing raids. Hitler was determined to bring them home, refit them and dispatch them to Norway as a continuing threat to Atlantic convoys, tying down the Royal Navy's Home Fleet of battleships at Scapa Flow. When the dangers of this move were pointed out by Admiral Raeder, the Navy's C.-in-C., Hitler shocked those assembled by ordering them to shape course up the English Channel.

This daring course of action was worked out in the closest detail. Early in February 1942, they were ready to go. The two big ships put to sea late in the evening, and were blessed by almost incredible good fortune, which they needed. The weather was on their side, and the RAF made almost incredible errors. One radar station was out of order, another identified the blips as an air/sea rescue operation; and it was not until two Spitfire pilots spotted them and then were pounced upon by a great number of German fighters that word reached the Admiralty that the ships were out, *and* by now close to the Straits of Dover.

Panic countermeasures were now called for: six Swordfish, commanded by Lieutenant-Commander Esmonde, who had led the first torpedo attack on the *Bismarck*, led them. They were all shot down by impenetrable flak or escorting fighters. (Esmonde was awarded a posthumous VC.) More modern torpedo bombers had no better success, and destroyers from Dover were all beaten back. It seemed then that the battle-cruisers were going to get through, but it was not to be so. As a precautionary measure, a minefield had been laid off the Dutch coast. It caught both ships. Strongly as they had been built, the *Scharnhorst* was holed and limped into Wilhelmshaven with 1,000 tons of water on board. The *Gneisenau* was so badly damaged that she took no further part in the war. So Hitler's instinct, of which everyone had heard so much, was not infallible, though Germany's propaganda machine worked overtime.

The *Tirpitz*, sister ship to the *Bismarck*, completed her trials in the Baltic by the end of 1941 and was dispatched to a north Norwegian fjord to act as a threat to Atlantic and, later, Russian convoys. She was joined later by the repaired *Scharnhorst* and the heavy cruiser *Lützow*, constituting a very formidable squadron.

The *Tirpitz* became the chief target for Allied attacks, mostly from the air, but also by midget submarines with delayed-action charges. These charges did not sink the great ship, but they put all her engines out of action and damaged her rudder, causing great quantities of water to enter the ship. Many of the gallant British sailors taking part in these raids were drowned or taken prisoner, and two officers received VCs. Four months later, when repairs to the ship had been completed, a dawn attack by modern carrier dive-bombers escorted by fighters put the *Tirpitz* out of action again, and killed 300 of her crew.

The *Tirpitz* was finally sent to the bottom in an elaborate exercise carried out by Lancaster bombers, with spare fuel tanks and carrying 12,000-pound 'blockbuster' bombs. They made three hits from a great height, causing her to capsize and sink. It was 12 November 1944. The *Scharnhorst* had not been even a secondary target for this attack. By the end of 1943, the Anglo-American convoys to Russia, routing around the northern tip of Norway to Murmansk, were becoming of increasing importance. The Russian armies were going over to the offensive, and the planes and tanks and other war material were sorely needed.

These convoys were fiercely attacked from under the sea by U-boats, and from the air by bombers and torpedo-carrying aircraft.

Admiral Sir Bruce Fraser had been C.-in-C. Home Fleet since May 1943. Among his responsibilities was the safe passage of these Russian convoys. In November and December of that same year, two successive convoys had reached Murmansk

without loss. Fraser, in close touch with the Admiralty, anticipated that the Germans, recognizing that these successes
amounted to a victory, would be determined to attack with
everything they had. The next convoy was due around
Christmas. Thanks to the superb code-breaking work carried
out at Bletchley, intercepted German signals confirmed this
conviction. Fraser was informed that the convoy had been
sighted by a German reconnaissance plane, and later that a U-
boat had been ordered into the attack. Most important of all
these intercepted signals was one ordering the *Scharnhorst* to
prepare to go to sea.

Fraser had wanted to give the British public a Christmas
present. Nothing would cheer them up more than the sinking
of the *Scharnhorst*. But it was not until 26 December that
Fraser was told that the *Scharnhorst* had 'probably' sailed
from her fjord at 6 p.m. the previous evening. He made his
dispositions accordingly. He had at his disposal the eight-
inch-gunned cruiser *Norfolk* (of the *Bismarck* pursuit) with the
Sheffield and *Belfast*, both with six-inch guns. These cruisers
were under the command of Vice-Admiral Robert Burnett.
Fraser flew his flag in the *Duke of York*, a new fourteen-inch-
gunned battleship, sister ship to the *Prince of Wales* and *King
George V*. He also had with him the *Jamaica*, a modern six-
inch-gunned cruiser which was capable of thirty-three knots,
and four destroyers, one of them manned, appropriately, by a
Norwegian crew.

The *Scharnhorst* and her accompanying destroyers were
commanded by Rear-Admiral Bey, who was driving north at
the best speed that the tumultuous seas and a full gale allowed.
He anticipated 'good hunting' on this icy cold Boxing Day. Then,
at 9.20 a.m., still pitch dark in this northern latitude, shells sud-

denly started falling about the *Scharnhorst*, and shortly after this the German ship found herself brightly illuminated by bursting star shells. Admiral Bey countered when his radar picked up the British cruisers. The *Norfolk*, *Suffolk* and *Sheffield* immediately became the target of the German eleven-inch guns. But this time British gunnery was superior to the German, and hits on the German battle-cruiser started a fire and knocked out the fore radar. When Bey reported this engagement to Admiral Dönitz back in Germany, he received the exhortation 'Strike a blow on behalf of the troops fighting on the eastern front'. Instead Bey now withdrew at full speed to the north under cover of a smoke-screen.

Admiral Burnett's duty was to shadow and report on the enemy, but he had been so heartened by his cruiser's early success that he set a course that could intercept the *Scharnhorst* before she could close on the convoy.

Soon after noon in the midday twilight, the *Scharnhorst* again showed up on the cruisers' radar, and they opened fire at extreme range and fired star shells to illuminate the dim target. This renewal of the engagement was not so one-sided. Like an angry, cornered beast, the *Scharnhorst* opened fire with three-gun salvoes, and at once straddled the eight-inch-gunned *Norfolk*, and, a few salvoes later, scored a hit at the base of her third turret, putting it out of action and killing a number of men. A second hit amidships did more damage and knocked out her radar.

When the *Sheffield*, too, was straddled, Admiral Burnett reduced the speed of his squadron, opening out the range.

Admiral Fraser at this time was steaming through the mighty Arctic seas, and made radar contact at 24,000 yards. It was already dark. The *Duke of York* as well as the cruisers fired numerous star shells. A survivor of the *Scharnhorst* later wrote:

> The flares hung over the ship for minutes on end with stark, pitiless clarity, the cruel brilliance sharpened by the fiery flashes of [our] own salvoes. The whole ship from bridges to foretop, masts and funnels were bathed in a ghastly pink to blood-red light. Smoke and cordite fumes clung to the ship, driven now by an almost following wind, and at times completely obscured visibility in the direction of the enemy.

The German battle-cruiser's high speed had many times saved her, and it appeared might do so again as she headed due east, pursued by the *Duke of York*, which was steaming at over twenty-nine knots through the heavy seas, while her escorting destroyers — all of them capable of thirty-six knots under ordinary conditions, were scarcely able to keep up. Shortly before 5 p.m. the *Scharnhorst* had reason to believe she was outpacing the enemy. All thoughts of the convoy had been driven out of consideration: she just wanted to escape the fourteen-inch gunfire of the British battleship. To cheer on his men the German captain had a message sent out: 'The heavy enemy units are turning away. The *Scharnhorst* has again proved herself.'

One of the turret gunners was heard to remark, 'Phew! — this time we only just made it!'

Admiral Fraser now recognized that the German ship might well escape unless she could be slowed down. Lacking a carrier with its torpedo planes (unlike in the *Bismarck* pursuit), his only possible answer lay in his destroyers.

Desperate measures were called for, and he now signalled them to go in. No one will ever know if they could have caught up with the *Scharnhorst* and carried out their duty if the *Duke of York*, which had continued firing her six forward guns at extreme range, had not had a stroke of luck. At 6.20 she made a single hit which by a million-to-one chance struck a boiler room and immediately reduced the speed of the ship by around ten knots. This signalled her end. The destroyers went in and pumped torpedo after torpedo into her. Strongly built as she was, she could not stand these blows and was driven to a standstill, although almost at the end she managed to get off intermittent, defiant salvoes.

Like the *Bismarck*, the *Scharnhorst* never lowered her flag, and like that great ship, she was pummelled to death, salvo after salvo of fourteen-inch and six-inch fire tearing her apart and setting off fires from stem to stern. She fired a last eleven-inch shell at 7.30 p.m.

Admiral Fraser in his dispatch on the battle wrote:

All that could be seen of the *Scharnhorst* was a dull glow through a dense cloud of smoke which the star shell and searchlights of these surrounding ships could not penetrate. No ship [he concluded] saw the enemy sink, but it seems fairly certain that she sank after a heavy underwater explosion which was heard in several ships at about 7.45 p.m.

Just thirty-six of the *Scharnhorst's* company of nearly 2,000 were dragged alive from the icy sea.

The Battle of North Cape was the last big-ship action in European waters in the Second World War. All the German pocket battleships had been either sunk or disabled, like the *Gneisenau*, and the threat of the big gun to Atlantic and Arctic convoys had been removed. A dangerous chapter in the war at sea was triumphantly over.

13

....

THE BATTLE FOR THE
PHILIPPINES,
JUNE–OCTOBER 1944

*Having provoked the world's greatest industrial power into war,
the Japanese found that once the United States of America had
cranked her potential might into full production, their enemy was
overwhelming. The U.S. offensive, begun at Guadalcanal, was to
consist of the steady, relentless island-by-island erosion of
Japanese positions throughout the Pacific. It was to be a war of
desperate attrition, and the United States was to find the Japanese
difficult to dislodge and their task a protracted and bloody one.
But for the Japanese, there was an inevitability to their gradual
defeat. They had staked much on their gamble in 1941 and, in
the end lost. The only possible recourse to avert the terrible
humiliation of defeat was a masterstroke that would destroy U.S.
sea power.*

*The Japanese Combined Fleet under Vice-Admiral Ozawa
had consisted of nine aircraft carriers supported by land-based
aircraft from Guam. Their objective had been the frustration of
the invasion of the Marianas by attacking Vice-Admiral
Spruance's Fifth Fleet, protecting the American invasion forces,
and Vice-Admiral Mitscher's Task Group 58 with its fifteen carriers and almost 1,000 aircraft. By the time Ozawa committed his*

fleet he had lost the advantage of his aircraft from Guam. The resulting eight-hour battle in the Philippine Sea of June 19, 1944, resulted in the destruction of over 300 Japanese aircraft, while two U. S. submarines, skilfully working within the Japanese fleet formations, sank the carriers Shokaku *and* Taiho. *The following day a third carrier, the* Hiyo, *was also sunk. The damage inflicted on the Imperial Japanese Navy was irreversible.*

By the fall of the year the critical moment had come when (surrender of the Japanese homeland being unthinkable), the holding of the Philippines was decided upon. If by a powerful counter-attack the Imperial Japanese Navy could inflict so terrible a reverse on the United States that they undermined American confidence, Tokyo could at least seek a peace which would save the Emperor's face. Accordingly, the Imperial Japanese Navy set out to challenge the advance of the Americans in the waters around the Philippines.

The Japanese attack was to be focused on the beachhead seized by the United States at Leyte Gulf on the October 20. Ozawa was to approach from the north and draw off Admiral Halsey's Third Fleet. Then, attacking through the archipelago from the west by way of the San Bernardino Straight, would come a heavy battle-group under Vice-Admiral Kurita. This would be joined by Vice-Admirals Shima and Nishimura with a second battle-group approaching from the southwest through the Sulu Sea. These forces would fall upon Kincaid's Seventh Fleet and the invasion craft in Leyte Gulf. It was a well-conceived battle plan, but it was also Japan's last gamble.

• • • • • • • • • • • • • • • • • • • •

AS A BONUS FOR the Americans after securing Guadalcanal and the adjacent islands, they shot down and killed Admiral Yamamoto a couple of months later. These were the circumstances: reading the Japanese code as if it were today's newspaper, the Americans learned that the great admiral, the instigator of Pearl Harbor, worshipped by the IJN and the Japanese people, was engaged on a morale-lifting tour of the Upper Solomon Islands. When he had completed his mission, he took off from Rabaul in a Betty to return to his headquarters. His chief-of-staff, Vice-Admiral Ugaki, accompanied him, but in a second plane.

All this was known to the Americans, even to the hour of take-off. Henderson Field had recently received a number of new P.38 Lightning fighters with a speed approaching 400 mph and an armament of cannon and machine-guns in the nose. They looked futuristic with their twin-boom, twin-engine configuration. Sixteen of them took off and headed for Yamamoto's headquarters on the island of Buin. The timing was precise. The low-flying P.38s caught the two Bettys on their final approach, jumping them at a few hundred feet, brushing aside their escort of Zeros and tearing the aircraft to pieces. Admiral Yamamoto died at once; his chief-of-staff survived, though gravely wounded.

The American combined chiefs-of-staff had long before agreed the policy for defeating the Japanese at sea and recovering all the many islands they had occupied in 1941/2. It was something entirely new in naval strategy. In essence, it was to push back piecemeal the Japanese occupying forces island by island to their homeland. If a target proved obstinate and might delay them, they would simply pass it by. This was known colloquially as 'island hopping'. In order to feed the voracious appetite of this policy, in which air power would be the leading factor, thousands of planes and dozens of carriers would be required. American industry and the provision of raw materials were quite capable of meeting these needs. The conversion of industry from peacetime conditions to wartime conditions, and the speed with which it was accomplished, was one of the wonders of the twentieth century. It was matched only by the Soviet Union's achievement under similar conditions from 1941 to 1945.

The first move was a thrust from the Solomon Islands and Guadalcanal north to the Gilbert and Marshall Islands. The island of Tarawa proved the hardest nut to crack. It was honeycombed with strong points defended by men prepared to commit suicide rather than allow this island with its priceless air base to fall into enemy hands. There were mines on the coral reef, then barbed-wire entanglements, also mined, along the shores, and machine-gun emplacements to mow down anyone who survived. The defences were like Germany's 'Western Wall' along France's northern coast in 1944. But thanks to the complete control of the air by the Americans, Tarawa was captured by the courageous Marines, although at the cost of more than 3,000 casualties.

Kwajalein in the Marshalls was the key island in this group. The Americans not only controlled the air but the sea, too. Sixteen-inch-gunned battleships were used for bombarding Kwajalein and other islands in the group.

So far, Admiral Nimitz's policy was working well. Thanks to 'overkill' in the air and on the sea (and on land, too, where the infantry usually outnumbered the enemy five or ten to one), American casualties were acceptably low.

The Marianas, by the Japanese 'back door', were a different matter. The Japanese High Command was now thoroughly alarmed and gathered together the remnants of its Navy into one giant task force. The supreme commander was Admiral Soemu Toyoda, flying his flag in the *Oyodo* in Hiroshima Bay. In command of the land-based planes from the islands still in Japanese hands was Vice-Admiral Kakuji Kakuda. He had approximately 1,000 planes under his command.

The Japanese had managed to gather together no fewer than nine carriers, including the new big fleet carrier, *Taiho* (flag), and eight more varying from fleet carriers to much smaller 10,000-ton escort carriers. In all they could launch nearly 500 planes from new Judy dive-bombers capable of twice the speed of the Vals to the standard Zeros, which had proved so effective in earlier operations. Admiral Takeo Kurita was in command of this powerful force, and also of a formidable squadron of battleships, nine in all, including the mighty *Yamato* and the *Musashi*. And finally, Toyoda commanded heavy and light cruisers — seventy-three ships in all.

There was one significant omission among the higher command of the IJN, and that was Admiral Nagumo. He had been effectively demoted owing to his failure at Midway and in the Solomon Islands battles.

Admiral Nimitz had renamed the Central Pacific Force the Fifth Fleet. This was under the command of Admiral Clifton Spruance, flying his flag in the heavy cruiser I*ndianapolis*. Task Force 58 was commanded by Vice-Admiral Mark Mitscher, flying his flag in the carrier *Lexington*. His task force was split into five groups with a combined total of fifteen carriers, confirming their speed of construction in American shipyards. It seemed only the day before that the Pacific Fleet possessed just one damaged carrier.

Spruance's battleship group, under the command of Vice-Admiral W. A. Lee, boasted nine modern sixteen-inch-gunned battleships, supported by five eight-inch-gunned heavy cruisers.

The Battle for the Philippines was the greatest naval battle in history, judged in terms of the number of ships taking part, the number of ships sunk, and the importance of its outcome. It included every form of naval warfare of the twentieth century: gunnery duels between battleships; destroyer battles at night and by day, as ferocious and sustained as any at the Battle of Jutland; submarines that stalked the depths, sinking many ships; and, finally, carrier warfare on a scale never dreamed of even by the most ardent enthusiasts of air warfare at sea.

That air power was going to dominate this crucial battle soon became evident. In a preliminary, precautionary operation, Admiral Mitscher launched hundreds of fighters from the flight decks of his carriers. The fighters were not Wildcats. The Grumman plants back home had produced a new but closely related fighter, the Hellcat, which was to become the standard ship-borne carrier fighter for the USN. The Hellcat was bigger and approximately 50 mph faster, with six rather than five half-inch guns. (Later versions were to carry twenty-millimetre cannon.)

The purpose of this preliminary operation was to destroy Japanese air power protecting the Philippines. Vice-Admiral Kakuda's fighters rose to the challenge, launching land-based Zeros from their airfields on Saipan, Guam and Tinian in the Marianas.

The fighting that followed was the first major test of the naval Hellcats, and the dog-fighting was on an heroic scale — larger than any previous fighter-to-fighter battle in the Pacific, and almost matching the dog-fighting in the Battle of Britain four years earlier.

The Americans had not only the advantage of an improved fighter, they also had better-trained pilots. The Japanese, in their efforts to match the number of American fighter pilots, skimped student pilots' training, which was further acerbated by the shortage of fuel and training planes. The Americans, however, lavished vast resources on the training of their pilots, with no shortage of fuel, planes and airfields. All this could be seen in the Zero—Hellcat dog-fights which seemed to stretch from horizon to horizon. Planes plummeted from the heavens, sometimes in flames. Parachutes spotted the sky white. As these pilots splashed into the sea, the US Navy pilots had a ten-to-one advantage over the Japanese of being picked up and brought home. The Americans had an air/sea rescue service second to none. The pilots were equipped not only with inflatable lifejackets ('Mae Wests') but a dinghy that automatically inflated when it struck the sea. The dinghy was equipped with emergency food, water-purification pills and flares.

The Japanese had none of these facilities. Life was cheap, and it would be the ultimate humiliation to be taken prisoner. The fact that the Zero had no self-sealing tanks of armour plate behind the pilot's head was another illustration of this philosophy.

When the dog-fighting at last ceased owing to falling fuel needles on both sides, thirty-six Zeros were in the water while just eleven Hellcats had been lost out of the 208 than had taken off.

The following day, 11 June, Mitscher dispatched bombers to shatter the airfields from which the Zeros had taken off. Then Admiral Spruance sent seven carriers north to deal with the more distant airfields on Iwo Jima and Chichi Jima.

Some of the Japanese ships had radar now, thanks to their

German allies, but again it was their catapulted seaplanes which delivered the most accurate intelligence. The Americans, on the other hand, had made the decision to discard all their catapult aircraft owing to their fire risk. Apart from his radar, with its limited range, Admiral Spruance had to rely on his submarines. They were not very helpful in this capacity, but two of them, *Albacore* and *Cavalla*, were well placed. The former not only sighted Ozawa's enormous advancing fleet but found herself within range of a large carrier. She was not zig zagging because she was launching her planes and therefore made a steady target.

The days of eccentric and unreliable American torpedoes were now over. At least one of *Albacore*'s torpedoes struck the carrier, which happened to be Admiral Ozawa's flagship. She did not sink at once, but later a fire broke out on the hangar deck, spread to the fuel tanks — and then, fatally, to the bomb stores — and the *Taiho* exploded. Fortunately, however, Ozawa had already shifted his flag to a heavy cruiser.

The other American submarine in the path of the Japanese fleet, the *Cavalla*, got her sights on another big carrier. She was the *Shokaku*, veteran of the Coral Sea battle and other engagements. The American captain fired a spread of three torpedoes. All of them hit the carrier amidships. She suffered the same fate as the *Taiho* only more quickly. Thus Admiral Ozawa had lost two of his biggest and best carriers before he had even sighted Admiral Spruance's main fleet.

But Ozawa still had plenty of carriers, and plenty of planes. Moreover, he had quantities of a new dive-bomber — the Judy, as it was code-named by the Americans. This Yokosuke D4Y1 made the Val look like something out of the 1920s. It had a speed of 340 mph, almost as fast as a Hellcat, and a range of 1,100 miles. It carried a 550-pound bomb under the belly and two smaller bombs under the wings. It was a two-seater, with one gun for the observer and two more for the pilot.

Having located the position of the Americans, Ozawa launched a strike of a mixed force of Judys and Zeros, some of the Zeros carrying a single bomb under the belly; these fighter-bombers filled the role of a pure fighter after dropping their bombs.

A second wave of over 100 fighters and bombers was ordered off soon after the first. When all these enemy aircraft began to smudge the radar screens, Admiral Spruance launched 300 Hellcats, which could climb to 20,000 feet in seven minutes. They faced the hordes of enemy fighters and bombers like battalions of infantry with bayonets fixed. The Judys and Zeros that did get through then faced a wall of flak, worse than any of them had seen before. The few Japanese pilots who succeeded in penetrating these two walls of defence — and there was no doubting their courage and tenacity if not their skill — made just one hit, and that was not on a carrier but on the modern battleship *South Dakota*, and it scarcely dented her thick steel armour plate.

A handful of Hellcats were shot down; the others returned to their carriers to refuel and rearm, for the Japanese had not yet exhausted their supply of planes, nor the air crews their enthusiasm.

It was the same story again as the sky was dotted with Zeros, Bettys and Judys. But not one of them got through, and by the evening the Americans claimed 275 aircraft destroyed in the biggest air battle of the Pacific war: thereafter it was referred to as 'the Great Marianas Turkey Shoot'.

Admiral Ozawa complained at the lack of intervention of Vice-Admiral Kakuda's land-based fighters and bombers: he had not been informed that they had been virtually wiped out several days before. Admiral Ozawa despaired when he did receive this information. As dusk fell, the Japanese Admiral took his force north-west and out of range of the American fleet.

Meanwhile, Admiral Spruance received better news than his counterpart: the landings on Saipan were running according to plan, with thousands of American Marines already ashore and penetrating inland.

Early the next morning, 20 June, Admiral Mitscher launched scouting planes, including Avengers, to try to locate the Japanese Fleet. The Americans had the latest radar, just as they could now use the latest invention, the proximity fuse, and other devices that the scientists back home provided. But when it came to locating a vast armada on the Philippine Sea, they were obliged to resort to the human eye. But it did the trick, belatedly. One of the Avenger pilots spotted Ozawa's armada in the late afternoon, and reported its position accordingly as 275 miles from Admiral Mitscher's Task Force 58.

The Admiral and his staff did some rapid arithmetic. A launch now from his carriers would inevitably entail a night landing on return. Although his latest air crews were well trained, they had no experience of landing on a carrier in the dark. On the other hand an opportunity like this might never recur. He gave the order to launch. It was a few minutes after four o'clock; the skies were clear but the sun was already uncomfortably low.

The deck crews ranged their machines on the flight deck; the air crews, lumbered with their Mae Wests and folded dinghies, climbed in, and with a roar that increased as more and more Hellcats, Dauntlesses and Avengers, with torpedoes under their bellies took off, climbed into the afternoon sky.

Admirals Mitscher and Spruance sent up a silent prayer for their success and safety — all 216 of them.

It was almost twilight when the pilots saw ahead of them the Japanese Fleet spread over a vast area of the ocean. Some of the pilots asked themselves why it had not been spotted earlier. The Zeros were waiting for them, but the Hellcat pilots were confident of their ability to deal with them. And they did so, while the dive-bombers and the Avengers went down with their bombs and torpedoes. The new Avengers were well named; they closed in on both sides of the big fleet carrier *Hiyo*. It was knocked out within five minutes, sinking later. The Dauntlesses, which had first proved themselves at Midway two years earlier, tore to pieces the carrier *Zuikaku* and left the carrier *Chiyoda* in a sinking condition. They also damaged a battleship and a cruiser.

When they climbed again to their cruising altitude, there was little light remaining. It was a long way back to their carriers, and the pilots glanced anxiously at their fuel gauges.

The air crews' anxiety about the imminent darkness was matched by that of Admiral Mitscher and his staff. As the radar blips told of his returning aircraft's approach, he ordered flares to be fired and searchlights to be switched on. This helped those air crews who had enough fuel to make it. But eighty, some of them damaged by flak, were forced to splash into the sea. Others crash-landed on the carriers' decks, and as soon as the crew were helped out their machines were hurled overboard in a gesture of extravagance the US Navy could well afford.

The rescue launches were soon out and going about their business, guided by the flares activated by the airmen in their inflated dinghies. The sea was warm, as it always is in these latitudes. By dawn they had picked up sixty-four of the eighty missing men; some of the missing could have been killed in combat.

So, at a negligible cost of American lives, they had all but wiped out Admiral Ozawa's carrier fleet — just one ship remaining afloat. And as for the planes that had taken off in defence of these carriers, the Admiral was left with only a handful of Zeros, Judys and Bettys. Admiral Mitscher was proved right; the risk had been justified. 'The Marianas Turkey Shoot' followed by the Japanese carrier losses was, in boxing terms, a blow to the right and a blow to the left.

Midway had been a decisive battle, but it could now be seen as a mere preliminary to the Battle for the Philippines, the most decisive carrier battle in history.

The Americans now had two options open to them. The first was to go for the jugular, bypassing all islands and heading straight for the heart of the Philippines — Leyte Island. The second, a less radical operation, was to reach the same destination from the islands of Pelelieu, Yap and Ulithi in the Caroline Islands. In the event, both alternatives were pursued.

The Japanese defence arrangements were equally complicated. Admiral Ozawa's carrier fleet, or what was left of it, was based on Formosa. He had four carriers and two battleship-carriers. He also had some light cruisers and destroyers.

Admiral Kurita was stationed near Singapore with a powerful battleship fleet — seven battleships including the 18.1-inch-gunned *Yamato* and *Musashi*. These were supported by a substantial force of cruisers, including twelve heavy cruisers — and, of course, many flotillas of destroyers.

When the Japanese received confirmation that Leyte was the enemy's main target, Ozawa with his carrier force came south from Formosa and soon clashed with the van of the approaching American carriers. A tremendous air fight ensued, with Hellcats battling with Zeros while Judys turned on their backs and went into their steep dive.

Before being shot down into the sea, one Judy dropped a 550-pound bomb in the centre of the flight deck of the carrier *Princeton*. It exploded in the hangar where, although every precaution had been taken, a fuel fire broke out, and spread to some Avengers and their torpedoes. The carrier was clearly doomed. Except for the fire-fighters, the ship was abandoned. The flames inevitably spread, but a cruiser came alongside and helped in the struggle with her own fire-fighters. But it was hopeless, and later two torpedoes were dispatched to put the *Princeton* out of her misery.

As night closed in, Admiral Nishimura was ordered by Admiral Kurita to drive up the Surigao Strait on the southern side of Leyte. The Admiral felt confident that he could deal with anything he met, knowing of the Americans' incapacity to fight in the dark. His first brush with the enemy involved a group of destroyers. Nishimura ordered star shells to be fired and then high-explosive shells. The American destroyers turned and fled at high speed, delaying only to fire a spread of torpedoes. The battleship *Huso* was hit, but by how many torpedoes no one will ever know. In fact the 30,000-ton battleship had her back broken. This led to fires and the ship went down half an hour later.

Admiral Nishimura was obliged to change his mind about the American capacity to fight in the dark. He could see the *Huso* ablaze behind him, and then he felt the shudder of two torpedoes striking his own flagship, and the *Yamasiro*, the

Huso's sister ship, was forced to slow to five knots. Worse was to follow. So far it had been radar-equipped destroyers stealing out of the darkness of the shoreline which had inflicted the damage. Now it was American battleships, fitted with new centimetric fire-control radar, which enabled them to fire with devastating accuracy. That finished off any hope of Admiral Nishimura and his force surviving.

The following morning, 24 October, Admiral Halsey's 3rd Fleet intercepted Admiral Kurita's surviving battleships as it was threading its way east through the islands. Dive-bombers, Avengers and Hellcats were launched for a major attack. The American air crews, looking down from 20,000 feet, observed the biggest ship they thought they had ever seen. And they were right — she was the *Musashi* which, with her sister ship *Yamato*, was the biggest battleship in the world.

Refusing to be awed by this sight, the pilots concentrated their attention on this 71,000-ton battleship. The Dauntlesses went down with their 1,000-pound bombs and one of them scored a hit. The *Musashi* scarcely shuddered. But when it was the turn of the Grumman Avengers, it was a different story. No one counted how many of the twenty-one-inch torpedoes exploded against her hull. But she was split open below the waterline, internal explosions followed and water poured in, and she was brought to a standstill. But like a mortally wounded elephant, the *Musashi* took a long time to die. In the afternoon another mass of Avengers closed about her, putting ten more torpedoes into her hull. But even then it was not until 7.30 p.m. that she rolled over and went down.

The American pilots attacked other battleships, too, and

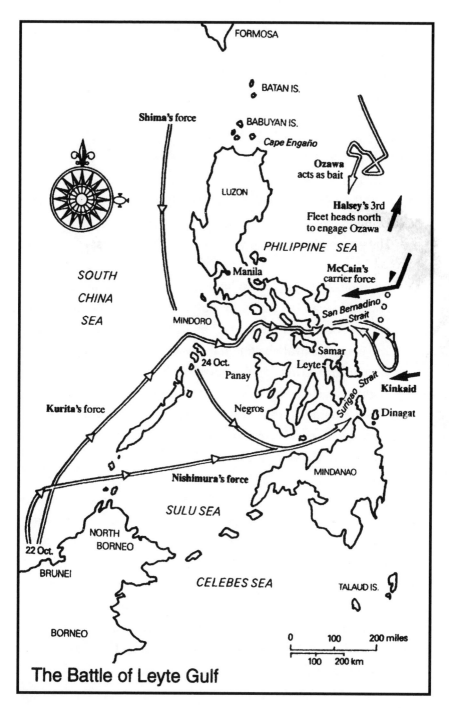

FORMOSA

BATAN IS.

BABUYAN IS.

Cape Engaño

Shima's force

Ozawa
acts as bait

LUZON

**Halsey's 3rd
Fleet heads north
to engage Ozawa**

PHILIPPINE SEA

SOUTH

CHINA

SEA

Manila

McCain's
carrier force

MINDORO

San Bernadino
Strait

24 Oct.

Samar

Panay

Leyte

Kurita's force

Negros

Surigao Strait

Kinkaid

Dinagat

Nishimura's force

MINDANAO

SULU SEA

NORTH
BORNEO

22 Oct.

BRUNEI

CELEBES SEA

TALAUD IS.

BORNEO

| 0 | 100 | 200 miles |

| 100 | 200 km |

The Battle of Leyte Gulf

such was their state of excitement that they reported four or even five battleships sunk — virtually a wipe-out of this Japanese force. Admiral 'Bull' Halsey, on 'sentry duty' in his flagship *New Jersey*, noted this news with satisfaction, and immediately after he had received it was passed a sighting report. Far to the north an enemy carrier force was speeding south. Reassured that the Japanese battleships had been neutralized, Halsey felt justified in leaving his post as guard of the San Bernadino Strait and going north to deal with the advancing enemy.

Halsey, recounting his position later, wrote this:

> Searches by my carrier planes revealed the presence of the Northern carrier force on the afternoon of 24 October, which completed the picture of all enemy naval forces. As it seemed childish for me to guard statistically San Bernardino Strait, I concentrated [my force] during the night and steamed north to attack the Northern force at dawn. I believed that the Centre force had been so heavily damaged ... that it could no longer be considered a serious menace to the Seventh Fleet.

It is possible to forgive Halsey for deserting his post; what is difficult to forgive is his failure to inform anyone of what he was doing. The consequence was that when the battleships that Halsey's airmen had claimed they had sunk suddenly materialized out of the San Bernardino Strait, it came as a fearful shock. The Japanese were faced by Rear-Admiral Sprague's carriers and destroyers, no battleships — and the carriers were small escort carriers, or 'Woolworth' carriers, so called because they were so cheap and quick to build.

On the face of it, Admiral Sprague's chances of lasting ten minutes against such a powerful force were extremely thin.

Sprague launched his Hellcats and Avengers but had to turn into wind to do so, thus shortening the distance between himself and the pursuing battleships. Moreover, his escort carriers could not even reach a speed of twenty knots. The Avengers and Hellcats did their best, but there were few of them and they faced a wall of flak.

The first phase of this contest became a destroyer/battleship duel. The American destroyer captains were in their element: this was what they had been trained for. They darted about, making smoke, launching their torpedoes, and making the battleships turn to 'comb' their tracks. But this uneven fight could not go on for ever. Their chief enemy was the Japanese destroyers — and there were plenty of them. A Japanese destroyer squadron surrounded the destroyer *Johnston* (2,100 tons, eight five-inch guns), which had exhausted its supply of torpedoes and had already been hit in the engine room, knocking out one engine. A cruiser joined the destroyers, harrying this single American destroyer.

For the next half hour this ship engaged first the cruiser on our port hand then the destroyers on our starboard hand [wrote a surviving officer] alternating between the two groups in a somewhat desperate attempt to keep all of them from closing the carrier formation. The ship was getting hit with disconcerting frequency throughout this period.

At 09.10 we had taken a hit which knocked out one forward gun and damaged the other. Fires had broken out. One of our 40-mm. ready lockers was hit and the exploding shells were causing as much damage as the Japs.

The bridge was rendered untenable by the fires and explosions, and Commander Evans had been forced at 09.20 to shift his command to the fantail, where he yelled his steering orders through an open hatch at the men who were turning the rudder by hand.

The most heroic bravery could not finally save the *Johnston*: battered into a mass of tangled steel, she went down half an hour later, with 186 of her officers and men. Two more American destroyers were sunk, but the others torpedoed and sank two Japanese cruisers. Admiral Kurita's battleships and cruisers sank with their heavy shells the escort carrier *Gambier Bay*. This unarmoured lightly built 'Woolworth' carrier struggled for a while against the damage caused by eight-inch and fourteen-inch shellfire. But it was too much for the 11,000-ton escort carrier, and she went down blazing. Two more of Sprague's escort carriers were hit but survived the onslaught.

Then, at 9.15 a.m., the entire Japanese pursuing force — battleships, heavy and light cruisers and destroyers turned through 180 degrees and disappeared down San Bernardino Strait. Whatever could be the reason for this? puzzled Admiral Sprague. The reason was that Admiral Kurita had mistaken the American escort carriers for fleet carriers, and he had witnessed the previous day what American dive-bombers and torpedo bombers had done to the giant *Musashi*, overwhelming her with a series of deadly attacks. It was not the loss of the *Musashi*'s guns — even though they were the biggest in the world — it was the loss of morale caused by the capsizing and sinking of this 'unsinkable' battleship which had caused Kurita to turn tail and flee.

* * *

These October days in 1944 were in stark contrast to 1941/2, when Admiral Nagumo was ranging virtually unhindered round the Pacific from Pearl Harbor to the Indian Ocean.

Whatever loss of morale Admiral Kurita might have suffered, it did not apply to the Japanese airmen. Towards midday, Admiral Sprague was astonished to see the sky above him spotted with Val dive-bombers. They came down in their usual steep dives. They were followed all the way by heavy and light flak. Those the gunners did not destroy on the way down were surely doomed at the point of pull-out, a dive-bomber's most vulnerable moment. But to the mixed horror and astonishment of all those above deck they did not pull out or drop their bombs — they just came straight on in an act of self-immolation. These were the first *kamikazes*, or suicide bombers. Two of Sprague's carriers were hit — one fatally. The *St Lo* was the first American ship to be sunk by *kamikazes*; there would be others in the weeks and months ahead.

Far to the north a more orthodox sinking of carriers was taking place. Admiral Halsey and his carrier admiral, Mark Mitscher, had at last found and were setting about the destruction of Admiral Ozawa's carriers. The Japanese Admiral launched all his Zeros, but there were pathetically few of them, and they were set on by Hellcats. But soon the few Zeros that survived had no home to return to. By the end of the morning of 25 October all of Ozawa's carriers were at the bottom of the sea after being torn apart by over 200 of Mitscher's torpedo and dive-bombers.

All this was crucial and commendable, but it left Admiral Kincaid in the lurch and open to massacre by Kurita's battleship force. After a series of messages of support, not only from Kincaid but also from Admiral Nimitz at Pearl Harbor, Halsey, who had been preoccupied with Ozawa's carriers, dispatched battleships, including his flagship *New Jersey*, at full speed to Kincaid's aid. By the time they arrived, the enemy had flown, back down San Bernadino Strait to safety.

The naval battle for the Philippines, dominated by the Leyte Gulf operations, marked the end of Japan's efforts to defend its vast new Pacific empire. It had been the greatest naval battle of the twentieth century; more ships were involved and more sunk even than at Jutland. There were further engagements but of a comparatively minor nature. Even the new British Pacific Fleet took part to add to the imbalance of power against the IJN. This move could be seen as the counterpart of the United States Navy's contribution to the British Grand Fleet in 1917/18. At that time the German Navy was disinclined to challenge any further the British Navy: it was the spirit of co-operation and comradeship which mattered.

Just as carrier-based air power won the battle for the Pacific, it was again air power which smashed Japan's industry at home. It was the new B29 'Superfortress', operating from air bases captured from the Japanese, which conducted these operations, culminating in the dropping of the first atomic bomb on the city of Hiroshima on 6 August 1945, killing about 120,000 people.

A second atomic bomb was then dropped on the city of Nagasaki, but some historians judge that this was to impress upon the Soviet Union that America had plenty of supplies of this dreadful weapon.

SELECT BIBLIOGRAPHY

CHAPTER 1: THE BATTLE OF TSU-SHIMA
Ballard G., *The Influence of the Sea on the Political History of Japan* (1921).
Blond G., *Admiral Togo* (1960).
Bodley R., *Admiral Togo: The Authorised Life* (1935).
Hough R., *The Fleet that Had to Die* (1958).
Novikoff-Priboy A., *Tsushima* (1936).
Semenov V., *Rasplata: The Reckoning* (1909).
Talk G., *Togo and the Rise of Japanese Sea Power* (1906).
Wright H., *A Life of Togo* (1907).

Royal Navy Attaché's reports on the Battle of Tsu-Shima, papers captured from the Russians by the Japanese and retranslated from the Japanese by G. V. Rayment. Fleet Orders of Rear-Admiral Z. P. Rozhestvensky.

CHAPTER 2: THE BATTLES OF CORONEL AND THE FALKLAND ISLANDS
Bennett G., *Coronel and the Falklands* (1962).
Churchill W. S., *The World Crisis*, Vol. 1, 1911—1914 (1923).
Hough R., *The Pursuit of Admiral von Spee* (1969).

Marder A. J., *From the Dreadnought to Scapa Flow*, Vol. 2 (1965).

Conversations with Rear-Admiral Dannreuther, DSO, RN, and Captain Steele, RN, both of HMS *Invincible*.

CHAPTER 3: THE BATTLE OF THE DOGGER BANK

Chalmers W. S., *The Life and Letters of Admiral David, Earl Beatty* (1951).

Haywood V., *HMS Tiger at Bay* (1977).

Hough R., *The Great War at Sea* (1983).

Marder A. J., *From the Dreadnought to Scapa Flow*, Vol. 2 (1965).

Young F., *With the Battle Cruisers* (1921).

CHAPTER 4: THE BATTLE OF JUTLAND

Admiral of the Fleet Lord Chatfield, *The Navy and Defence* (1942).

Sir Julian Corbett/Sir Henry Newbolt, *History of the War*. 'Naval Operations' (1920—31).

Dreyer, F. C., *The Sea Heritage* (1995).

Hough, R., *First Sea Lord* (1969).

Hough, R., *The Great War at Sea* (1983).

Admiral of the Fleet Earl Jellicoe, *The Grand Fleet, 1914—16* (1919).

von Hase, G., *Kiel & Jutland* (1927).

John Winton, *Jellicoe* (1981).

Conversations with the late Professor Arthur J. Marder.

Conversations with the late H. E. Dannreuther, May 1968.

CHAPTER 5: THE BATTLE OF THE RIVER PLATE

Churchill, W. S., *The Second World War*, Vol. I, 'The Gathering Storm' (1948)

Macintyre, D., *The Naval War Against Hitler* (1971)

Roskill, S. W., *The Navy at War* (1960)

The Oxford Companion to the Second World War (1995)

Conversations with Admiral Sir William Tennant, RN.

Conversation with the one-time British Naval Attaché in Montevideo.

CHAPTER 6: THE BATTLE WITH THE *BISMARCK*

Bradford, E., *The Mighty Hood* (1959).

Campbell, J., *Jutland* (1986).

Churchill, W. S., *The Second World War*, Vol. III 'The Grand Alliance' (1950).

Kennedy, L., *Pursuit* (1974).

Mullenheim-Rechberg, B., *Battleship Bismarck* (1981).

CHAPTER 7: THE BATTLE OF CAPE MATAPAN

Admiral of the Fleet Viscount Cunningham of Hyndhope, *A Sailor's Odyssey* (1951).

Hough, R., *The Great War at Sea* (1983).

Macintyre, D., *The Battle for the Mediterranean* (1964).

Winton, J., *Cunningham* (1998).

CHAPTER 8: THE BATTLE IN THE SOUTH CHINA SEA

Arthur, M., *The Navy to the Present Day* (1997).

Churchill, W. S., *The Second World War*, Vol. III 'The Grand Alliance' (1950).

Hough, R., *The Hunting of Force Z* (1963).

Conversations with Admiral Sir William Tennant, RN.

CHAPTER 9: THE BATTLE FOR THE PACIFIC

Gray, E., *Operation Pacific* (1990).

Hough, R., *The Longest Battle* (1986).

Lord, W., *Day of Infamy* (1957).

Macintyre, D., *The Battle for the Pacific: Opening Rounds* (1966).

CHAPTER 10: THE BATTLE OF MIDWAY

Frank P., & Harrington, J. D., *Rendezvous at Midway* (1967).

Lord, W., *Incredible Victory* (1967).

Macintyre, D., *The Battle for the Pacific* (1966).

Tuleja, T., *Climax at Midway* (1960).

CHAPTER 11: THE BATTLE FOR GUADALCANAL

Cutler, T. J., *The Battle of Leyte Gulf* (1994).

Gray, E., *Operation Pacific* (1990).

Hough, R., *The Longest Battle* (1986).

Macintyre, D., *The Battle for the Pacific* (1966).

The Oxford Companion to the Second World War (1995).

CHAPTER 12: THE BATTLE OF NORTH CAPE

Gray, E., *Operation Pacific* (1990).

Hough, R., *The Longest Battle* (1986).

Macintyre, D., *The Battle for the Pacific* (1966).

The Oxford Companion to the Second World War (1995).

CHAPTER 13: THE BATTLE FOR THE PHILIPPINES

Churchill, W. S., *The Second World War*, Vol. V 'Closing the Ring' (1952).

Cutler, T. J., *The Battle of Leyte Gulf* (1994).

Frank P., & Harrington, J. D., *Rendezvous at Midway* (1967).

Gray, E., *Operation Pacific* (1990).

Hough, R., *The Longest Battle* (1986).

Lord, W., *Incredible Victory* (1968).

Lord, W., *Day of Infamy* (1957).

Macintyre, D., *The Battle for the Pacific* (1966).

The Oxford Companion to the Second World War (1995).

INDEX